To
Andy

Not another bloody aeroplane book!

With all best wishes

TOMORROW
MAY NEVER COME

The remarkable life story of

'STEVIE' STEVENS

Lancaster pilot and

beloved school teacher

This edition first published 2021

Cover and page design by Mark Postlethwaite

All photographs via the authors and ww2images.com

Publishers: Wing Leader Ltd www.wingleader.co.uk

Printed in Leicester, England by Spectrum Printing Services Ltd

TOMORROW MAY NEVER COME

The remarkable life story of

'STEVIE' STEVENS

Lancaster pilot and
beloved school teacher

by

Jonny Cracknell and Adrian Stevens

CONTENTS

ABBREVIATIONS:

RAF RANKS AND ARMY EQUIVALENTS

ROYAL AIR FORCE	BRITISH ARMY
ACM: Air Chief Marshal	General
AM: Air Marshal	Lieutenant General
AVM: Air Vice Marshal	Major General
A/C: Air Commodore	Brigadier
Gp Cpt: Group Captain	Colonel
W/Cdr: Wing Commander	Lieutenant Colonel
S/Ldr: Squadron Leader	Major
F/Lt: Flight Lieutenant	Captain
F/O: Flying Officer	Lieutenant
P/O: Pilot Officer	Second Lieutenant/Subaltern
W/O: Warrant Officer	Regimental Sergeant Major
F/S: Flight Sergeant	Company Sergeant Major
Sgt: Sergeant	Sergeant
Cpl: Corporal	Corporal
LAC: Leading Aircraftman	Lance Corporal
AC: Aircraftman	Private
AOC: Air Officer Commanding	GOC: General Officer Commanding

C-in-C: Commander-in-Chief

CO: Commanding Officer

RAAF: Royal Australian Air Force

RCAF: Royal Canadian Air Force

RNZAF: Royal New Zealand Air Force

DEDICATION

This book is dedicated to the memory of Stevie's friends Johnny Pickett, Dickie Newcomb, George Martin DFM and Johnnie Smith, and to all the other members of 57 Squadron lost on operations.

FOREWORD

This is the story of an incredible, inspirational, caring man, who I was proud to call my friend. While much of the book rightly focuses on his experiences in the Royal Air Force's Bomber Command during the Second World War, Stevie Stevens led a life that enriched the lives of innumerable others before, during and after the War.

The Stevie I knew always put the needs of others before his own, and it is that quality that runs like a golden thread throughout the narrative of his long life. Whether doing anything he could to look after his young schoolmates who got into trouble, doing his utmost to take care of his Lancaster crewmates as they flew into battle night after night during the darkest days of the War, or going 'above and beyond' what was required in his later career as a beloved teacher, Stevie's first thoughts were always for the well-being of others.

Stevie was an unassuming, self-deprecating man (a quality he shared perhaps with all the men and women who served in the air, on the ground, at sea, at home and overseas during WW2). He would never have dreamt of describing himself as a 'hero' but, as you will read, that is what he was. 'Stevie's Story' lays bare in vivid detail the stresses, fears and seemingly impossible odds of survival Bomber Command crews faced — it takes true heroism to overcome such fears and to continue to fight as Stevie and his comrades did.

But this is also the story of Stevie's life after he left the Royal Air Force. A life he shared with his beloved wife Maureen and his son Adrian for over 70 years. Stevie felt that he had been blessed to survive his time with Bomber Command and gave thanks in his own inimitable fashion by making a life where he could help others, which he did in spades as a teacher who inspired innumerable pupils for almost 40 years.

Perhaps it is that post-RAF life that represents Stevie's most vital and fitting legacy. A life filled with love for family and friends, a life spent trying to help others and, I think, the type of life that all his companions who perished with Bomber Command would have aspired to lead had they survived the War.

Group Captain David Houghton

President, 57 & 630 Squadrons' Association

INTRODUCTION

In the last years of his life, my father became, much to his surprise and amusement, something of a media celebrity. In 2018, the year in which the RAF celebrated its hundredth anniversary, he was asked, as one of the last surviving Lancaster pilots from the Second World War, to feature in the promotion RAF 100 Heroes on Facebook and Twitter. He felt he couldn't refuse, but he said to me in the way that was so typical of him, "They really were wrong to use the word 'hero'. I'm no hero, I was just doing my bit." The many people who posted comments thought differently, and soon afterwards, the RAF arranged for the broadcaster Dan Snow to interview my father at his home in Norwich. The interview subsequently appeared as a podcast on Dan Snow's History Hit website under the title The Unheard Tapes of Bomber Command, and reached a nationwide audience.

My father had no time for celebrity culture, and no interest in promoting himself. He agreed to do the interview because he wished to give people an authentic account of what it was like to serve in Bomber Command in 1943, at the time he did his tour of operations with 57 Squadron. Throughout his long life, the friends who had flown with him remained vivid presences in his memory. Many of them laid down their lives at a tragically early age in the struggle for freedom and the survival of democracy. Four of them to whom my father felt especially close are commemorated at the RAF Memorial at Runnymede, among the thousands of Bomber Command aircrew who have no known resting place.

My father wished to commemorate not only the friends he had lost, but also my mother, Maureen, who passed away in 2017, just a day before what would have been their seventy-fourth wedding anniversary. They had met while she was serving as a Radio Telephone Operator in the WAAF, relaying instructions to pilots from Ground Control at airfields across wartime Lincolnshire. Like my father, she became a reluctant celebrity in old age. When my parents celebrated seventy years of marriage in December 2013, their story went viral across the media, and was even broadcast on local radio stations throughout America. Although my mother hated talking about it, she had rubbed shoulders with history. It was Maureen, speaking from the Control Tower at RAF Scampton, who gave Guy Gibson and the other pilots who returned from the Dambusters raid their landing instructions. My father had been posted to Scampton to begin his tour shortly before the Dams raid. He watched 617 Squadron as it took off on what would become the most celebrated mission in the history of Bomber Command, and when he began to date my mother, he had to beat off competition from some of Guy Gibson's pilots. When my mother passed away in 2017, the main daily newspapers ran lengthy tributes, and she was given a half-page obituary in the *Times* – an expression of appreciation which would have astonished her, and which she would have thought quite undeserved.

For my father, 'freedom' and 'democracy' were not empty words; they were the values for which he and the young men of Bomber Command had laid their lives on the line. I remember going with him to cast my vote for the first time at the 1970 General Election. I had been moving between Cambridge and Germany, and my father had kept me registered on the electoral role in Norwich, where I had been born and gone to school. We walked up to the local polling station together, and on the way, he said to me, "I'm glad you came back to vote. A lot of my friends gave their lives so that we could do this, and a lot of them were younger than you." As I marked my ballot paper, I had a lump in my throat.

I had the same kind of lump in my throat as I worked on this book. The story it tells is remarkable, a memorable piece of history in its own right, but it would not have seen the light of day without the tireless energy and enthusiasm of my co-author, Jonny Cracknell, and the support and creative expertise of Mark Postlethwaite, the publisher, who knew and liked my parents. My father came to Jonny's attention thanks to the very social media of which he was so sceptical. In 2019 and 2020 Jonny visited him at Saxlingham Hall, the beautiful nursing home in Norfolk where he spent the last year of his life, and did a series of interviews with him. My father had kept an extensive written record of his time in the RAF, and he asked me to collaborate with Jonny to help turn his reminiscences, letters and diaries into a story that would be accessible to readers born long after Bomber Command had passed into history.

As he was a natural storyteller, he made things easy for us, and the parts of this book Jonny and I have written do no more than provide a narrative frame, and a timeline for his reminiscences. I was able to read him an early draft, and he gave me an extensive and detailed verbal commentary on it which he continued to elaborate until, quite literally, speech failed him. This book is written as he wanted it to be written. The title *Tomorrow May Never Come* was chosen by him, and the voice that tells the stories that form the book's centrepiece is his voice, in all its uniqueness. Luckily, that voice is not confined to print. Readers might like to know that my father can be seen and heard in person not only on the History Hit website, but also in a moving video made by Sean Johnson which was posted on YouTube on 6 May 2020 under the title A Lancaster Pilot's War: The Story of Sidney "Steve" Stevens DFC, AE*.

Inevitably, the main focus of this book is on the years between 1941 and 1947, the period of my father's full-time service in the RAF. He continued to serve in the RAFVR on a part-time basis until 1961, but long before then, he had embarked on a vocation which he found every bit as challenging in its own way as piloting a Lancaster. For almost forty years he taught Science and Maths at schools in Norwich, giving children from ordinary and often underprivileged homes opportunities they might never otherwise have had. When he passed away on 11 April 2020, tributes appeared across the local and national media, and on 8 May, the seventy-fifth anniversary of VE Day, the *Times* printed a whole-page obituary of him which it had held back specially to mark the occasion. But the most heartfelt expressions of thanks came from his former pupils. He was a war hero who had played his part in ridding Europe of the curse of Hitler; but the men and women he had taught in Norwich remembered him as a charismatic and inspirational teacher who had lit up their lives with his kindness, infectious good humour and passion for learning. Their expressions of thanks and appreciation would, I know, have made him smile. He was a man who, both in war and in peace, placed his life in the service of others, for the greater good. This book is his legacy.

Adrian Stevens

A BOY FROM NORTH DEVON

Sidney George Stevens, known to his family as Sid, but to everyone else as Steve or Stevie, was born on 14 December 1921 in the picturesque market town of Great Torrington in North Devon. Torrington is built on a hill rising steeply above the River Torridge. The hill, known as Castle Hill because it was the site of a castle in the Middle Ages, affords visitors spectacular views over a landscape of rolling green fields and hedges. The countryside around Torrington is the setting of Henry Williamson's classic novel *Tarka the Otter*, first published in 1927. Stevie read it as a boy, and it remained a firm favourite of his because of its powerful evocation of the Devon of his childhood.

Stevie's father, George William Cecil Stevens, and his mother, who was christened Florence Mabel, but always called 'Doll' by her family and friends, lived in a small terraced house at the bottom of Mill Street, which climbs steeply from the bridge over the Torridge up to the centre of Torrington. Doll had been told that Stevie would be born in February 1922, but he made an emergency landing in Mill Street several weeks prematurely. Stevie liked to tell the story with his own inimitable brand of humour:

> *My mother was planning to do some Christmas shopping in Bideford with a friend. She told her friend she couldn't go as she had a dose of wind. It turned out that I was the dose of wind. I was so ugly, small, fragile, and hairless that she said I looked more like a monkey than a child!*

As an older brother born the year before had only survived for three hours and died before he could be christened, Stevie's early arrival created a panic. His grandmother, a devoutly religious woman, rushed up Mill Street to fetch the Vicar, desperate that history should not repeat itself. Before they arrived, one of their neighbours looked in:

> *Being a kindly and practical man, he decided to try an earthly remedy. He ran back to his house, fetched a bottle of brandy, and gave me a tablespoonful of warm brandy and milk. This was so much to my taste that I decided I'd rather like to live. The Vicar duly christened me in the chamber pot, and I went contentedly off to sleep.*

Later in life, Stevie reflected on what it was like to grow up in Torrington in the 1920s in the aftermath of the First World War:

Stevie as a baby in the garden of the house in Mill Street, Torrington

There was scarcely a family in my home town, Torrington, which had not had at least one of its members killed or wounded during the First World War. Returning soldiers were allowed six weeks to draw the dole and after that they had to fend for themselves. Many of them were suffering from shell shock, now known as Post Traumatic Stress Disorder. An Old Comrades Club was started, and this later became the British Legion. There veterans were able to meet and discuss their experiences. The country they had saved had promised them a 'Land fit for Heroes' to live in. Instead, like their ancestors the 'Heroes of Waterloo' commemorated by the Monument on Castle Hill, they were left in poverty or struggled to make a living.

Torrington had been known for glove making since Tudor times, and Stevie's mother Doll worked for one of the factories that made gloves:

In some ways, Torrington was fortunate because it had several industries. There were three gloving factories, mostly employing female labour. Much of the work was done by women who worked at home for very low wages. Most houses had a sewing machine designed for glove making. They were treadle operated because there was no electric power. The light in nearly all the cottages was provided by paraffin lamps. These varied from beautifully designed lamps with twin wicks and richly decorated glass bowls to very small 'Kelly lamps' which were made of metal and had a lead-weighted base so that it was almost impossible to knock them over. Every house also had a supply of candles which were far less expensive to buy than lamps. It was by the yellow, flickering Kelly lamp that much of the machine work was done. Standing on the white scrubbed table, it was the centre of all reading and working activity. Apart from the gloving industry, there was a small and smelly tannery, several small farms, and the Torridge Vale factory in the neighbouring village of Taddiport, which collected milk and produced butter and cream.

Stevie's father Cecil, whose own father had died when Cecil was a boy, left school at the age of thirteen to work on the Railway, starting as a cleaner, moving on to become a fireman, and finally an engine driver:

The Railway was the main employer for men. Torrington was the terminus for trains running from Waterloo. As a terminus it had engine sheds where locomotives were serviced, a turntable where the engines were turned around in preparation for the return journey, and a small shunting yard with sidings which handled local passenger and goods trains. A single branch line also ran to collect clay from Claymoor, passing through pretty little stations at Watergate, Meeth, and Merton. There was a junction at which passengers could join the Great Western Railway to travel on to Cornwall. There were no Sunday trains, and on Sunday mornings, the waiting room was turned into a lecture room.

Railwaymen were proud craftsmen. Their brass buttons were always brightly polished, as were their shoes and cap badges. There was a precise hierarchy. A boy would join the railway as a cleaner, usually at the age of 14 when he left school. This was the hardest and grimiest job on the railway. Steam engines were a formidable size — wheels, pistons and connecting rods all had to be thoroughly cleaned, as did the main body of the engine. In the course of cleaning the boy learned the names of its complex parts. He helped with cleaning out the huge deposits of ash from the fire boxes, and then there were carriages to clean, brass to polish everywhere, and endless amounts of dirty, hard work. Yet when it was completed, boy cleaners took as much pride in the sparkling brassware and clean footplate as did the fireman and engine driver.

After several years, the cleaner became a fireman, whose exhausting job it was to shovel the coal into the fire box. This job had its special skills. If the fire did not burn hot enough, steam could not be generated to drive the engine, and the wrath of heaven fell on the fireman if a train was late. Passenger locomotives on the Atlantic Coast Express were the most demanding, and the firemen toiled ceaselessly, shovelling tons of coal to keep the engine running at speed. In summer the heat from the fire and foot plate was exhausting, while in winter cold draughts overcooled sweat-filled shirts, and the wet coal stuck and was difficult to handle. On tank engines it was just as bad; often the trains ran tender first, with rain, sleet, and coal dust blasted into the eyes of the driver, and this created additional misery for the fireman. At the end of a shift, oil and coal dust begrimed overalls and every square inch of skin, and the train crew had to climb the hill to the town. In their houses, there was only a tin bath to wash in, and water had to be heated in kettles and pots on the iron stove.

Cecil was determined that when Stevie left school, he should find a job that was both cleaner and less physically demanding:

"Don't work on the Railway, it's a dirty job," he would say to me in his broad Devon accent. "When you need to get a job, find yourself one where you can wear your best shirt."

If life for the railwaymen was hard, it was equally hard for their wives. The house in Mill Street where Stevie was born had an outside wash house with an old copper in which his mother did the household laundry and cleaned his father's overalls. Stevie could see it from his bedroom window:

Stevie with his parents

By day my little back bedroom window was warm and sunny, and now I was growing taller, I could look out of the bottom pane of the window without standing on the chair. Just within sight was the outside wash house with an old copper in which the sheets, pillowcases, towels and tea cloths were boiled every Monday.

First the copper was filled with cold water carried by a bucket from our only kitchen tap. Then a fire was lit underneath it, burning old boxes, tree branches, cardboard, old shoes and anything else that was combustible. Thick smoke would erupt from the chimney, greyish blue at first, then blacker as the various pieces crackled under the copper, and finally a column of grey decorated by an occasional spark as the draught really got going. After a while, the copper could be heard bubbling, and Mum would take off the wooden top and put in handfuls of shredded soap which would soon foam and flow out over the top, smelling clean and fresh, and occasionally hissing on the cast-iron door of the fire below. The clothes would then be fetched and tipped into the boiling soapy water and, red faced, Mum would poke and agitate the linen with a long white well-used copper stick. She would leave it to boil and return to the kitchen to make a cup of delicious hot brown sweet tea. I would go down the steep stairs to join her, and sit on her soapy aproned lap and drink my own tea, and eat a biscuit on the special days when such treats were available.

Then Mum would go back into the wash house and fish the washing from the copper with her copper stick and drop it into a galvanized iron bath. She would carry the bath to a mangle and turn the huge cast-iron handle while feeding the linen into the rollers. Streams of soapy water would be squeezed from the linen to fall into a bucket below. Much would miss the bucket and flow over the cobbled yard, forming innumerable streamlets. Meanwhile the washing was put into another bath and buckets of cold water thrown over it. Once again, the washing was mangled and this time dropped into blue water. Mangled yet again, and scrubbed on a scrubbing board, it was then taken up some steps to be pegged on the clothes line which ran the length of the long, walled garden.

When they started school, Stevie and the other children living in Mill Street had to trek up the hill to the centre of town:

There was a little girl called Betty who lived a couple of houses higher up the hill than me, and when I went to school in the morning, she would come with me. She was a little younger, and she had a habit of wetting herself. When this happened, the teacher would say:

"Sidney Stevens."

"Yes Ma'am."

"Would you like to take Betty home?"

"Oh yes, Ma'am."

She was, of course, my favourite teacher! I would take Betty home, then go on to my own house further down the hill, and shout through the letterbox to ask my mother to make me a pie, please. At other times, I used to help other children in trouble who were sent home. Because I lived at the bottom of the hill, the teacher would say, "You can take him home and come back later," so I would take whoever it was home, then I would often have another hour or two at home myself. It's strange to think of the responsibility that was put on very young children back then.

A young Stevie with friend

Times were hard, and for many of the children growing up in Torrington, poverty and hardship were the norm:

Several of my school friends were dressed in rags, and the annual Sunday School Treat organised by the Parish Church was a big moment in their lives. A visit to the seaside, though it was only ten miles away, was one of the highlights of the year for many of my school mates.

When Stevie was eight, his younger brother Denzil was born, and Stevie started his first job working part-time for a grocer, delivering goods to customers. *'I was not very keen on carrying large parcels for old ladies, but I really enjoyed weighing out tea, sugar, currants and dried fruits into small blue bags.'* Blessed with a naturally sunny and cheerful temperament, Stevie made a very favourable impression on the grocer, Jack White, who remained a lifelong friend, and constantly tried to lure him into becoming his business partner when Stevie made return trips to Torrington.

At this time, Stevie was also being given the musical training which was to stand him in good stead for the rest of his life. Being gifted with a fine singing voice, he joined the choir of the Parish Church in Torrington as a treble, and soon began to give solo recitals, which included such popular pieces as *Wings of a Dove*. Years later, the older people in the town would recall those recitals, and remark what a beautiful voice he had. He also joined the Wolf Cubs, and started to develop the strong spirit of adventure and self-reliance that would ease his passage into the RAF.

In 1932 Stevie won a scholarship to the grammar school in the neighbouring town of Bideford, some eight miles north of Torrington. To get there, he had to walk a mile and a half in the morning to catch a train, and then walk another mile from the station in Bideford:

> *There were no school meals, so I took sandwiches in my satchel. There was no hot or cold running water, and there was nowhere to hang coats, so when it was pouring with rain, we had to leave our dripping raincoats in a concrete-lined room. At that time there was one old building, and the rest of the school was accommodated in First World War huts. They let in the rain, and you can imagine that during the winter it really was a dreadful place to be. School finished at 4pm, but the train to Torrington did not leave until 5pm, and on a wet, cold evening I might not arrive home till 6pm.*

Stevie's difficulties were compounded by the fact that he was not keen on team sports:

> *I never played football or any team sports enthusiastically. I remember I got a really nasty leg injury playing rugby. I couldn't walk properly, which meant I had to catch an earlier train every day, or else not go to school at all. At the end of the term, my report asked, 'Has he tried hard enough?' Though there were only about two hundred boys in the school, nobody noticed that my leg injury had made it difficult for me to get to school!*

But Stevie did retain one very positive memory from his year at Bideford Grammar School. In August 1933 he was one of a party of nineteen from Bideford who went on a school cruise on board a troopship, the *SS Neuralia*. The cruise took them from London to Norway, Denmark, Germany, and Holland. Stevie and the other boys slept in hammocks and messed on the troop decks. Reveille was at 6:30, hammocks had to be lashed and stowed by 7:30; dinner was at 12:30, tea at 16:00, and supper at 20:30; hammocks were drawn and slung at 21:30; the Last Post was sounded at 22:00, and Lights Out was at 22:15. Stevie would always maintain that the military-style discipline on the *Neuralia* prepared him for his next voyage on a cruise liner eight years later, when he crossed the Atlantic in December 1941 to do his flying training in California.

In the summer of 1933, the family moved from Torrington to London, as Stevie's father had decided to take a cleaner and better-paid job with Southern Railway, driving electric trains:

> *My father moved to London, and as I'd already got a scholarship in Devon, I was transferred to a grammar school called The Henry Thornton School by Clapham Common, which was fairly posh, but not too posh. It was close enough to the Thames for boating, and some of the more elegant boys used to dress up in blazers, trousers, badges, and sailor suits—that's the sort of place it was. Of course, houses were much more expensive in London than in Torrington. When we moved to Clapham, we lived in a flat, then we managed to find a house further out in South Norwood that was cheaper to rent. It was much easier for me to get to school than it had been in Torrington, and the day was much less exhausting.*

Two years later, on 9 August 1935, at the age of 13, Stevie joined the 1st Balham Hill Boy Scout Troop. On the enrolment card bearing his name and the Scout motto 'Be Prepared' was a message from Baden Powell, the founder of the Scout Movement: *'You are now a Scout. So, sleeves up — and tackle your job!'* Stevie relished his time in the Scouts, and was soon taking himself off on camping expeditions during weekends in the summer. In May 1937 he was one of the Scouts who lined the processional route at the coronation of King George VI and sold commemorative programmes.

Stevie as a Boy Scout in 1936

On 29 March 1936, he was confirmed at his local parish church, St Luke's Woodside, where he became a server. A deeply spiritual man beneath his smiling and humorous exterior, Stevie was a firm believer in the power of prayer, and would remain a practising Anglican for the rest of his life.

He took the School Certificate in the summer of 1937 before his sixteenth birthday, passing with credit in English, History (English and European), French (written and oral), and General Physics. Always supremely articulate, and with a rare gift for language, he had hoped to stay on in the Sixth Form to study English, French and Latin, and study at university, '*but my father was then earning £3.10s a week, and could not afford it.*'

When he left school, his Form Master at the Henry Thornton, Mr. A.H. Collins, supplied him with an excellent reference, dated 22 July 1937:

> *I have known S.G. Stevens for the past four years, and I have been his Form Master for the last one of them, during which he was selected to serve as Form Monitor. It gives me very great pleasure to testify to his more than average intelligence, his utter trustworthiness, and reliability. His work has always been most diligent, neat and careful; and he has performed his duties as Form Monitor to my complete satisfaction. I am certain he will prove a valuable acquisition in any post to which he may be appointed.*

Helped by this recommendation, Stevie got the first job he applied for:

> *I applied for a job in the Estates, Housing and Valuations Department in Croydon, and was appointed from a short list of 20 to start work at 12s 6d a week. This was raised to 15 shillings in 1938, and then to 17s .6d when I was promoted to the permanent staff.*

By the time he started work in 1937, Stevie was certain that Hitler was bent on war and that Chamberlain's policy of appeasement would fail:

> *I was an ardent cinema goer, and watched the build-up of German forces on the news reels week after week. I kept on seeing pictures of Nazis on the march, and tanks, aircraft, and troops taking part in military exercises, and I watched reports of the enormous success of the German Air Force in the Spanish Civil War. It was quite clear that Hitler had set out to dominate the world, and while young idealists in this country were talking about disarmament, in Germany 'guns before butter' was the watchword. When Mr Chamberlain, with his umbrella, wing collar, thin body, and droopy moustache came back from his meeting with Hitler in Munich waving his pathetic little piece of paper, I decided to do something useful in the war I was sure was coming.*

LONDON AND THE BLITZ: LIFE AS AN ARP CONTROLLER

In 1938, Stevie volunteered for the RAFVR (Royal Air Force Volunteer Reserve), but was turned down because, he was told, 'public school types' were preferred. Instead, he joined the Air Raid Precautions Service (ARP). The ARP had been set up in 1937 after the Government accepted the advice of the military that the mass bombing of cities was highly likely in the event of war. As tensions with Hitler's Germany rose, the ARP was put in control of Britain's air raid defences, and hundreds of thousands of people across the country hurried to join it. Stevie recalled:

> *At this time there was a request for volunteers to help with the Air Raid Precautions Service. When I reached the age of 16, I was eligible, and I volunteered to train as a Controller. It was envisaged that if war broke out and bombing started in earnest, all sorts of public services would suffer severe damage. Experience of the Spanish Civil War showed the disruption caused by damage to electricity, gas and water supplies, shattered sewers, broken railway and tram lines, and roads blocked with the rubble of bombed buildings. Fire was a frightening certainty, and we were all very worried about the effect of poison gases on civilians and on morale as a whole. All ARP volunteers had a series of lectures on recognition of tear gas, mustard gas, chlorine and others. Respirators and anti-gas clothing were issued to us, and indeed the entire civilian population was issued with gas masks.*
>
> *At the outbreak of war, all areas were constantly patrolled by Air Raid Wardens. When bombs dropped, the Wardens sent damage reports to the local Air Raid Control Centre, and it was at one of these Centres, in Melfort Road, Thornton Heath, that I was employed. When the reports arrived, they were given to an Incident Plotting Officer, who plotted the type and position of the bombs on a large map. The Controller alerted the Fire, Gas, Electricity, Unexploded Bomb and Drainage services, while the Medical Officers' representative sent ambulances or cars to pick up casualties, and the Engineers' representative sent out light or heavy rescue parties to get people out of shattered buildings.*

When Hitler launched the Luftwaffe in an effort to break Britain in 1940, Stevie found himself playing a key role as a Controller in the ARP Centre at Thornton Heath. He had vivid memories of witnessing the Battle of Britain in the skies over London in the summer of 1940, and of living through the long days of and nights of the Blitz which followed:

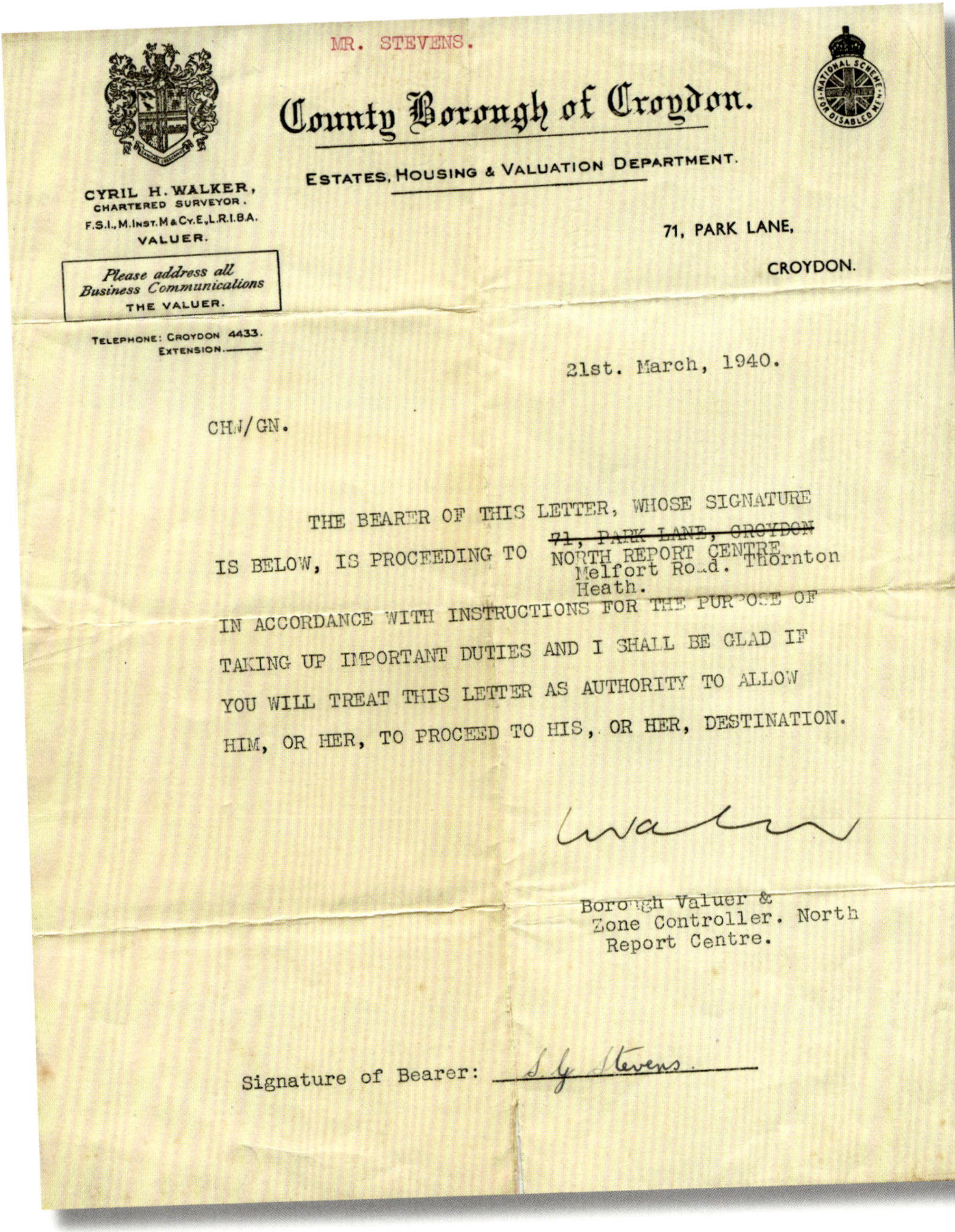

MR. STEVENS.

County Borough of Croydon.

ESTATES, HOUSING & VALUATION DEPARTMENT.

CYRIL H. WALKER,
CHARTERED SURVEYOR.
F.S.I., M.INST.M.&CY.E., L.R.I.B.A.
VALUER.

Please address all
Business Communications
THE VALUER.

TELEPHONE: CROYDON 4433.
EXTENSION.——

71, PARK LANE,

CROYDON.

21st. March, 1940.

CHW/GN.

THE BEARER OF THIS LETTER, WHOSE SIGNATURE IS BELOW, IS PROCEEDING TO ~~71, PARK LANE, CROYDON~~ NORTH REPORT CENTRE Melfort Road. Thornton Heath. IN ACCORDANCE WITH INSTRUCTIONS FOR THE PURPOSE OF TAKING UP IMPORTANT DUTIES AND I SHALL BE GLAD IF YOU WILL TREAT THIS LETTER AS AUTHORITY TO ALLOW HIM, OR HER, TO PROCEED TO HIS, OR HER, DESTINATION.

C Walker

Borough Valuer &
Zone Controller. North
Report Centre.

Signature of Bearer: S. G. Stevens.

Letter to County Borough of Croydon confirming Stevie's ARP appointment March 1940

The German heavy bombers weren't the only danger. The spent ammunition cartridges that used to shower down over London could do a lot of damage if they hit you. They came down in showers in the early days, but after a time our air defences got better, so the raids weren't quite so heavy. You could see all the German bombers coming over quite clearly. In and around Croydon, we saw lots of action overhead. The Spitfires and Hurricanes were our fighter aircraft, and the Hurricanes were a very much better aircraft than we often give them credit for, but of course, the Spitfire pilots had all the glamour — the boys with the scarfs round their necks, waving at their girlfriends from the air!

A girl I used to go to work with was standing in a queue waiting for a bus when the girl beside her suddenly collapsed. She had been killed by a stray bullet from an aircraft. Another time, my cousin and I went up to a nearby airfield, just to have a look, and a German fighter pilot opened up his machine guns on us, so we promptly dived under a hedge, then we ran into a farmhouse and hid under a table until the fighter disappeared. That was my first experience of air warfare.

It was so common then seeing death — windows were blown out; sewage pipes were blown up and houses were reduced to rubble. Strangely enough, those of us who had been trained for ARP work were so busy ourselves that we didn't have time to worry about what was going on, or how people were managing.

While Stevie was on duty at Thornton Heath Control Centre, beginning an eight-hour night shift, he received a message that his own house in Macclesfield Road, South Norwood, had suffered a direct hit:

A message came through during my shift to say that my own house had been bombed. There were so many bombs reported in the area that I stayed on duty until I was relieved at about 6am, when my shift finished. I cycled back home over fire hoses and rubble. When I arrived at my road, sure enough, my house had received a direct hit and was just a ruin. Ironically, my mother had just come back from Torrington, where she had been staying with her sister, because she thought things were getting quieter. She and my father and my uncle, who had popped in for a cup of tea, were all in a shelter, badly shaken.

We had a large, sturdy farmhouse table and when they heard the bombs coming down, they had got themselves underneath it. The bruised face of my father, the white bomb dust in my mother's hair, and the broken leg of my uncle, who had not managed to squeeze all of his body under that table, etched themselves in my mind forever.

As I was on my way to the ARP Centre, the lady who lived next door had asked if I would like some tea. Tea was rationed, so I stopped and had a quick cup with her, and then off I went. The house in which she lived had also been destroyed in the bombing. The next I saw of this poor lady, she had been smashed into her own front door – it was like a cartoon from a comic with jam all over the place, but in reality, it was anything but funny. The bomb blast had turned her into smelly human paste.

Stevie (right) with his colleague Douglas Wand at the Thornton Heath North Report Centre in 1940

I came out of our house at the end of the raid, when the sirens were sounding the All Clear. Everything for which I had worked and saved was pulverised except for a torn shirt, a pair of Boy Scouts shorts and a school prize dated 1935. They were my sole possessions, apart from the clothes I was wearing. I looked up at the empty sky and said to myself, "You bastards, what a bloody awful thing to do, I'll get my own back on you for this." I knew straight away then I wanted to be a bomber pilot; not many people wanted to fly bombers, but I knew I did, and I was determined that I would.

After the bombing of the family home, the drivers who worked with Stevie's father on the Railway drove trains for him while he was recovering from his injuries so that he would not lose two days' pay. Stevie's mother moved back to Torrington to live with her sister; his father went to lodge with his brother-in-law, and Stevie himself was given full board and lodging by a sympathetic neighbour for fifteen shillings a week.

FROM LORD'S CRICKET GROUND TO CARLISLE: EARLY DAYS IN THE RAF

With his parents' full approval, Stevie applied again to join the RAFVR. This time, with the country fighting for survival, and the RAF in urgent need of recruits, he was accepted, and enlisted as an 'Aircrafthand/Pilot' on 3 April 1941:

My parents thought joining the RAF was the right thing to do. They seem to have convinced themselves I was bound to survive! They always used to say that being a pilot was a job for public school boys, and that ordinary grammar school boys like me wouldn't be considered, but by 1941 things had changed. Most young men wanted to be pilots, and so volunteers flooded in, and the selection process creamed off the best. As with all expanding organisations, there was some chaos. Regular airmen suddenly found themselves promoted to corporals, and many loved their temporary power over the new entrants.

Stevie joined up at the most unlikely place — Lord's Cricket Ground, where the RAF had established an emergency reception centre:

My flight was formed at Lord's Cricket Ground. I sat with several others and watched a game of cricket. It seemed a marvellous way to join the RAF. Our first surprise was when we were asked to go to a place underneath the stands. We stood in a row and were asked to lower our trousers and pants and raise our shirts. A doctor walked rapidly in front of us and we were told to tidy up and to return to the cricket. This was my first FFI (Free-from-Infection) medical examination.

We were marched from Lord's to a superb new block of flats in St John's Wood. It had an imposing exterior, but was totally bare inside. We were told to "Nip along to the hut around the corner and collect blankets." We formed a queue and collected two blankets. We put one blanket on the floor and rolled up our clothing to form a pillow. Only the Corporal had a bed, in a small room about the size of a cupboard.

Stevie soon had reason to be grateful for the training he had received in the Scouts:

It was hard sleeping on a bare floor, but we were young and fit and not bothered. We were marched to Regent's Park Zoo for our meals, which were so bad that you had to be very hungry to eat them. We had classes in Morse Code, and tests involving Maths, night vision, colour vision and aptitude.

Kitted out in his RAF uniform in August 1941

I was surprised to find my night vision was above average. Several lads were weeded out and departed when the results were announced. Funnily enough, I found the most useful bit of pre-war training was the Boy Scouts—because you learnt First Aid and how to make yourself comfortable when you hadn't got much stuff around you. When I joined the RAF, I already knew Morse Code, which we'd learnt in the Scouts, and I knew a bit about camping — how to make yourself comfortable in awkward positions, which I did. It wasn't supposed to be training for war, but it was very useful.

Supervision, Stevie recalled, was surprisingly lax. It took some time before the new recruits were issued with uniforms, and some were quick to take advantage:

Before we were issued with uniforms, one or two lads went home for a day, and we covered up for them. We had no uniforms and were never checked by Service Police, so we were able to disappear for short periods without anyone noticing. One day there was a sudden clothing parade and we were issued with our uniforms and accessories. One lad whose name was Adams collected his uniform and queued up again calling himself Vince, as Vince had gone home for the day. Adams was about 5ft 8ins tall, whereas Vince was over six feet. When the tailor called the next day, he asked Vince why his uniform was such a bad fit. Vince said it was the only one near his size, and the Sergeant had told him to take it. The tailor sent him to the stores with a chit to refit. This covering up for others was part of our early team spirit.

Life for the newly bonded recruits was sometimes fun, but it could also be dull and dispiriting:

One pouring wet day, we were marched to a football field and stood there hapless. We were wearing overcoats which were soon soggy and leaden; then, soaking wet, we were marched to a cinema where an Air Commodore appeared on stage and demonstrated inflatable dinghies and life jackets. He seemed to find it entertaining, but we airmen, soaked through and cheesed off, saw little point in the exercise.

The medical examinations, blood tests, and vaccinations that were an integral part of RAF life for the new recruits were also something of a trial:

We had several medical examinations, injections and blood tests. The injections were crude and usually involved the same needle being used many times. One vaccination gave me a violent headache which lasted for several days. I did not report sick, as I felt I might fall behind in my training, but I had a sore arm for several months and the scab was still there the following Easter.

Despite this, Stevie got through the induction process with relative ease, and was posted to the Initial Training Wing at Paignton:

I was assessed again at 'Above Average' in night vision and did well at the aptitude tests. When our postings arrived, I was sent to an Initial Training Wing at Paignton. We travelled comfortably by train and I was delighted to be in Devon once again. We were billeted in the Hydro Hotel and I had a room overlooking the sea. We went for a meal and had lashings of bread and margarine and large mugs full of really strong tea.

We were quite a pleasant group and got on very well together. After breakfast we went on parade on the sea front where Drill Corporals had us marching about, saluting, forming columns of three and turning about until several hats fell off. We were told to "Ram your 'ats on your 'eads like crash 'ats!" Then we were marched to a lecture room where a Flight Lieutenant briefed us on what was expected of us in the next six weeks.

The course was demanding. At the end of an intensive six weeks of lectures, Stevie and his fellow recruits had to sit a series of examinations. Many of them failed, and those who did were removed from flying training:

The syllabus was formidable, and we had much to learn and many tests to pass before we were able to begin to fly. I still have one of my old note books and see that we were required to pass tests in signalling, which involved receiving and transmitting in Morse Code (at least eight words a minute by key and four words a minute by lamp), airmanship and theory of flight, navigation including working and applying triangles of velocities on Mercator's Charts, plotting true and air positions, cylindrical and modified polyconic projections, Air Force law, hygiene, aircraft recognition, and

Stevie, pictured second from the right, at Paignton in 1941. Next to him is Vince – you can see why his 5ft 8in uniform didn't fit!

elementary armaments. We took tests along the way, and failure often meant remustering from pilot to other aircrew duties. After six weeks, we had a final series of examinations, and about four in ten failed.

Stevie passed, and was given leave. When he returned to Paignton, he took courses in Maths and Navigation, and was also introduced to clay pigeon shooting:

We were sent on nine days leave but were recalled within a week. Our numbers were already much reduced and, as we had finished the course, there was little to do. However, arrangements had been made for clay pigeon shooting, and we spent many happy hours being taught by experts. There were also opportunities for further study. Some of us brushed up our mathematics and we were able to spend time on plotting navigational courses and working through air and ground speed calculations.

From Paignton, he was posted to Carlisle. When the train taking him north reached Crewe, he had his first encounter with the Navy:

We boarded a train at Paignton to take us to Carlisle. It seemed a long journey, but we were well equipped with sandwiches. We stopped at Crewe and queued at a tea urn. To our surprise, a large group of sailors barged in.

There was a scuffle, and Military Police pushed us back on to the train. After the train left the station, three large sailors came up the corridor carrying a bucket of tea for us! They said they were broke after their leave, so some had caused the scuffle while the rest took a spanner to the urn and poured tea into buckets to drink on the train. We RAF prided ourselves on having initiative, but the Navy showed us a thing or two that day!

Stevie was attached to number 15 EFTS (Elementary Flying Training School) Kingstown at RAF Carlisle. Initially based at RAF Redhill in Surrey, 15 EFTS had relocated to Carlisle in June 1940 following the mass evacuation of the British Expeditionary Force at Dunkirk:

We were transported to the airfield at Carlisle, and billeting officers took us to various houses. I was delighted to be taken to a pleasant house where I lived with a Local Government Officer, his wife and two daughters. I was made very welcome and taken up to a neat and tidy bedroom which had a very comfortable bed. Tea was brought up to me before transport picked me up at the door each morning. I spent comfortable evenings in the living room with the family and we became very friendly. It was a splendid set up.

Stevie went for his first flight on 17 October in a Miles Magister, the two-seater monoplane used for basic training.

The Miles Magister basic trainer monoplane

In an intensive period of training with a series of instructors in the month which followed, Stevie was introduced to the aircraft's cockpit layout and controls. Then he was taught the techniques of straight and level flying; climbing, gliding, and stalling; medium turns; taxiing; taking off into wind; powered approach and landing; gliding approach and landing; spinning; action in the event of fire, and abandoning the aircraft.

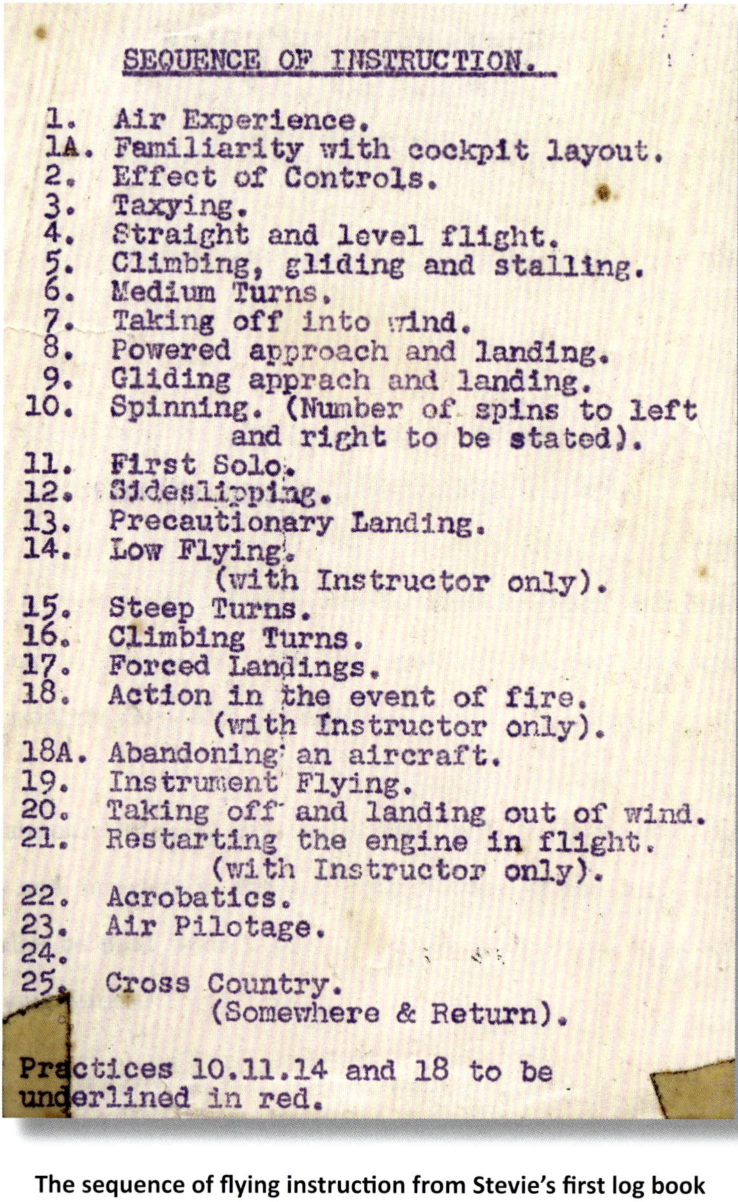

SEQUENCE OF INSTRUCTION.

1. Air Experience.
1A. Familiarity with cockpit layout.
2. Effect of Controls.
3. Taxying.
4. Straight and level flight.
5. Climbing, gliding and stalling.
6. Medium Turns.
7. Taking off into wind.
8. Powered approach and landing.
9. Gliding apprach and landing.
10. Spinning. (Number of spins to left and right to be stated).
11. First Solo.
12. Sideslipping.
13. Precautionary Landing.
14. Low Flying. (with Instructor only).
15. Steep Turns.
16. Climbing Turns.
17. Forced Landings.
18. Action in the event of fire. (with Instructor only).
18A. Abandoning an aircraft.
19. Instrument Flying.
20. Taking off and landing out of wind.
21. Restarting the engine in flight. (with Instructor only).
22. Acrobatics.
23. Air Pilotage.
24.
25. Cross Country. (Somewhere & Return).

Practices 10.11.14 and 18 to be underlined in red.

The sequence of flying instruction from Stevie's first log book

In a letter to his parents written on 28 October, Stevie reported:

Our flying instructors are very patient, and run over things time after time without getting annoyed. My flying is going quite well now, although my landings are still bad. I was hoping to go solo tomorrow, but I do not think I am good enough yet, and I am sure you would rather have a slow son than a dead one.

Less than a week later, on 2 November 1941, he was taken for a test, and then, after some 15 hours of training, he made his first solo flight. His training continued until 17 November, with Stevie practising map reading; instrument flying; side slipping, steep turns and climbing turns; restarting the engine in flight; and precautionary and forced landings. In the period between 17 October and 17 November, he clocked up some 21 hours of dual flying, 15 hours of solo flying, and 2 hours of instrument flying.

Looking back on his time at Carlisle, Stevie reflected:

At the airfield the course was intensive and quite strict, and they didn't let everybody through. I had my first flight in a Miles Magister aircraft on 17 October and did my first solo flight on 2 November. At first, I had been very nervous, but I gained confidence with experience. It's something you never forget, that first solo flight.

Early in the first phase of training you had to learn what to do if the plane got out of control. The easiest way was to go up to a certain height, then shut the engines off and just let it fall out of the sky, kick it about a bit, and then come out of a spin. When it started spinning, you had to take the necessary action to pull it out by using opposite rudder, put the stick forward, switch the engine on, and go straight down into a dive. The first time I tried this, the instructor told me to go up to about 5,000 feet. So, I went up to 5,000 feet, looked over the side and thought, I don't like that much. So, I went up to 6,000, having decided that it was better to give myself another 1,000 feet or so before I started. The next thing an aircraft came spinning down past me. It went straight into the ground and the pilot was killed. I watched that poor chap go down, and said to myself, "Right I'm going to have another 1,000 feet and if it doesn't start up, I'll just jump out."

The official stamp in Stevie's log book which certified the completion of his initial training on 18 November 1941, noted that he had '*shewn aptitude as a pilot navigator*', and recorded that there were no '*special faults in flying which must be watched*'.

Aged just 19, Stevie suited up for his very first flight in 1941

ON THE FRINGES OF HOLLYWOOD: FLYING TRAINING AT WAR EAGLE FIELD, SOUTHERN CALIFORNIA

The weeks that followed opened up a new world for Stevie. He was informed that he had been selected for further flying training in the United States, and he spent the Christmas of 1941 at sea, making the perilous Atlantic crossing to Canada:

> *I was quite surprised to find out that I had been posted to America. We crossed the Atlantic to Canada at Christmas time on a very crowded troopship. Fortunately for me, I'd been on a troopship before the War as a boy at Bideford Grammar School, so I'd got used to rolling my own hammock, and I'd also remembered to take with me some salt-water soap because you can't normally get any lather in cold water. There were also the tricks that the toilets could play! The toilets were in a line from port to starboard, and when the sea was calm, you'd pull the plug and the toilet would flush. But when the sea was rough and the ship was rocking from side to side, the water would slop all over you if you were caught sitting down, and you got a nasty drenching!*

The *SS Bergensfjord*, the ship which took Stevie across the Atlantic to Halifax, Nova Scotia, was a Norwegian ocean liner which had been launched in 1913. She was requisitioned by the War Ministry in November 1940, and converted into a troopship. By the end of the War, she would ferry around 165,000 Allied service personnel across the Atlantic between Britain and America.

The *SS Bergensfjord,* which took Stevie across the Atlantic

In a letter Stevie wrote to his parents on Boxing Day 1941, headed *'Somewhere at Sea'*, he noted:

> *When we awoke, the sea was still rocking the ship, causing many of the lads to be very sea sick. I was quite OK and did not even feel squeegee. To be honest, I quite enjoyed the experience, and I think I should have joined the Navy if the RAF had not wanted me. There certainly seems to be an awful lot of water in the Atlantic, and it seems incredible that we could spend so many days and not see land. All we see is the sea, one other very ancient ship, and two fussy destroyers charging about all over the place to protect us.*

He reported that on Christmas Day, he and his shipmates had been served a special dinner, and that there were parties and concerts all over the ship:

> *It was very good indeed – goose, potatoes, peas, carrots, chicken soup and mixed fruit pudding. We are having a concert, or rather several concerts all over the ship this evening. The one to which I am listening is a sailors' concert and they are all thoroughly enjoying themselves, singing and larking about. We get canned beer from the wet canteen which is made by Barclays and tastes very much like the lager I used to enjoy at The Norbury and The Greyhound.*

Less than a month before the *Bergensfjord* docked in Halifax on 1 January 1942, America had joined Britain in the War. The Japanese had attacked the American Pacific fleet in Pearl Harbour without warning on the morning of 7 December 1941, and four days later, on 11 December, Hitler had declared war on the United States.

While Stevie was in America, he kept a day-by-day diary which gives a fascinating insight into his impressions and experiences in the months between January and August 1942, when the US was getting itself on a war footing and beginning a ferocious struggle with the Japanese Empire in the Pacific. When Stevie disembarked at Halifax, Nova Scotia, late in the afternoon of 1 January, and boarded the train which was to take him to his dispersal unit at Moncton, New Brunswick, the first thing that struck him was that there was no blackout in Canada:

> *The good ship 'Bergensfjord' steamed into Halifax bearing me and many others into a new world. Farewells were taken of all the ship acquaintances, and in the late afternoon we were disembarked and placed on a train to go to Moncton, New Brunswick, our dispersal unit. We were greatly impressed by the size of the engine, although the coaches were very hot. There was no blackout, and we were highly delighted to see cars dashing about with unshielded headlamps, street lamps, lights from the windows of houses, and all these were reflected by a carpet of snow.*

On his first day at Moncton, Stevie discovered to his great delight that there was no food rationing either. On 2 January, he noted in his diary:

The barracks too are most pleasing, being centrally heated and spacious, with excellent shower bath accommodation. This morning after a fair breakfast of porridge, bacon and mash and coffee, we had a pay parade. We had an excellent dinner of soup, beef, potatoes, carrots and macaroni, and as much bread and butter as was required. We had a medical inspection, and then tea of scrambled eggs on toast, bread and butter, and super strawberry jam and apples.

Three days later he wrote to his parents:

I wish you could come over here so that you would realize how nice it is not to have to worry about the blackout and to be able to have as much sugar, butter, meat and fruit as you could possibly eat.

Stevie was to spend a fortnight in Moncton, occasionally being assigned to fatigue duties, but otherwise reading, writing letters, going to the cinema, and being entertained by a variety of friendly Canadians.

On 4 January, he learned that he would be doing his advanced flying training in California:

We were split up into Flying School sections this morning, and I find, to my delight, that I am going to No. 2 BFTS (British Flying Training School), at Lancaster, California. This is about 40 miles from Los Angeles and near Hollywood.

On 17 January, some two weeks after their arrival in Moncton, Stevie and the other cadets assigned to No. 2 BFTS boarded a Canadian Pacific Railway train to start the long transcontinental journey from the east coast of Canada to the west coast of the United States. The journey took five days. They left Moncton in freezing cold, crossed the province of New Brunswick to Trois Pistoles on the St Lawrence River, where they stopped for long enough to do some bobsleigh runs; from there they continued on via Montreal, Toronto, and Detroit to Chicago. In Chicago they changed trains, running south through Kansas City to El Paso in Texas. From El Paso their journey took them to Alamagordo in New Mexico and Yuma in Arizona, then on to the Pacific coast of California. On the train from Chicago, they struck up an easy camaraderie with a group of young Americans who were on their way to join the Marines and the US Army Air Corps:

At Chicago we were transported by a fleet of taxis to the Southern Pacific railway station. There were many Americans on the train on their way to join the Marines and the Army Air Corps, and we were soon on the friendliest of terms with them. We sat up late into the night drinking beer and whisky, far more than was good for me, I think, as I acquired peculiar ideas of the train's motion, but slept very soundly.

Among the party of cadets crossing North America to join No. 2 BFTS was a young man from Chelmsford in Essex, Ivor Davies, then still only eighteen years old. Just after Stevie passed away on 11 April 2020, it emerged that Ivor Davies was the father-in-law of his solicitor, Alisdair Liddle. Like Stevie, Ivor kept a diary, and compiled a photographic record of his time in America. He, Len Gray, and Stevie were not part of the same social circle, but they would rub shoulders daily in California. They completed their training course together, and were presented with their Wings at War Eagle Field at the same passing-out parade.

Unfortunately for Stevie, he fell ill on the journey. When the train arrived at Colton in California on 22 January, he was diagnosed with mumps, and taken to the isolation ward of the nearby County Hospital in San Bernardino. Dr Martin, the doctor assigned to treat him, and the staff of the hospital did everything they could to make him feel welcome, and made a great fuss of him:

Dr Martin visited me every day and kept me well supplied with magazines and chocolates. He was quite a fairy godmother. The staff doctors and nurses, too, contributed magazines and anything else I wanted, and I made many outside friends.

When Stevie was discharged from hospital on Monday 9 February, Dr Martin invited him to stay at his home and took him out for dinner:

We had shrimp cocktails, salad, then the most luscious steak I have ever tasted, and afterwards chocolate pudding. We drove slowly back and admired the oranges growing on either side of the road, and so to bed after talking until well after midnight. What can one say about such generous hospitality? Adjectives fail me.

This was only the start. Dr Martin was determined to make Stevie feel welcome and show him something of California. The following day he took him for a drive through the mountains, and introduced him to many of the people living in the neighbourhood:

The scenery was really marvellous. I was introduced to quite a number of the local people, and they were a fine lot and were obviously genuinely pleased to do anything they could to help me. The generosity of the Americans has to be experienced to be believed, it is really too amazing for words. We returned to an excellent dinner of fried chicken, and afterwards Dr Martin and I spent a long time talking about the War, the Anglo-American relationship etc., and so to bed.

On Wednesday 11 February, Dr Martin and his wife drove Stevie to Los Angeles. They stopped to give him an impression of the city, then took him on to Lancaster and War Eagle Field. After a journey lasting several weeks that had taken him from England across the Atlantic to Canada, and from the eastern seaboard of Canada to southern California, Stevie was finally able to begin his advanced flying training with No. 2 BFTS.

War Eagle Field was situated some five miles from Lancaster, on the fringe of the Mojave Desert. It was not attached to the US military, but run by the

Stevie outside Dr Martin's house in San Bernadino, February 1942

Polaris Flight Academy, a civilian flying school which had been contracted in 1941 to train cadets from the RAF and the Royal Canadian Air Force. Although the training programme proved highly successful, it continued only until December 1942, when the last RAF trainees were presented with their Wings. From the beginning of 1943 until the end of the War in 1945, War Eagle Field trained cadets from the United States Army Air Force.

Unusually in view of the fact that they were training military personnel, the War Eagle Field flying instructors were all civilian pilots; but they were very experienced, with thousands of flying hours between them, and they were well respected by the cadets. Typical of them was Tex Gentry, with whom Stevie did much of his training in May and June 1942. Gentry, who was 31 at the time, had himself done his first flight with one of the instructors at the Polaris Flight Academy when he was just 17 in a Curtiss JN-4 Jenny, an open-cockpit First World War biplane. He gained his Wings two years later, and clocked up many hours doing displays, exhibitions, and charter flying before joining the Polaris Flight Academy in January 1942, just before the arrival of Stevie's cohort.

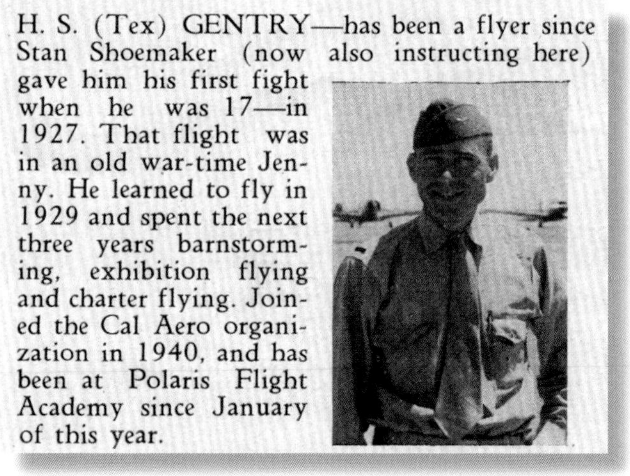
H. S. (Tex) GENTRY—has been a flyer since Stan Shoemaker (now also instructing here) gave him his first fight when he was 17—in 1927. That flight was in an old war-time Jenny. He learned to fly in 1929 and spent the next three years barnstorming, exhibition flying and charter flying. Joined the Cal Aero organization in 1940, and has been at Polaris Flight Academy since January of this year.

Experienced flying instructor Tex Gentry, taken from *Salute* Magazine

Forced to start some three weeks behind his fellow trainees because of his attack of mumps, Stevie did his first flight at War Eagle Field on 12 February in a Boeing Stearman PT-13B biplane. It was a stiff test in an unfamiliar aircraft, which involved taxiing; take off; landing; climbing; gliding; stalling; spinning; medium turns, steep turns, and gliding turns. But Stevie was full of confidence. He wrote to his parents that evening:

> *'I am about three weeks behind on the course now, but I think I shall be able to pull up on the others without too much trouble. Stearmans differ a bit from Magisters, but I do not think it will take me very long to solo. I was surprised to find that some of the lads who have been here three weeks have not yet solo'd.'* In his diary he noted, *'Went up for a first flip on Stearmans this morning and made quite good progress. My landings were quite good,*

RAF trainees being shown a Boeing Stearman PT-13B

and I feel I should solo in about four hours.' The next day he added, *'Some more flying today in which my instructor confirmed my belief.'*

13 February, Stevie's second day of flying, was marred by a tragic accident. LAC Maier Ben Himelstaub, a Polish Jew who had escaped from Poland when it was overrun by the Germans and joined the RAFVR, was killed when he walked into the spinning propeller of one of the Stearmans. Stevie noted in his diary: *'Tragedy was added to the day by a cadet being cut up by a prop.'* Himelstaub's body could not be shipped back to England, so he was buried with full military honours in Lancaster Cemetery. He is still remembered at the annual ceremony held to mark Veterans Day in America, when a Union Jack is placed on his grave.

Stevie's prediction that it would not take him long to solo turned out to be accurate. He had his first solo flight on the Stearman, on Monday 16 February, only four days after beginning his Primary Training. Flying from War Eagle Field over the Mojave Desert was, of course, very different from flying from Carlisle, and it brought fresh challenges:

The first thing you needed to be able to do was control the aircraft, and the second thing was to look for an emergency landing ground wherever you were. Easy enough in America because you had about a million miles of desert! Except sometimes people landed in the desert and didn't know where the hell they were; then they would need to set light to the aeroplane to get a smoke column going to get rescued. There was one bloke who went off on a cross-country run, mistook his course and finished up in Mexico. Mexico was not in the War at the time, so he was put under arrest, and did not get freed until Mexico joined the Allied coalition against Germany.

On 5 March Stevie had his first experience of night flying, and it reinforced his determination to become a bomber pilot. In his diary he noted, '*I did my first night flight in the evening and I thought it was great fun. I am even more sure now that I want to fly a heavy night bomber.*'

He went on to observe:

We barely did any night flying in America. They always had masses of lights turned on, and we were flying over the desert, so you could see for miles. I remember the instructor saying, "When you've taken off, make sure you look behind you to check you are going in a straight line." What we found was when you turned around to see what was going on behind, it was very difficult to then keep the aircraft straight and level, so we just took off and flew straight ahead to the point we were aiming at with the compass — but the Americans obviously looked back to see where they had been!

There were another couple of 'firsts' recorded in his dairy. On 25 March, he noted, '*First formation flying today, and I was fascinated to be flying so near other planes.*' And on 26 March, '*First cross-country this afternoon. In the evening, which was really wondrous, with bright moon and sparkling stars, I performed my first night solo and so happily.*'

During his time at Moncton, Stevie had struck up what would be a lifelong friendship with a fellow cadet, Len Gray, whom he describes in his diary as '*a canny Scot*'. Len and Stevie were posted to War Eagle Field together, and after Stevie was discharged from hospital and settled in at War Eagle Field, they were soon enjoying a busy social life at weekends, and making many friends among the local community.

On Saturday 21 February, Len arranged a blind date with two American girls, Shirley and Mary, who lived in the nearby town of Whittier. The four of them got on well, and quickly developed an easy friendship. Stevie noted,

'Shirley, Mary, Len and I drove all over the countryside, and had a thoroughly enjoyable time.' On Friday 27 February he and Len hitched a series of lifts from War Eagle Field to Los Angeles, where they visited the *Green Jade* and the *Brown Derby*, two fashionable bars frequented by Hollywood film stars. They stayed overnight in a hotel named *The Bonnie Brier* on Hollywood Boulevard, then made their way to Whittier. They spent a day rambling with Shirley and Mary, and went to the cinema in the evening to see Diana Durbin and Charles Laughton in *It Started with Eve*. After spending the night in the *William Penn* hotel, they rejoined Shirley and Mary, and the four of them '*made a ten-inch record and two six-inch records of our adventures. We had dinner at Shirley's house, and then Mary drove us to see the beauty spots we had missed seeing before. Shirley's father drove us and the girls to Lancaster, where we bade them a fond adieu.*'

The following weekend, they met up again with Shirley and Mary, and on Sunday 8 March, Shirley drove them to Long Beach:

> *We were subjected to many curious stares on the Beach, but had a thoroughly good time motor-boating, auto scooting, shooting, ghost training, etc. We had an excellent lunch and returned to Shirley's house. We went out again and had pots of ice cream at 'The Spinning Wheel'. Len and I then departed, returning to Lancaster in two very long hitches, and so to bed having spent another jolly weekend.*

Stevie with Mary and Shirley at Long Beach, 8 March 1942

They continued to meet with Shirley and Mary at weekends, alternating flying with pleasure. On 21 April Stevie completed his Primary Training on the Stearman, and he and the other pilots selected to progress to Basic Training, the next stage of the course, were given a week's leave.

On Saturday 25 April they found themselves rubbing shoulders with Hollywood film stars. Along with eight other RAF cadets and ten trainee pilots from the US Army Air Corps, they were invited to a party at the mansion of Mr Harvey Seeley Mudd in Beverly Hills. Harvey Mudd was a wealthy mining engineer. He had founded the Cyprus Mining Corporation in 1916 with his father, and when his father died in 1926, he took over as its chairman. The Corporation developed copper mines in Cyprus, and copper became Cyprus's largest export, making Harvey Mudd's fortune. Stevie's diary records the occasion:

> *'We were driven to Benedict Canyon Drive No.1240, the residence of Mr Harvey Mudd, by Flight Lieutenant Martin Green. Attended a party where we met the film stars Basil Rathbone and Nigel Bruce and a host of celebrities. A very jolly time was had by all.'* In a letter written shortly afterwards to his parents, he added, *'It was a warm afternoon and most of us wanted to swim, but had not brought our costumes. However, some bright person suggested that we could easily improvise costumes with towels and safety pins, and this we did. We provided quite an interesting contrast against the girls with their perfectly cut habits, but we enjoyed ourselves immensely. Quite a revolutionary pattern for Hollywood!'*

Martyn Green performing in Gilbert and Sullivan – taken from *Salute* Magazine

Flight Lieutenant William Martin Green, the Station Adjutant at War Eagle Field who drove Stevie, Len, and the other RAF cadets to Harvey Mudd's party, was an internationally famous Gilbert and Sullivan singer, better known under his stage name Martyn Green. Born in 1899, he had served in the Army during the First World War and sustained a serious leg wound from which it took him a year to recover. Undeterred, he embarked on a highly successful singing and acting career, and in the 1930s he became the principal comedian of the D'Oyly Carte Opera Company. He had already made a name for himself in America before Stevie encountered him, having received rave reviews for his performances in the D'Oyly Carte's New York Gilbert and Sullivan seasons in 1934 and 1939. He broke off his singing career to volunteer for the RAFVR in April 1941, and was posted to War Eagle Field as the RAF Administrative Officer when the training programme started there. When the programme ended, he went on to serve in Iceland, India, and Burma, and left the RAF in September 1945 with the rank of Squadron Leader. He resumed his singing career, but in 1953 he moved to America, where he was in great demand, and appeared in a series of films and stage plays. He spent his final years in Hollywood, where he died in 1975, close to his old RAF stamping ground at War Eagle Field.

Later, Stevie would recall:

> *Harvey Mudd had a large swimming pool. There were containers, each with two bottles of champagne, right the way around the pool. He had uniformed staff coming round, and when you'd drunk your half, they threw the rest of it in the swimming pool and gave you another one. It was quite incredible. The drink was unlimited and the food excellent. He looked after us very well, I don't know why – perhaps he just liked our British accents!*

Stevie (left) relaxing in Harvey Mudd's swimming pool at his Hollywood residence. Harvey Mudd himself is in the centre.

This was probably not the only reason Harvey Mudd invited Stevie and the other trainees to his party. With the US now allied with Britain in the struggle against Germany and Japan, prominent Americans, including Hollywood film stars, were eager to be seen to support the War effort. The RAF for its part was keen to foster good relations with its American hosts, and between March and December 1942 War Eagle Field produced a magazine called *Salute*. Its aim, in the words of the Foreword to the first issue, was '*to let the world know of our existence and activities*'. The June 1942 issue celebrated the first anniversary of No. 2 BFTS and the Anglo-American alliance of which it had become a symbol:

> *Over 50,000 flying hours ago, No. 2 BFTS was born. Those 50,000 hours indicate work done, training accomplished, friends made with American men and American methods. Those 50,000 flying hours have been carefully entered into the log books without a single flying fatality. Those 50,000 hours, too, have a significance that cannot be recorded: they express cooperation between nations as well as between men. They add to the meaning of Alliance, and that as we make war as friends, so shall we write the peace.*

The same issue contained a letter from the President of the Polaris Flight Academy, Mr. C.C. Moseley:

> *Much has been written about the RAF training programme at Polaris Flight Academy and other American flight schools, created under the lend-lease program.*
>
> *It seems to me, however, that one of the most significant features has been overlooked in these articles. I refer to the fact that the British aircraftsmen who have come here during the past year have proved to be the most effective ambassadors of good will ever to bring our two great nations into close understanding and friendship.*
>
> *You gentlemen, and those who have preceded you, have brought a new accord between Britain and the people of the United States. During the past year, we have been together both professionally and socially. We have acquired a new understanding of people from Britain: you have similarly secured a more intimate understanding of the people of America. You have found that 'Main Street' not 'Wall Street' is the real America.*
>
> *By your exemplary conduct, you have won our admiration and respect. The War ultimately will end, but those who came here as Leading Aircraftsmen and return home as military pilots are creating an international accord that will endure forever.*

As these words show, Stevie, Len, and the other young RAF trainees posted to War Eagle Field found themselves in the vanguard of the great alliance which would defeat Germany and Japan. In their day-to-day contacts with their American hosts, both professional and social, they did much to help cement what Churchill would dub the special relationship between Britain and the United States.

After the party at Harvey Mudd's Beverly Hills mansion, Stevie and Len again stayed at the *Bonnie Brier* hotel, and as they were walking down Hollywood Boulevard, they were approached by Anna Neagle, one of the leading English film stars of the time, who recognised their uniforms:

> *In the evening Len and I were walking along Hollywood Boulevard when to my delight and amazement we met Anna Neagle. She had just come out from England, so we were able to hear some more recent news from her. She was very quiet and unassuming, but had a beautiful voice which thrilled me very much.*

Anna Neagle was the professional name of the English stage and film actress Florence Majorie Wilcox. When Stevie and Len met her, she was in Hollywood to make the film *Forever and a Day*, which co-starred Ray Milland, C. Aubrey Smith, Claude Rains, Charles Laughton, and Buster Keaton. When shooting finished, she returned to England. In 1949 she was voted the most popular film actress in Britain. She also appeared to great acclaim in numerous stage roles, and was made a DBE in 1969 for services to the theatre.

For the rest of their week's leave, Stevie and Len hitchhiked to Santa Barbara. Then as now, Santa Barbara was home to the very rich, and they were entertained, wined and dined by a succession of well-heeled Americans and British expats. They were invited to stay at a ranch, did some horse riding and swimming, went to the cinema, and were taken to watch a baseball match. They also visited the Spanish Mission, and there they made the acquaintance of the well-known newspaper and radio journalist Alistair Cooke. He was in California preparing a series of programmes for the BBC on the American War Effort, broadcasting talks to the Empire, and writing for *The Times*:

> *He asked us, "Where are you from?" and Len in his dour Scottish accent replied, "We are from hum (home)". Alistair Cooke grinned and said, "I have Scottish ancestry too," and started talking to us. He took us up into the mountains in his car to admire the scenery, and then drove us down to the sea, where we had an excellent lunch seated on a bench under a palm tree.*

I'd told him that I had worked as a controller in ARP in London and that my house had been bombed, and this prompted him to take us to the ARP Centre in Santa Barbara, which had been set up in the Court House. We were shown around by an obliging Local Government Officer with whom I compared notes on Air Raid Precautions. I talked to him about the procedures we had put in hand to deal with bombing, and discovered that they'd got the same forms printed out as we had in England. Our experience of the Blitz had helped them to prepare.

When Alistair Cooke died in 2004, the manuscript of his travels in wartime America was discovered among his papers. It was published in 2006 under the title, *Alistair Cooke's American Journey: Life on the Home Front in the Second World War*. The back cover of the English first edition, published by Penguin, features a photograph of Stevie and Len sitting with Alistair Cooke. The caption under the photograph described them simply as *'British fliers'*. When friends contacted him to tell him that he was pictured with Alistair Cooke on the back cover of the book, Stevie wrote to Penguin and identified Len

Len Gray and Stevie with Alastair Cooke, 27 April 1942

and himself as the unnamed airmen. In the second edition of the book, a new caption was inserted under the photograph, in which Stevie and Len were identified. Stevie was given a copy of the American edition, which contained a second photograph of him and Len, and they each received a warm letter from Alistair Cooke's son, John Byrne Cooke, thanking them for contacting Penguin and saying how delighted his father would have been to know that they had survived the War:

I can't tell you how pleased I was to learn of your communications with Stuart Profitt at Penguin. I'm certain my father would have been absolutely delighted, as I am, not only to know that you both survived the War, but that you have kept in touch with each other and have lived full lives.

News of Stevie's first-hand experience of ARP work spread. Three days after visiting the ARP Centre in the Santa Barbara Court House, he was having lunch with the president of a local bank and the coordinator of the Civil Defence Services, and informing them that their Report Centre was set up on similar lines to his own Report Centre in Thornton Heath. Later that day, they invited him to a Wardens' Meeting:

They had just had a lecture on the effects of bombing when I appeared on the scene, and when I was introduced, I was asked to give a talk on dealing with air raids. I spouted on the subject for about twenty minutes and got a pretty good reception. One man went as far as to say he had learned more from my talk than he could have learned from hours of lectures, but I am sure he was just being super-polite.

The devastation wreaked by the Luftwaffe during the Blitz had been well publicised in America, and by the time Stevie arrived in California, numerous charities had been formed under the umbrella of the British War Relief Society to offer non-military aid (food, clothes, medical supplies, etc.) to Britain. During their stay at Santa Barbara, Stevie and Len attended a fête organised by the local branch of the British War Relief Society as guests of honour.

A few days later, on 4 May 1942, Stevie wrote to his parents:

I have not mentioned the British War Relief Society, have I? A lot of people in Santa Barbara voluntarily work hard for a few hours every day at making bandages, collecting metal and tin foil, and generally doing all they can to raise money for Britain. They usually remain anonymous as far as Britain is concerned, but they certainly have my very deepest respect and gratitude for the hard jobs they do without as much as an encouraging letter of thanks to

Stevie with Len Gray at a 'Bundles for Britain' rally, Santa Barbara, 1 May 1942

> *help them along. They also run a canteen where members of the Forces can get free sandwiches and drinks.*

From Santa Barbara Stevie and Len made their way to Los Angeles, and from there to Whittier, where they spent the weekend with Shirley and Mary, making another excursion to Long Beach before returning to War Eagle Field and the serious business of flying.

Stevie was feeling confident. In his letter to his parents he noted: *'I did quite well in our examinations at the end of the Primary Course, coming out 4th in a crowd of about 50, so naturally I feel quite pleased about it.'* On 5 May Stevie began Basic Training in a Vultee BT-13 Valiant. The Vultee was more powerful than the Stearman he had flown in Primary Training; it had a 450hp Pratt & Whitney radial engine, and flying it necessitated the use of wing flaps. The Vultee had fixed landing gear and operated without hydraulics, so that the wing flaps had to be manually cranked.

Stevie's summary of his first flight in a Vultee was, *'Much perturbed by the great amount of work there is to perform.'* But on the following day, 6 May, he wrote in his diary: *'Went up for second trip in Vultee and had a pretty good time, finding that I was getting procedure taped off.'* On 8 May he did his first solo flight in the Vultee, and *'felt quite happy about it.'* The following days saw him practising steep turns, climbing turns, and aerobatics, after which he progressed to formation and cross-country flying. On 27 May he did a cross-country trip as First Pilot with Tex Gentry, noting:

> *I had quite a pleasant dual cross-country to Johannesburg and Lake Arrowhead and back to Polaris. Lake Arrowhead looked particularly beautiful, the water was blue and clear, and the scenery very pretty.*

Two days later he went on his first cross-country solo:

> *A solo cross-country today with other cadets to Doggett and Needles (400 miles), which I thoroughly enjoyed. Many and varied were the conversations we carried out over the radio: "Hello One Zero Three calling, have lost my map, where am I?" "Are you sure you're on the right course?" "Where are you?"*

The following day, 28 May, all the trainees were assembled for a group photograph:

No.2 BFTS, Polaris Flight Academy, 28 May 1942. Len Gray and Stevie are fourth and fifth from the left in the second row.

Stevie pictured on the wing of a Vultee BT-13 Valiant

A few days later, on 3 June, Stevie flew with Tex Gentry to the US Army Air Force training base at Oxnard:

> *Flew dual to Oxnard, which is a US Air Force Primary School. I was amazed to have a lad come up to me, salute, and say, "May I look at your plane, Sir?" Spent quite a pleasant afternoon there, then I returned to Polaris and performed some solo formation flying, which I thoroughly enjoyed.*

On the weekend of 6-7 June, Stevie and Len spread their wings in a more metaphorical sense, and made their way to Pasadena on a whirlwind blind date:

> *We met Barbara and Margaret Craighill and spent a pretty amusing afternoon together. After dinner Barbara drove us down to the Mexican and Chinese markets, where we rambled around for a long time. Then we went on to Hollywood, and later returned and had supper at a drive-in, which we thoroughly enjoyed. We had breakfast at Barbara's house, and we were entertained by Barbara playing the harp. In the afternoon we went for a picnic in the mountains, which was thoroughly enjoyed by everyone. Then we rushed back to camp and bed.*

Another view of Stevie on the wing of a Vultee BT-13 Valiant

Stevie's hectic social life did not detract from his flying. Four days later, on 11 June, he successfully completed his Basic Training on the Vultee. On Saturday 13 June, he and his fellow trainees were taken by bus from War Eagle Field to Los Angeles, where they took part in a military parade in support of the Allied war effort. After that, they were given a week's leave before proceeding to Advanced Training, the third and final element of the course.

Stevie and Len made their way to Santa Barbara, where they stayed with an English couple, the Lejeunes, with whom they had become friendly. On Sunday 14 June they went to a garden party held by the Canadian Legion where they met many of the people who had befriended them on previous visits. On Monday 15 June, a Scot by the name of Mrs Simpson drove them up to Braemar Ranch in the hills above Santa Barbara overlooking the Pacific. There they met Major McEwan, who had been a cavalry officer in the First World War. *'He had a very pretty step-daughter and niece, and Len and I were soon paddling happily in the Pacific with them.'* The following day, Mrs Simpson again drove them up to Braemar Ranch, taking them for lunch on the way:

> *Major McEwan again made us very welcome, and Patsy, Jean, Len and I went for another swim in the Pacific. Mrs Simpson drove us back to town after a few beers with the McEwans on the porch of their ranch. In the evening we met a lieutenant in the Marines and got quite happy at various cocktail bars, before finally finishing up with hamburgers and ice cream at 2am.*

Stevie and Len Gray at the McEwans' Ranch, Santa Barbara, 18 June 1942

On the Wednesday they watched the filming of a naval battle using model boats, and then went sailing. The following day they moved on to the home of a Mr and Mrs Grant, who lived in Hope Ranch, a community known for horse riding, which lies along the coast immediately to the west of Santa Barbara. The Grants, who put them up for the rest of the week, gave them lunch, then took them for another visit to Braemar Ranch:

> *Major McEwan lent Len and me a couple of .22 rifles, and we did some shooting. In the evening we went up to a hill overlooking the sea, and the Major prepared an excellent barbeque of leg of lamb, washed down by copious pots of lager beer.*

BBQ at the McEwans' Ranch, Santa Barbara, 18 June 1942

On the following day, a Mrs Perkins, another resident of Hope Ranch, arranged a buffet supper for them:

> *It was quite a classy affair, with evening dress worn by the guests. Two very charming and beautiful girls, Barbara Hitchcock and Margaret Balcom, had been invited to accompany us, and we thoroughly enjoyed ourselves. Later the four of us went to see the film 'This Above All', and after a few drinks the girls drove us back to the Grants' house. Mrs Perkins had given us ten dollars so that we could enjoy the evening, and we returned just over a dollar to her!*

> *The next day we went to look over the horses performing in a junior horse show, and in the afternoon, we went to the show itself. Then we rang up*

Margaret Balcom, and arranged to meet up with her and her sister Barbara. The four of us painted Santa Barbara a very mild shade of pink. We had a couple of drinks at a most exclusive club, the Coral Casino, and then went for a drive along the coast, which looked very pretty in the moonlight. After that we had a most sumptuous dinner at a Spanish-type restaurant named 'El Pasao'—fruit cocktails, soup, fried trout, salad sweets and wine. We did a spot of dancing, and then the girls took us home.

On the Sunday, we went on to Ventura, where we were treated to a fried chicken lunch. We stopped at a ranch in Fillmore and picked some oranges, then made our way back to Lancaster.

Back at War Eagle Field, Stevie wrote to his parents to tell them the story of his leave:

Here I am back in camp again, with my arms rather a deep brown and the skin peeling off my nose — the only souvenirs I have of a most enjoyable leave that has just ended. Len and I have had the time of our lives. This leave differed quite considerably from the last in that we met many more people of our own age, most of whom were wealthy and ran their own cars, and most of them were horse owners too. Really, we could not have wished for anything better!

At the end, he added:

We have just started on our final stage of the course, with the Wings exam only four weeks away, so you can imagine there is plenty to distract my attention.

Stevie would continue his busy social life with Len at weekends, with more excursions to Whittier and Santa Barbara. His diary stops on 5 July (its covers and the pages for the rest of 1942 are lost) but it seems that at some point during that month, he and Len were again the guests of Harvey Mudd, and that their partying put them at risk of a late return to War Eagle Field. Many years later, Stevie reminisced:

The next morning, we were a bit late going back, so Harvey Mudd said to us, "You'd better borrow one of my aeroplanes to get back, or you'll be late on parade tomorrow morning." So, he lent us an aeroplane. He'd never seen us fly before, but we flew back to our airfield with his pilot on board to return the plane. I got my ear clipped for that, because if we'd had an accident, the RAF would have had to foot the bill! But that was life in California in 1942.

Fun though the weekends may have been, Advanced Training at War Eagle Field required total concentration and commitment, and Stevie had to master a third and final aircraft: the Harvard AT-6. The Harvard had a bigger engine than the Stearman, and a retractable undercarriage, but Stevie did not take long to get the hang of it. After an hour and a half of instruction, he did his first solo flight in a Harvard on 24 June, and progressed quickly to Aerobatics, sometimes solo, and sometimes with Mr Bonzo, his principal instructor for Advanced Training. In July, the last month of the course, he went on to do intensive periods of instrument flying, formation flying and night flying. This included flights with fellow trainees, in which he would sometimes be First Pilot, and sometimes Second Pilot and Observer.

On 19 July, Stevie wrote to his parents:

> *We have just finished quite a busy week of flying, and I have now finished all my night flying on this course. We did some night cross-country flying last Tuesday, Wednesday and Thursday, and it was really quite good fun. At first, I got the impression that I was going to fly into the mountains instead of over them, and this was quite peculiar, as we had a good 2,000 ft clearance over most of them. On Thursday evening we flew on a night cross-country which would correspond to a flight (in distance) from London to Salisbury and back, though we were flying more than three times faster than the train, principally over the desert.*
>
> *We have quite a number of cross-country flights to do still, and some instrument and radio-beam work, and then the flying training is over. Next weekend we get our Wings examination, which promises to be a stiff one, and we are all trying our hardest to do some swatting, but this becomes very difficult because of the heat, the radio in the next hut, and our last leave over here.*

He added:

> *Apparently, no more British courses are coming to this School for training, so I just got in at the right time, as I am sure there cannot be a more pleasant training camp anywhere. I shall have a great many stories to tell you when I get back of the very fine times the Americans have given us.*

On 31 July, Stevie did his last flight in a Harvard with Wing Commander George Greaves, the RAF Chief Flying Instructor at War Eagle Field. This flight, which Stevie described in his log book as a *'check ride'*, marked the formal completion of his Advanced Training. Soon he would be presented with his Wings. On 5 August 1942, he wrote an excited letter to his parents:

> *You will no doubt be pleased to hear that, at long last, I have passed my flying and ground examinations, and will very shortly—in about half an hour as a matter of fact — get my WINGS!*

Stevie receives his Wings at War Eagle Field, 5 August 1942

Personalised Brass Polaris Flight Academy Graduation Badge given to Stevie at the Wings presentation ceremony

I heard on Saturday night that I had passed the Navigation Theory and Plot, which relieved my mind considerably. Len got through as well, and he and I spent a very jolly final weekend in Santa Barbara. When we returned, we found that we had passed the rest of the subjects as we had anticipated, so naturally we felt very happy. Well over 40% of our original mob fell by the wayside, so we who have got through consider that we have done pretty well.

15.00 hrs or 3 p.m

Well, I have just been presented with my Wings and Stripes, and so now I feel absolutely on top of the world! The camp, or my room in particular, seems to be crowded with people, and this is not very conducive to letter writing. Anyway, I'm too excited to write any more, and I have to keep fingering my Wings to make sure that it is not all a dream.

Ivor Davies, the fellow trainee who would become the father-in-law of Stevie's solicitor, received his Wings at War Eagle Field at the same parade. This picture, made available by Ivor's family, shows Ivor at the salute at the moment of his presentation. Stevie is standing in the row immediately behind him. He is fourth from the left, waiting to go forward to be presented with his own Wings.

Ivor Davies gets his Wings. Stevie is waiting to be presented in the row behind, fourth from the right [Photograph: Alisdair Liddle]

Hollywood autographs from the August 1942 edition of *Salute* magazine

The issue of the War Eagle Field magazine *Salute* which appeared in August 1942, at the time that Stevie, Len, Ivor and the rest of their cohort gained their Wings, contained a two-page spread under the caption: *Happy Landings And Good Luck from Hollywood.* Among the Hollywood celebrities whose autographs were reproduced were: Charles Boyer, Basil Rathbone, Herbert Marshall, Moira Shearer, Reginald Gardiner, Anna Lee, Spencer Tracey, Cary Grant, Gladys Cooper, William Edmunds, Conrad Veidt, William Powell, Nigel Bruce, Edmund Gwenn, Alfred Hitchcock, Tyrone Power, Ronald Colman, Brian Aherne, Joan Fontaine, Mary Pickford, and Kay Francis. In reaching out to the newly qualified British pilots who had been its neighbours and were now about to be thrown into the War in Europe, Hollywood was doing its bit to cement the special relationship.

Among the trainees Stevie met at War Eagle Field was LAC William 'Bill' Reid, who graduated shortly before him, in June 1942. Bill Reid would go on to serve with 61 Squadron in Bomber Command. On the night of 3 November 1943 his Lancaster LM360 was attacked twice by enemy fighters en route to Düsseldorf. The Navigator was killed, the Wireless Operator fatally wounded, and Bill Reid himself and his Flight Engineer suffered multiple injuries. But Bill, having memorised the course, pressed on to the target, completed his bombing run, and flew back home navigating by the moon and the pole star. In and out of consciousness, he somehow managed to land at RAF Shipdham in Norfolk. He was awarded the Victoria Cross. The last sentence of his citation summarises the extraordinary bravery of his actions that night.

Bill Reid, later Victoria Cross recipient, at War Eagle Field in 1942

> *Wounded in two attacks, without oxygen, suffering severely from cold, his Navigator dead, his Wireless Operator fatally wounded, his aircraft crippled and defenceless, F/Lt Reid showed superb courage and leadership in penetrating a further 200 miles into enemy territory to attack one of the most strongly defended targets in Germany, every additional mile increasing the hazards of the long and perilous journey home. His tenacity and devotion to duty were beyond praise.*

For Stevie, Len Gray, Ivor Davies and the others who completed their flying training successfully, War Eagle Field turned out to be a very fortunate posting. Arriving as they did soon after Pearl Harbour and America's entry into the War, they were welcomed wherever they went, not only as allies, but as friends. Never since the War of Independence can relations between Americans and Britons have been warmer than in the opening months of 1942. But for all the opportunities presented by social life, a posting to War

Bill Reid's battered Lancaster LM360, photographed the morning after his return from the Düsseldorf raid for which he was awarded the VC

Eagle Field was not a dream ticket to America for all the trainees. Between weekends, the course was very demanding; standards were high, and so was the failure rate. Of the trainees from Stevie's intake at No. 2 BFTS, only just over half graduated, with over forty per cent failing to complete training. Tragically, some found the shame of failure unbearable:

> *I remember one trainee whose father had bought him a very nice silver cigarette case for his 21st birthday. He failed the course and was posted to Canada, and when he arrived he hanged himself. It was very sad, but lots of people could not bear the shame of failure; there were a number of suicides, but he was the only one I knew personally.*

The RAF did its best to compensate. Those who did not manage to become pilots were trained for other duties. Many served as Flight Engineers, Navigators, Bomb Aimers, Wireless Operators or Gunners in Bomber Command, and it was not at all unusual for them to be commissioned before the pilots who were the captains of the aircraft in which they flew. While wearing Wings may have conferred glamour and prestige, it was by no means always a fast ticket to promotion, and Stevie and many others had to work their way up through the ranks, and do lengthy stints of operational flying before they were promoted.

When Stevie and Len departed from California, they left a gap in the lives of their American friends. Mary wrote to Stevie from Whittier on 18 November 1942:

> *I was so happy to receive your letter on Monday. It sounded so natural, it seemed as though you were here talking to me personally, which reminds me of last Sunday when Shirley and I decided we would listen to those records we all made quite some time ago. We were all gathered in a group awaiting that familiar joke about the two seagulls 'Peter' and 'Paul' and Len's Scottish 'burbling' when, to our great disappointment, we discovered that the records are worn down so much that we were only able to catch a few words here and there. Evidently, we didn't cut the records deep enough when we made them. The next time you and Len take a flying course at Lancaster, we will know better.*
>
> *The good old state of California is about the same as when you were here. Perhaps a little colder, but the desert is just as barren. Shirley is doing her part for defence. She is now working at Douglas Aircraft on the swing shift — 4pm. to 12am. I don't see very much of her during the week, but we are nearly always together at weekends (as usual). She wants you to relay Len's address so that she may write to him.*
>
> *At present I am secretary to the Head of the English Department here at Whittier High School, but I intend to go into a defence plant as secretary in a short time. It seems to be the regular thing to do in this part of the country.*
>
> *Well, Stevie, that about covers the news for this time. I sincerely hope that everything goes well with you and your parents. If by chance you should stumble across Leonard, give him my regards and best wishes.*
>
> *Let me know from time to time how things are going with you. I do enjoy receiving your letters. Best of luck!*
>
> *As ever,*
>
> *Mary*

Stevie would never return to California, and he would never again see Mary or any of the other friends he made there again. But his time in America left a deep impression on him. His face would light up whenever he reminisced about the kindness and generosity shown to him, the magnificence of the mountain scenery, or the sheer joy of flying from War Eagle Field. Years later, he would record the delight he experienced '*in flying over California, bounded by the Pacific, the backbone of the Rockies, and the impressive Desert around Death Valley'*; and in his last days, he spoke with great affection of Dr Martin, who had treated him in hospital, taken him into his home, and given him the psychological boost he needed to embark on his flying training weeks behind schedule. As for Mary, she and Stevie clearly had a genuine affection for each other, and had they met at a different time under different circumstances, their lives might have turned out very differently. But in August 1942, the Allies were on the back foot, and the outcome of the War was very much in the balance. Singapore had fallen to the Japanese; General MacArthur, the Commander-in-Chief of American forces in the Pacific, had been forced to abandon the Philippines and retreat to Australia; and Hitler had defeated France, overrun much of Europe, and made huge inroads into Russia. Mary and Stevie, like millions of other young men and women, found themselves caught up in the struggle for humanity and civilisation; and they were both in their own way determined to do their bit to serve the greater cause. The Americans rightly call their generation the Greatest Generation. We are, all of us, in their debt.

War Eagle Field was deemed surplus to requirements at the end of the War, and trained no more pilots; it was purchased by Los Angeles County, and today houses a prison complex known as the Mira Loma Detention Centre. But many of the original buildings are still standing, and the runways on which Stevie, Len, Bill Reid, Ivor Davies and the others learned their craft are still easily identifiable.

Proudly sporting their Wings, Stevie and his fellow trainees left War Eagle Field on 6 August, and made the return transcontinental train journey from California to Moncton. They arrived at Moncton on 11 August, and on 22 August they boarded a ship at Halifax to take them home. But they were forced to return to port after they were involved in a collision with an American destroyer. They had to wait until 5 September to be ferried back across the Atlantic in the *Queen Mary*, and it was not until 11 September that they finally docked at Gourock in the Firth of Clyde.

There were to be no more sumptuous meals and none of the other perks of life at War Eagle Field. Returning to England with its blackout and rationing was, Stevie noted, *'a shock'*. He now had to decide whether to convert to fighter planes or heavy bombers. True to his intention, he volunteered for bombers.

Len Gray, second from right, went on to fly Whirlwind fighters with 263 Squadron, seen here at RAF Warmwell in the summer of 1943

Len Gray opted for fighters. After completing his further training, he was posted in March 1943 to No. 263 Squadron at RAF Warmwell in Dorset, which flew Westland Whirlwinds, twin-engine fighter bombers designed for low level attack. On 24 October 1943 six Whirlwinds from 263 Squadron were detailed to carry out reconnaissance on the Cherbourg shipping lanes. They photographed *SS Münsterland*, a 6,000-ton German merchantman, in the Inner harbour at Cherbourg, and Len was among the pilots detailed to make an immediate attack on it. He was hit by flak during his bombing run. Falling out of the formation, with his starboard engine smoking heavily, he was seen to ditch his stricken aircraft, and was reported in the Squadron records as *'missing under circumstances which give hope that he may still be alive'*. In November news came through that he had been captured and interned as a POW in eastern Germany. Len made his escape as the Red Army approached, and the German camp guards themselves started to flee. He eventually made it home, and he and Stevie remained in touch, reminiscing about their time at War Eagle Field, until Len passed away in February 2012.

BACK IN ENGLAND: BECOMING A LANCASTER PILOT

By the time Stevie signalled his intention to fly heavy aircraft, he had logged over 237 hours flying time, but all of his training up to that point had been on small single-engine aircraft. Before he could begin operational flying, he had to do several more months of intensive training to master the very different techniques involved in piloting bombers. In September 1942, less than two weeks after returning from America, he was posted to Number 12 AFU (Advanced Flying Unit) at RAF Grantham in Lincolnshire, to begin the process of conversion.

On 24 September he did his first flight in a twin-engine aircraft, the Airspeed Oxford:

The Airspeed Oxford was a low wing monoplane of wood and fabric construction powered by two Armstrong Siddeley Cheetah engines. The maximum permitted speed in a dive was said to be 270 mph, but we cruised around at a stately 120-140 mph. It was a pleasant aircraft to fly, although we were warned that its stalling characteristics were vicious. After the single-engine aircraft I had been flying in America, the controls seemed heavy, and I missed the freedom of being able to loop, roll, and do aerobatics. On the other hand, visibility was excellent, and we could do much longer cross-country flights.

RAF Airspeed Oxfords were a perfect introduction to twin-engine flying

After a week on the Oxford, flying from Grantham's main airfield at RAF Spitalgate, Stevie went solo. Within two weeks he had clocked up 29 hours on the Oxford, and on 15 October he was sent on detachment to No. 1514 BAT (Beam Approach Training) Flight at RAF Coningsby in Lincolnshire.

His task at Coningsby was to familiarise himself with the Beam Approach System, a homing device operated from the control tower at airfields to help pilots land in poor visibility. Radio beacons transmitted signals to aircraft as they came in to land. The main beacon, located at the end of the runway, transmitted a signal in the form of a narrow beam. In Stevie's words:

> *The beam was so arranged that if you were on the right of it, it sent a series of dashes, while if you were on the left, it sent a series of dots, and if you were on course, a steady note was transmitted. At about six hundred yards from the end of the airfield, a low-pitched series of pips was sent, and at about two hundred yards further along, another series of pips was transmitted at a higher frequency. Just before the perimeter of the airfield, there was a 'cone of silence' where nothing could be heard. At this point, the aircraft should be about 50-100 feet above the runway, with wheels and flaps down ready to land.*
>
> *I spent a week at Coningsby doing nothing except flying on the beam. At the end of that week, I had learned to identify a beam, fly down it and land without aid from anyone, and this boosted my confidence.*

On returning to Grantham on 22 October, Stevie began night flying, which entailed taking the Oxford on cross-country flights from Grantham's satellite airfield at RAF Harlaxton. Night flying in Lincolnshire proved to be very different from the night flying Stevie had done from War Eagle Field. Whereas in California the visibility had been excellent, in Lincolnshire it was often very poor, and landing in the dark on ill-lit runways was a hazardous business which required skill, steadiness, and nerve:

> *Night flying was carried out under rather spartan conditions from an airfield called Harlaxton. We either flew an aircraft there in daylight and waited until it was dark, or travelled by bus. Wearing full flying kit, we lounged around on camp beds in unheated Nissen huts until our turn came to fly. As there were more pilots than aircraft, we often had to wait several hours. When one was cold and tired with a 2am wait until take off, neither temper nor concentration was at its best, and on occasion the weather was appalling.*
>
> *At this time, large numbers of beacons had been erected all over England. Some of these were red, and some, known as 'lighthouses', flashed white.*

We used to take off, fly to one of these beacons and set a compass bearing, then fly to another. Sometimes we would visit three or four beacons, then return to the one near our airfield, wait until the conditions were right, and land. This could be fun on a clear night, but when the visibility deteriorated, it could become very trying. Each beacon flashed a different letter of the Morse Code; sometimes the dim flash of a beacon through the murk could be misread, and this made it easy to mistake the particular beacon that marked the base. I remember being caught in a snow storm, circling a beacon when I could see it, and concentrating like mad on the bearing of the airfield from the beacon. On another occasion, I was horrified to find myself flying towards the glow of the rising moon under the impression that I was headed for a 'lighthouse'.

The dangers of landing at night imprinted themselves indelibly on Stevie's mind:

The lights we had to land by were paraffin lamps known as 'Goosenecks', which were just ordinary watering cans filled with paraffin and lit from a long wick pushed in through the spout. Goosenecks were lined in a row in the shape of a T to mark out the average runway, and they were quite a long way apart. We used to land with them on our port side, the left-hand side. The light from them was very weak. There was a chap I knew quite well, a happy character, who was doing night flying with me. After I'd got down, he said, "Good, my turn now." I got out, he took over the aircraft, and the next thing I knew, he'd been killed! He'd been coming in towards Grantham and seen some little blue lights. They were actually dimmed railway signal lights, but he mistook them for Goosenecks and flew into Grantham Station, and that was the end of him.

A gooseneck paraffin lamp (bottom right) marking the runway for a IX Squadron Lancaster on a particularly murky day

Bomber Command losses were high at the end of 1942, and the there was an urgent need for replacement pilots, so on 30 November, after twenty hours of night flying, Stevie was posted with a group of other pilots from Grantham to No. 14 OTU (Operational Training Unit) at RAF Cottesmore in the East Midlands without completing the full Oxford conversion course. At Cottesmore, he would convert to a proper heavy bomber, the Vickers Wellington. The Wellington, which had been commissioned as a long-range bomber by the Air Ministry in 1936, remained in service throughout the War.

Stevie provides a vivid account of being posted to Cottesmore:

> *I was posted to No. 14 OTU at Cottesmore with a group of pilots to convert to Wellingtons. On a dreary cold November afternoon, the train disgorged us at the small railway station. The pilots who had been commissioned unloaded an array of cases and trunks from the First Class compartments. Those of us who were Sergeant Pilots travelled Second Class. We each had two kit bags, one crammed with flying kit, the other with a spare uniform and personal belongings. The Officers looked smart, with pressed tunics and trousers and polished shoes; us Sergeants with our shoddy thick tunics and trousers and heavy boots looked much more rumpled.*
>
> *I never did discover how the commissioning system worked. People who were made officers were always one up, but we had all done the same training and progressed to the same point, so that the distinction between commissioned and non-commissioned pilots seemed artificial and rather unfair.*

Pilots posted to RAF Cottesmore [Photograph: Eve Janocko, daughter of Anthony Gobbie]. Notice the haloes inserted by Anthony Gobbie above the heads of the pilots he thought had been lost. Luckily, he added Stevie's halo in error!

(Of the pilots pictured with Stevie, Whittam, Hodgkinson, Gobbie and Josling, whose name is misspelt as Gosling, were subsequently posted with him to 57 Squadron at Scampton. Gobbie and Hodgkinson had already been commissioned by the time this photograph was taken. Whittam was described by Stevie as *'an ex-Army corporal, seeming more experienced and older than the rest of us'*; Gobbie he remembered as *'self-assured'*; Hodgkinson as *'dapper and slim, with a trim moustache'*; and Josling as *'a Cockney, squat, and a very good natural pilot'*. Benny Goodman, who is still alive at the time of writing, went on to fly with the famous 617 Squadron.)

A truck arrived at the nearby railway station to transport them to the airfield:

> *Everyone piled in. The truck stopped first at the Officers Mess, then went on to the Sergeants' Mess. The Sergeants' Mess was crowded, as it was home to Navigators, Bomb Aimers, Wireless Operators and Air Gunners as well as Pilots. The new arrivals were billeted in Married Quarters some distance from the Mess. There were two beds in each of the larger rooms, and a single bed in the smaller rooms. Pilots usually had the single rooms, while other aircrew doubled up. The quarters were freezing. There was no coal for the fires, and the bathroom taps sported icicles. Some Canadians in residence before us had removed most of the banister rails and some of the cupboard shelves, and used them to light a fire in the living-room grate. It was a relief to return to the smoke-filled fug of the anteroom, where a fire blazed. In the dining hall we were given a mug of tea and slices of thin bread and margarine.*

At this point, the Group Captain in command of RAF Cottesmore entered the Sergeants' Mess to address the new arrivals. Stevie and his fellow pilots were distinctly unimpressed:

> *Into the anteroom swaggered a short, fat, heavy Group Captain, an old man in his fifties. "Sit down," he said, and then he gave us a speech which made out hearts sink. "Welcome to Cottesmore. I am sure you will be happy here. I rely on you Sergeants to set an example of discipline to the airmen. You will always have bright buttons and brilliant boots. You will salute all officers, and I expect you to salute me even when I am in my car. When I am in my car, I shall always fly my pennant. If that pennant flies, you salute the car, even if you do not see me." Then off he rolled.*
>
> *"What a bloody fool," said Johnny Pickett, a New Zealander who had trained at Spitalgate with me. "I often wondered what madness drew me to Pommie Land, and now I know. I've come all the way round the world just to salute that self-important old fart."*

Next, we were addressed by a Squadron Leader. "I am the Chief Ground Instructor," he said. "For the next two weeks you will be attending lectures and ground demonstrations. The pilots will concentrate mainly on learning all about the Wellington, but will also be expected to brush up on navigation and signalling, and will be able to use the Air Ministry Bombing Trainer. Other aircrew will go to specialist lectures. At the end of the fortnight, you will be part of a crew, so mix and talk together during your free time, and select the people you would like to fly with. You will find your appropriate lectures listed in Daily Orders. That is all, gentlemen."

At this point, the realisation dawned on Stevie that as captain of a heavy bomber, he would be responsible not only for his own safety, but for that of the crew flying with him:

The bar opened and us pilots bought ourselves a round and surveyed the scene. Before today, we had only messed with other pilots. During the past year we had learned to fly a variety of single-engine aircraft and gained our Wings. But now we would learn to fly Wellingtons and become aircraft captains responsible not just for ourselves, but for a crew.

The first night Stevie and the other new arrivals spent at Cottesmore did nothing to lighten their mood:

Johnny Pickett and I and 'Jos' Josling, another Sergeant Pilot who had come with us from Spitalgate, had a couple of pints and returned to our freezing quarters. During the first night we were there, we heard a tremendous explosion followed by a noise that sounded like a pre-War Crystal Palace firework display. Flares lit up the sky and gouts of smoke shot into the air, making patterns on the rose-coloured low clouds. After ten minutes the noise stopped, and the sky was black, save for the odd flicker. We did not realise what this was until the next morning, when we heard that someone had misjudged a landing, crashed his Wellington, and killed the whole crew. When an identical display occurred the following night, everyone knew exactly what it was.

Training on Wellingtons and learning the skills of night flying was a hazardous business, and it cost many lives. '*The casualty rate at this stage of training was high,*' Stevie noted,' *and continued to be so during the whole of the War.*' The atmosphere in which formal instruction began on the day after their arrival at Cottesmore could hardly have been worse; it provoked anger and resentment among Stevie and his fellow trainees:

Most of the lectures for pilots took place on the first floor of an administrative building. On the stairway were plastered large pictures of pilots under the

Training on Wellingtons at night was a hazardous business

caption: HE HELPED HITLER! Each photograph showed a pilot who had been involved in an accident. The Group Captain and the Chief Ground Instructor, a pompous prig, clearly imagined that shaming and humiliating these men would reduce the number of flying accidents; but we all thought they might more usefully have displayed their own pictures as Hitler's helpers. Nothing could have been better calculated to lower our morale.

One of the first lectures was interrupted by the sound of a slow drum beat. Stevie and his fellow trainees stood and looked out of the windows. '*We saw a coffin being escorted by a funeral party of airmen slow marching. I reflected that thirteen had been killed already, and that I had not yet flown a Wellington.*'

One officer Stevie did come to know and admire at Cottesmore was Donald Falconer, then the Commander of 'A' Flight:

He was a compact man with sleek dark hair and a sharp nose, a DFC who combined leadership with automatic discipline and a splendid sense of humour. Returning from the first 1,000 Bomber Raid, he had let down through cloud near March. A Halifax came down on top of him, and its props sheered through Falconer's cockpit. He was tossed clear, but his crew were killed. He went back for a second operational tour as Wing Commander with 156 Squadron, and was lost on a Berlin trip on 30 December 1944. I remember him with pride, and his non-flying colleagues and superiors with anger and disgust.

The familiarisation exercises Stevie had to undertake before actually taking the controls of a Wellington were difficult and demanding:

During the first two weeks, pilots concentrated on complex cockpit drill required to fly this more complicated aircraft. We had to learn about fuel supply and how to control it, and how to deal with the lubrication. We put on blacked-out goggles and learned the position of every knob, lever and switch by touch. We also brushed up on our navigation and on Morse Code signalling procedures, examining the Browning machine guns, and sat in the turret rotating them through their vertical and horizontal axis. Then we had lectures on the Mark XIV bomb sight and spent a little while on the Air Ministry Bombing Trainer.

But there were lighter moments.

We also did quite a lot of clay pigeon shooting. I enjoyed this and was pretty competent, but I found it difficult to shoot clays when a 12-bore shotgun was mounted in a rear turret!

While all this was going on, Stevie began the surprisingly informal and haphazard process of assembling a crew, or 'crewing up':

The methods of crewing up were crude. It wasn't done by posting from above, which was how the Americans did it; they just put people's names down and allotted them to a particular crew, and that was it. But we were made to choose. We mixed together for a couple of weeks during break times and in the Mess and just got talking. All we knew about each other was that we had done a course as a Pilot or Navigator or whatever and passed it. Someone would come up and ask, "Would you like to be my Pilot?" or, "Would you like to be my Engineer?" That's how we formed crews.

Stevie was soon to discover that crewing up was not without its pitfalls, and that first appearances could be deceptive:

The first Navigator I had was a public school ex-Guards officer. He was well over six feet tall, well-spoken, and very smartly dressed. When he unpacked his trunk and produced a gun case with a pair of Purdey guns, I was very impressed. He took me to Oakham and introduced me to his wife, who later drove us back to camp in their Bentley! Next morning in the Mess he came up to me and said:

"Oh, morning, Skipper, I'd like to be your Navigator."

I asked him, "Well, can you navigate?"

"Oh, yes, top of the class, no trouble at all," he replied.

I took off from Cottesmore one day and flew to Ely, which was easy to spot because of the Cathedral. I circled Ely for a bit, then said, "Where are we Navigator?"

"Just a moment, Skipper!"

About ten minutes later he said, "Ely, Sir."

I said, "Right, well you've got to do it quicker than that when we're over Germany!"

When we came back, he couldn't find the airfield either, but fortunately, I knew Cottesmore, so I landed without his help.

He came over and said, "Oh, sorry about that, Skipper."

I said, "Did you have a map by any chance?"

"Oh no, I thought I could find my way without one."

When I landed, my Wireless Operator said to me, "I don't want to worry you Skip, but look at the note I got from the Navigator," and he'd written, 'GET ME A FIX FOR CHRIST'S SAKE'. I didn't fly with him again! I went to see my Flight Commander. It was difficult to get rid of him, as everyone thought he was such a fine chap, but as a Navigator he was useless. He got shot down on his first raid about fifty miles off track, but he survived, and I saw him again after the War.

Luckily for Stevie, he was to find a far more competent Navigator in Flight Sergeant Ernie Howes. Ernie Howes had been a Post Office engineer in civilian life, and Stevie would later describe him as *'unflappable, the quiet, steady old man of the crew who stayed in his light-proof compartment beavering away'*. On numerous occasions on operations, Gee (the radio navigation system used to estimate the aircraft's position) and H2S (the ground scanning radar system) failed, but Ernie Howes, calm under pressure, always managed to find the way back to base. He was the only member of Stevie's crew who flew with him uninterruptedly throughout his tour, and in January 1944 he would be awarded a DFC on Stevie's recommendation.

Stevie's Wireless Operator, Ken Brown, was, in Stevie's words, *'a very nice chap, a Yorkshire lad with a pronounced accent, relatively short with a smooth face who looked like a cherub.'* Stevie's Rear Gunner, Bernie Townsend, was an Australian, whom Stevie remembered as *'slim, quiet, and reflective'*. He would fly with Stevie on nineteen of his missions. Stevie's Bomb Aimer, Dickie Newcomb, had come all the way from Chile to join the RAFVR:

He was amazing, much taller than I was, fair-haired, well spoken, and extremely good-looking. He came from Chile to fight in the War and had relatives in London who he'd go and stay with during leave. His father owned a farm as big as Rutland, and he was richer than the rest of the crew.

He didn't pass the Pilot's Course, but he was a very good Bomb Aimer. He never lost his temper and never got too excited. It's not easy, lying flat by the bomb bay with flak coming up at you, to give clear directions to the pilot on the bombing run, but that's what he did, time and again. He told me he was very disappointed when he got crewed up with me, as he thought I laughed too easily and didn't take the War seriously enough. It wasn't until we'd done about a dozen trips together that he realised I wasn't that bad a Captain after all!

After Stevie had completed his familiarisation course, he and his newly assembled crew were posted to RAF Saltby, the satellite station of RAF Cottesmore, to train on Wellingtons:

To begin flying our aircraft, we shifted from Cottesmore to another airfield at Saltby. This was a very newly constructed airfield which had been a racecourse. It was extremely muddy, and the living quarters were a long way from the airfield. Consequently, we used to ring up the airfield from the Mess every morning to see if there was going to be any flying. Usually the answer was "No," so we would ring up again at about midday, and usually the answer was once again "No!" After two or three days of doing this, several of us decided that nobody would notice if we left the airfield, and we took to going into Nottingham.

One snowy afternoon I rang up from a pub called the Black Bull at Nottingham to ask if there was any flying. "Yes," came the answer. "What time?" "Oh, get up here in about an hour." Panic stations; we rushed for a train to Grantham and took a taxi to Saltby. When I reported to the Flight Commander, he said "Sorry about that, the weather has changed, so there won't be any flying." Heaving a sigh of relief, we made our way to the Mess.

The weather was bad in December when they arrived, and it remained bad over Christmas:

Christmas 1942 came and went. There was not enough beer in the Mess for a real thrash, but I remember looking around in an odd moment and wondering how many of us would be around to celebrate the next Christmas.

Stevie had to wait until 28 December to do his first flight in a Wellington. He noted that his instructor, P/O Lockyer, *'flew smoothly and instructed well, and I soon felt at home at the controls.'*

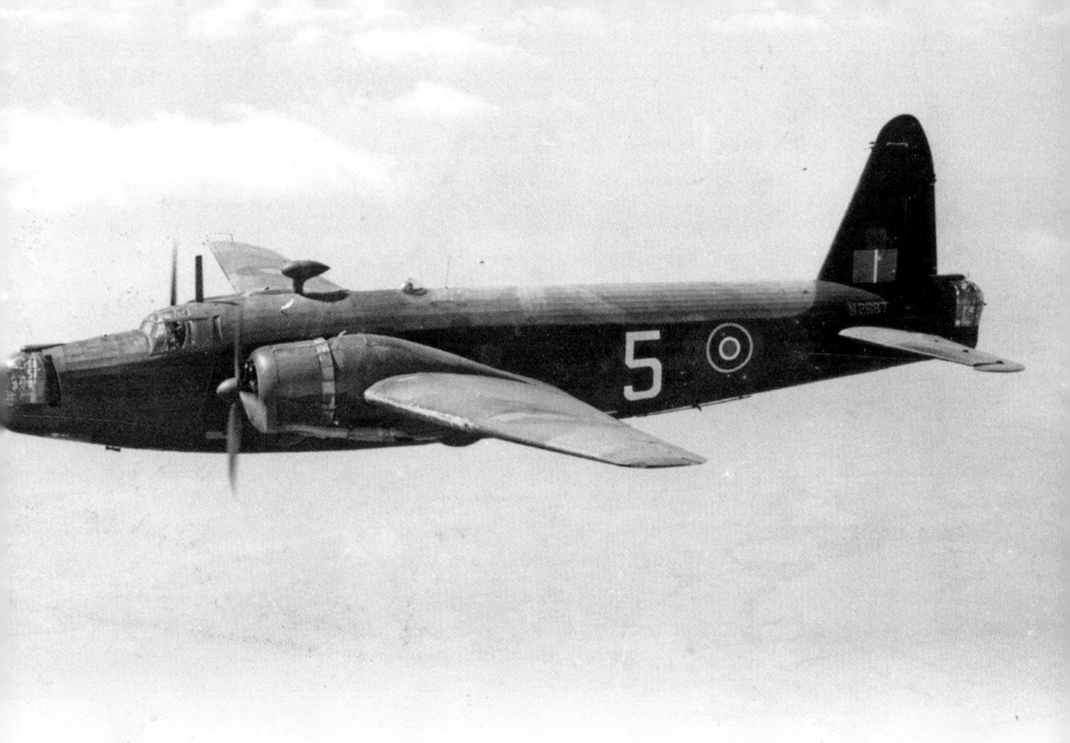

A veteran Wellington Mk I that flew with many OTUs

But learning to fly Wellingtons posed challenges of a kind Stevie had not encountered before:

The early production Wellington Mark ICs were pretty grim aircraft by the time they arrived at OTUs. The engines were derated, and you had to make up your mind up at 500 ft whether you were going to land or not because its Pegasus engines weren't powerful enough to get you back up below that, and you'd go on losing altitude. This led to a local instruction that overshoots were not to be attempted below a height of 500 ft. The runway was marked at night by a thin line of Gooseneck flares arranged in a T shape, and an inexperienced pilot was in real trouble if he made an inaccurate approach. If he did try to overshoot, he might well crash, and if he did not, he would probably prang.

Stevie did his first solo flight in a Wellington with his crew on 15 January 1943, after just six circuits and landings as Second Pilot. Flying conditions had continued to be poor, with foul weather drifting in from the North Sea producing a very low cloud base and poor visibility. On 16 January Stevie took off from Saltby, but by the time he had completed his circuit, low cloud was covering the airfield, so he was unable to return, and had to try to locate another base at which to land:

The weather was filthy, with low cloud and drizzle. I set off for Coningsby, and asked the Wireless Op to put up the aerial, only to find that it was missing. A Lysander emerged and flew alongside me; the pilot fired a Very pistol, then glided slowly back into the cloud. I followed him, thinking he was intending to lead me to an airfield; in the event, I broke cloud at about 500 ft, and found myself above a lake or reservoir, so I smartly opened the throttles and managed to climb again.

I had been airborne for three hours by this time, it was getting dark, and I was wondering whether to bail out the crew when, through a gap in the cloud, I saw RAF Waddington. As the transmitter was not working, I could not contact Flying Control, but I looked at the wind sock and the landing lights, and saw that I was as near as dammit on a downwind leg. I throttled back, lowered the wheels and flaps, and steamed in on a very high approach, landing about half the way down the runway and heading directly for the bomb dump. Luckily, there was sufficient pressure in the brakes to stop with about fifty yards to spare. The Flying Control Officer told me he had been yelling at me not to land, and had loosed off a red emergency flare, as he had been sure I would finish up in the bomb dump. Then within half an hour, the weather magically cleared, and I was able to return to Saltby. Later I happened to meet the pilot of the Lysander, who told me that he, too, had been lost and was running out of fuel. When he saw me looming out of the murk, he had fired his Very pistol to signal his distress, and had gone on to crash-land in a field near the lake.

Flying training progressed to include high-level and low-level bombing runs, gunnery practice, and 'Bullseyes'. A 'Bullseye' was an exercise in which a crew was given a target and a flight plan to simulate an operational sortie prior to doing the real thing. By 6 March, 1943, when he concluded his training at 14 OTU, Stevie had flown a total of 87 hours on Wellingtons, 36 of which had been night flights.

While training at Saltby, Stevie witnessed a horrific accident caused by the pilot misjudging his landing approach in the way earlier described. Fifty years later, the memory still haunted him:

I had taxied a Wellington to a point near the end of the runway along the perimeter track. Another Wellington was on the approach through low cloud to land. He seemed to be wallowing, wheels and flaps down, and then stalled. Just as he reached the end of the runway, he crashed into a contractor's lorry, and the whole lot quickly ignited. I could not turn around the perimeter track as the ground was too soft on either side, so I was stuck, and had the fire extinguisher ready to protect my aircraft from possible burning debris. The ashen face of Sgt Bradshaw, the pilot, and his trembling hands remain etched on my mind to this day, as does the small pile of wreckage left after the fire and the metallic clinking sound made by cooling metal.

Sergeant Bradshaw was the sole survivor; his entire crew was killed. Stevie noted:

Losses on OTUs were so high that Courts of Inquiry were hastily convened, and many of the records were untidy and hurriedly written. Often little attempt was made to contact witnesses, and consequently some of the records were inaccurate. Although I was within yards of the crash, I was not asked to give evidence, and I was not surprised to discover that the crash site was entered in the record as Cottesmore, not Saltby.

On 11 April 1943, Stevie and his crew were posted to No. 1654 Conversion Unit at RAF Wigsley in Nottinghamshire. Their first flying was done in an Avro Manchester. The Manchester had been designed to meet the Air Ministry's request for a twin-engine bomber, but it had a very short service life. Its engines were underpowered, and it proved unreliable. Unsurprisingly, only two hundred and nine entered into service. The first prototype flew in July 1939, and the first operational mission involving Manchesters took place in February 1941. Production ceased in November that year, and the Manchester was withdrawn from front-line service at the end of June 1942. It was used for training purposes until the end of 1943, its sole advantage being that its interior layout resembled that of the Lancaster, which was in essence a Manchester remodelled by the Avro company, and equipped with four engines.

Stevie was unimpressed by the Manchester:

Not many people flew the Manchester, only a two-engine aircraft, and it was not a success. The engines were heavy and very liable to oil up, and the aircraft used to dip into the ground when you were taxiing. You had to use both engines to turn it around with the drag. It was hard work and difficult to taxi, and its rate of climb wasn't anything like the Lancaster. If you were lucky, you got to 11-12,000 feet on the Manchester, whereas the Lancaster would do 20,000 plus.

While training on Wellingtons, Stevie had a crew of four: his Navigator, Ernie Howes; his Wireless Operator, Ken Brown; his Rear Gunner, Bernie

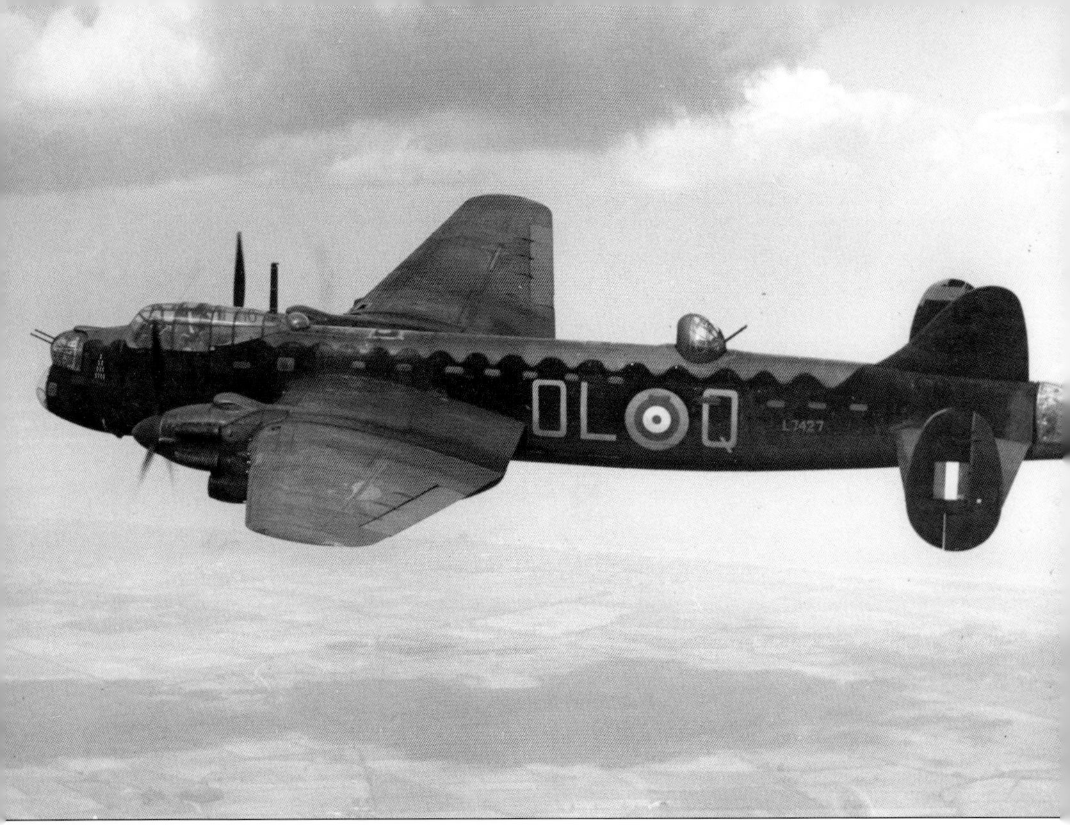

The unsuccessful Avro Manchester - forerunner of the mighty Lancaster

Townsend; and his Bomb Aimer, Dickie Newcomb. But the Manchester, required a crew of six in addition to the pilot, and at Wigsley, Stevie was joined by a Flight Engineer and a Mid-Upper Gunner.

Stevie's Mid-Upper Gunner, George Martin, was a Frenchman for whom he quickly developed the utmost respect and affection:

He was a very interesting chap, and I had a soft spot for him. First of all, he nearly lived in the armoury when he wasn't in bed with some girl or other! He'd go to the armoury in the morning and shoot the guns to make sure they were all synchronised. He was very, very good, and his commentaries were always very precise. He was an exceptional Gunner. When he spotted German fighters, he would not only give me their position but also estimate their speed, which was very useful when taking evasive action. He also devised a small flash pistol to temporarily blind attacking fighters.

He bowled over so many women that I was quite surprised that the babies in the area weren't smoking pipes and wearing little moustaches. One night we went to a dance, and I occupied the bar in my usual way and let the rest get on with stamping about. He came up to me with an attractive woman and asked if I'd mind looking after her while he danced with her daughter. I said, "Alright George," so he danced with the daughter, then came back and told me her mother wanted to go outside for a moment. It was some time before he brought her back, and he told me later he had gone to bed with her. When the dance finished, he took the daughter off to bed with him as well, and said afterwards that he'd had a very good night!

On one occasion, he didn't come back in time for an operational briefing, which left me in a bit of an awkward position, because if you didn't report all crew for duty, and had one missing, it attracted attention to that person and didn't do much for the morale of the rest of the crew either. I thought, 'I'm certain in my own mind that if George could get back, he'd be here,' so I just said all were present and hoped to God he'd get back in time. Time crept on and we got into our flying suits, and then, with just five minutes to spare, he came running in with sweat dripping from him. "Sorry Skipper, I missed the train," he said. He had actually gone off to do me a favour. I was always moaning because there were no records of classical music to listen to, and George had taken himself to London and somehow managed to get hold of a record player and some 78 records of classical music and operatic arias sung by Gigli, the leading Italian tenor of the time. Though we were at war with Italy, George's little buying spree got us into the habit of listening to Gigli to help us wind down when we got back from ops!

In sharp contrast to George Martin, the Flight Engineer who was first allocated to Stevie made his heart sink:

He was covered with unprepossessing boils, and he had such defective eyesight he wore goggles with prescription lenses. In the Manchester he seemed to grab the throttles for support and was sick all over the throttle controls. I was so unimpressed that his name is neither in my log book nor my memory. He went for a medical and vanished.

Stevie and his crew only had five flights in the Manchester, between 11 April and 13 April, and it was then that his first and nameless Flight Engineer disappeared, never to return. On 17 April, Stevie did his first flight on a Lancaster as Second Pilot, and on 19 April, after four hours of instruction, he did his first solo flight. Fortunately for him, he was joined at this point by a replacement Flight Engineer to whom he instinctively warmed, and with whom he would develop a lifelong friendship: Eric Blanchard. Writing to Eric 67 years later, in April 2010, Stevie told him simply that when he took over as Flight Engineer, *'it was like a miracle'*.

Eric Blanchard for his part never forgot joining Stevie's crew. In an interview with the Imperial War Museum, he recalled their first flight in a Lancaster on 19 April 1943, and the birthday celebrations which followed it:

> *My Pilot, Sergeant Stevens, who had trained on Wellington bombers in the Heavy Conversion Unit, had to learn how to fly the Lancaster bomber. It was quite exciting. On my 21st birthday my father sent me a £5 note, which was a lot of money then, and my mother had sent me a home-made sponge cake. We sat underneath our Lancaster, somebody produced a penknife, and we all had a little bit of cake. We went for a short flight and came back, then we went to a pub in the village nearby — out of beer and the hatch came down! We went back to the Sergeants' Mess, but we were too late there, too. The hatch went down again, so we never did get to have that birthday drink!*

Although Stevie would become an expert Lancaster pilot, he had to go through a steep learning curve:

> *I thought, that's a pretty big aircraft, and it was, of course, much bigger. You had to use four engines to taxi, though the four throttles were fairly easy to move with the palm of your hand. Once you got it where you wanted it, you could just tighten a screw and the throttles would remain in that position. You had plenty of power, but when you were taking off with a bomb load and you had the wind coming across, the tail would swing, and it was quite difficult. You had to make absolutely certain you were strapped into the seat and really push hard on the rudder and sometimes use the trimmer as well, just to keep the thing straight on the runway. As soon as you'd started, the aircraft would take the air, but not stable air, and quite often it would blow off track, so you had to push hard to get back to where you wanted to go.*
>
> *You also had to be very careful with lights; some people forgot in their excitement they had taxi lights on. You hardly ever used the main lights for taxiing because it just put too much light around the airfield, so you would use the minor lights on the side for taxiing out. Once you were in the air, you would turn all the lights off altogether, but just occasionally you would just flash a few of them on so that other people would know where you were, or if someone was trying to formate on you. When that happened, you would have a quick look to make sure it had four engines and was one of your own.*

But the exhilaration of flying the Lancaster soon took over, and on 26 April, Stevie and his crew went on a practice cross-country run which would provide him with his most treasured memory of flying:

A Heavy Conversion Unit Lancaster similar to that taken by Stevie and his crew on their training flight to Cornwall

> *We started somewhere around the beginning of the River Severn and went all the way down to Land's End, then back again. It was a beautiful day, the visibility was perfect, and I flew the aircraft as high as I could get it, at about 20,000 ft. We could see both the north and south coasts of Cornwall, and it was really glorious. It was that moment which brought home to me the point of it all: to stop the Germans stamping their dirty great jackboots all over this wonderful country of ours.*

After just seven daytime flights, totalling some seven hours with an instructor, and less than two and a half hours solo, Stevie and his crew switched to night flying. By 30 April, they had notched up eighteen hours of daytime and eighteen hours of night flying in the Lancaster, and the time had come for them to move on to operational duties.

Stevie photographed in May 1943 ready for Ops

OPERATIONS

MAY TO OCTOBER 1943

IN THE FRONT LINE: STEVIE'S TOUR OF OPERATIONS

On 1 May 1943 Stevie and his crew were posted to RAF Scampton in Lincolnshire, and joined 57 Squadron. Stevie took an immediate liking to Scampton, and his tour of operations with 57 Squadron would remain a deep source of pride for him for the rest of his life:

> *The welcome to me and my crew was cordial. We were comfortably billeted, having a whole Married Quarters to ourselves, and the Sergeants' Mess was superb, probably the best in England. It had a comfortable ante room and a splendid dining room with waitress service. Two veteran Warrant Officers were having a drink at the bar and welcomed me cordially. The following morning, we reported to 'A' Flight, where Squadron Leader Leland gave me a friendly greeting, and F/O Grey showed me around. My crew and I were one of six replacements, as several crews had been taken from 57 Squadron for the newly formed 617 Squadron.*

Wing Commander Hopcroft, the CO of 57 Squadron, also had a brief word with the newly arrived pilots, drumming into them that their lives depended on their ground crew. '*He was always reminding us of the importance of the ground crew,*' Stevie recalled, '*and would say, "Your life depends on your bloody ground crew. Get out there in the cold and wet when they are doing an engine change, and show your appreciation."*'

Stevie was quick to appreciate just how dependent he was on his ground crew:

> *My Flight Commander asked me to take one of the Lancasters across to a temporary engineering tent on the other side of the airfield. I got in this aeroplane, but though I'd taxied several Lancasters before, suddenly I found I just couldn't turn it. I did all the checks, the brakes and so on, then had to stop. Out came Flight Sergeant Booth with a couple of the ground crew with some chocks to put down. He hopped in and started the outer engines. I had been trying to taxi on just the two inner engines, which was all we had practised. I soon realised that once you got any kind of cross wind in a Lancaster, you needed all four engines to taxi. I thought, my God, my first time on a new station and I can't even taxi the blasted aircraft! I was afraid I might get chucked out before I'd even started. But in fact, what had happened to me was fairly common, and I was thankful to discover that I wasn't the first pilot to make that particular mistake.*

Wing Commander Hopcroft (centre) the C/O of 57 Squadron, who stressed the importance of the ground crews to all new pilots. The Lancaster behind is his own 'Frederick II' ED707.

Years later, he would describe in haunting detail the process of checking that everything was right with his aircraft before he took off on operations, quoting lines from Pope's *Rape of the Lock*:

> *'Thence by a soft transition we repair*
>
> *From earthly vehicles to those of air.'*
>
> *Come with me in the twilight to our old airfield. Walk with me in the dark around my Lancaster. Check what you can in the failing light. The pitot head must be uncovered, or we shall know neither height nor airspeed. Walk under the propellers, there is plenty of room. Look at the tyres, check for creep (tyres moving around the rim). Look at the ailerons, make sure the fixed locks are removed. Check the elevators for locks, and check chocks. Now, up the short ladder on the starboard quarter. It is nearly dark in here. Look at the rear turret. Imagine being crammed in here, cold and isolated, swinging from side to side, searching each part of the sky. In addition to the turret revolving, the aircraft will bank from side to side for hour after hour.*

Lonely, cold, black, looking for the shadow of the German fighter which will spit death at you unless you spot it first. Look up at the mid-upper turret. Can you imagine its arc of swing when the pilot banks the aircraft? Could you remember port from starboard if you were describing the flight of an attacking fighter? Pass the bunk (for casualties) on to the Wireless Op's cabin with its very small curtained window. The Navigator's cabin, already getting cluttered with its new Gee set, is full of maps, compasses, ruler, calculator (not electric!), slide rule, parallel rule, Mercator and Gee charts, star chart, and clock. Then the pilot's seat. Stow your chute and make sure it is fixed. Left leg up first on to the seat. Wriggle, stretch, adjust the seat and the rudder pedals. Strap in shoulder and lap harness. Wriggle again. You may be strapped there for eleven hours. No, you can't go for a pee! Dark, isn't it? No lights allowed. You must preserve that night vision. Any light would be seen miles away by a German. Look at all those luminous needles. Do you know what each one means? Can you sweep your eyes over the dials and recognize any unusual indication? You will do that thousands of times tonight while your eyes also sweep forwards, upwards, downwards, and sideways. Put your head in the blister and look towards the rear. The Flight Engineer has checked everything in detail. The Bomb Aimer has checked the bomb sight and the front turret.

Despite his early mishap with taxiing, Stevie's luck was in. On 11 May, his Flight Commander, Squadron Leader Johnny Leland, presented him with ED946 DX-E-'Easy', a spanking new Lancaster Mark III. This was the latest model. It had four Packard Merlin 28 engines manufactured in the United States, and these were very powerful, being capable of delivering 1,420 hp each on take-off. Stevie would never forget his delight at being given such a fine aircraft. Writing in 2000 to commemorate the anniversary of his fifty-seven-year association with 57 Squadron, he recalled:

A new Mark III Lancaster, ED946 DX E-'Easy', was delivered. I was asked to taxi it to the Flight Dispersal, and a little later, I took it for an air test.

"What did you think of it, Stevens?" Leland asked me.

"Apart from a few snags, absolutely bang on, Sir," I said.

"Right," he said, "it's yours!"

I was amazed and delighted. I still remember the duck-egg-blue finish on the inside of the cowlings and the superb tool kit, which was kept under the beady eye of Flight Sergeant Booth, whose smart appearance and great efficiency set an example to all the ground crew. Corporal Swinchatt, our engine fitter, was also very impressed with the tool package, which he thought was better than any he had ever used before.

Like most of the Bomber Command pilots who flew the Lancaster, Stevie retained a lifelong affection and admiration for the aircraft Sir Arthur Harris once called his *'Shining Sword'*. Looking back on his time as a Lancaster pilot, Stevie wrote:

> *I can remember very well the first aeroplane I ever saw. We all turned out one day from school in Torrington, looked up at the sky, caught sight of an aeroplane. It was only a biplane, but we were very excited. There was a small patch of cloud and the plane went right through it. We were all saying to each other, "It will come down now, it's hit that cloud!". I never dreamed then that I would one day be flying one myself, nor that when I did, it would be an aircraft as wonderful as a Lancaster with a crew of six for which I would be responsible.*
>
> *The Lancaster was an incredible aircraft, just superb. It was infinitely better than any other heavy aircraft. It was designed as a bomb carrier, unlike the aircraft which were converted from passenger liners into bombers, and weren't really up to the job.*
>
> *It was a very stable aircraft once you got it going. If you didn't get the engines synchronised, there would be a horrible droning noise. We used to tune the two inner engines by ear, so that we could hear they were running at the same speed. Then we would look look through the whirling propeller blades from the inner engines to the outer, and adjust them until all the engines were doing the same revs. It was a fairly crude way of doing it, but it was no good using the rev counters as they weren't accurate enough. We also had automatic pilot on the Lancaster. One chap I knew swore he did nearly all of his tour by setting the automatic pilot and just letting the aircraft go. But I think he was just shooting a line; either he was very lucky or wasn't ever seen by an enemy fighter.*
>
> *The Lanc's limitations were a consequence of its being built as a bomb carrier. It carried the maximum size and weight of bombs the air frame could support, and the crew had to fit around it. There was a long and devious method of getting into the Pilot's seat. The Navigator and Wireless Op were in very cramped, light-proof cabins. Somehow or other they managed to manoeuvre into them with their Mercator charts and navigational equipment. There wasn't really a decent second pilot's seat for the Flight Engineer, and the rear turret was isolated from the rest of the aircraft. The Rear Gunner had to enter through a small door, and leave his parachute outside. In an emergency, he had to push himself out and strap it on, which could be very difficult in an emergency. When Lancasters were hit, relatively few of their crews survived, compared with other aircraft.*

Another one of Stevie, taken in May 1943 just before Operations

If you were taking off with a full bomb load and a strong cross wind, and the aircraft blew off course, it was very difficult to correct. On one occasion, a chap nicknamed 'Lofty', one of our armourers, was standing by a Lanc when suddenly another Lanc came drifting across the track in a cross wind. There was a massive BANG, and he got blown right out of the airfield. Thankfully, he survived.

Stevie and his crew would soon find themselves in the front line, and E-'Easy' was to prove its worth in battle.

Early in March 1943, Air Chief Marshal Sir Arthur ('Butch') Harris, the Commander-in-Chief of Bomber Command, had launched the Battle of the Ruhr, a concerted series of air attacks on the complex of industrial cities in the Ruhr Valley which provided Germany with much of its manufacturing base, not to mention vital supplies of coal, steel, and chemicals, and much else.

It is important to bear the historical context in mind. On 18 February 1943, shortly before Harris launched the Battle of the Ruhr, Goebbels, Hitler's Propaganda Minister, had delivered a speech in Berlin in which he made the war aims of Nazi Germany brutally clear: the Führer was committed to 'total war' regardless of the cost in human life and suffering, whether in Germany itself, or in the European countries it had invaded and occupied.

The Battle of the Ruhr did not win the War without the need for bloody land battles, as Harris hoped it might, but it did pave the way for victory. The RAF dropped over 30,000 tons of bombs on Germany's industrial heartland (twice the power of the Hiroshima atomic bomb), permanently stopping any increase in armaments production. The series of raids on Hamburg alone led to the mass exodus of over 800,000 people, and interrupted the city's industrial production for two months, pulverizing its shipyards and nearly 600 factories crucial to military supply, and stopping construction work on twenty-five U-boats.

The German Air Ministry described the skies as 'the real front line', and took the decision that the mass of fighters must be deployed for home defence. The need to respond to the attacks launched by Bomber Command meant that two million workers had to be employed in the German aircraft industry, which in 1943 absorbed over 40 per cent of Germany's war production, while only some 6 per cent went on the tanks which were in desperately short supply. Realising that the failure to repel the RAF's bombing raids meant that Germany would lose the War, General Hans Jeschonnek, the Chief of Staff of the Luftwaffe, committed suicide in August 1943, and even Goebbels noted gloomily in his diary, 'We find ourselves in a situation of hopeless inferiority.'

Germany, although suffering a string of heavy defeats at the hands of the Red Army, could not supply the men or material it needed on the Eastern Front because of the vast resources required to counter the Bomber Command offensive. As Robert Tombs points out in his book *The English and Their History*, the bombing campaign starved the Eastern Front of men and weapons, giving the Red Army the vast superiority in tanks and artillery that enabled it to grind down the Wehrmacht. More than 900,000 soldiers were needed to man the German air defences, far more than fought at Stalingrad in 1943 or Normandy in 1944, and around 55,000 anti-aircraft guns were deployed, including nearly 9,000 of the 88mm guns which were the most formidable weapons in Hitler's armoury. Looking back on his own experience of fighting in the front line of the air war, Stevie remarked:

> *By 1943 the barrage of heavy flak which protected every major city was formidable. To approach any city, especially those producing armaments, our soft-skinned aircraft had to penetrate that barrage, which often formed belts several miles deep, every time. The heavy 88mm gun was a superb weapon for anti-aircraft and anti-tank use, but so many of these guns were deployed to deter the RAF that the Russian Front was starved of the one weapon which might have stemmed the Russian tank advance.*

Deadly as the 88mm guns were, Rommel had only thirty-five of them at his disposal when he faced Montgomery in the Western Desert; and in the crucial battle of Kursk in July 1943, which fatally crippled the Wehrmacht, the Red Army was able to deploy twice as many tanks and four times as many artillery pieces as the Germans. Despite the perilous situation on the Eastern Front, some 70 per cent of Germany's fighter planes had to be kept in the West to guard against air attack, and in April 1944 the Luftwaffe could put up no more than 500 planes against a Russian force of some 13,000, which gave the Red Army overwhelming air superiority.

In 1943 Bomber Command was in effect the British front line in Germany. Confronted by a formidable defensive network of anti-aircraft batteries and fighter squadrons, it suffered terrifyingly high losses. When Stevie joined the Battle of the Ruhr, less than one in five of Bomber Command's aircrew were completing the standard thirty-trip tour of operations, and he and his newly formed crew were all too well aware that their chances of survival were very slim:

An abandoned German 88mm Flak gun in the desert. This formidable weapon was mainly kept for home defence against Allied bombers, thus keeping it away from the front lines in both North Africa and Russia.

I was always astonished at the lack of panic among the aircrew who flew on tours. Only Captains of aircraft went to the first briefing, and we'd be told the amount of fuel we were to use, the height at which we were to fly, and not much else. It wasn't until it got to the main briefing when all the crews were there that we saw a big chart showing the target, what route we were going to fly, and the enemy defences, and we had to try and make a mental note of it all. You weren't allowed to write it any of it down on paper. It was pretty obvious that we couldn't all survive, and when you looked around the table at a briefing for 18-20 crews, you knew darn well the next day that at least two or three wouldn't be coming back, and perhaps more. As the Captain, you would come out and try to make a joke or a comment just to lighten the mood and to keep up the morale of your crew. Many would go out after briefing, light up a cigarette or take a lucky pee against the tail wheel. The Tannoy would click, and we'd be sitting outside, waiting for it, but pretending not to be interested.

I never smoked, but nearly all the boys would light up when we finished a raid and were waiting to be picked up and taken to debriefing. But smoking could be dangerous. One night when the Squadron was on ops, a Sergeant on ground crew said to a couple of airmen, "This hangar floor is filthy – clean it before the boys come back." Two of them got to work, then two more joined in, and they got some petrol to scrub the floor with. Unfortunately, one of them lit a cigarette and BANG, the whole hangar went up just like that! One of the poor airmen was killed.

The terrors of the air war were indelibly imprinted on Stevie's memory:

When we approached the target, heavy flak would explode and hurl the aircraft about, while from below, light flak would hose up menacingly. Generally, we tried to avoid taking violent action to avoid flak due to the risk of collision and didn't worry too much unless we could hear it explode, see close bursts, or smell it. We had light-proof compartments, but if we got hit by flak or enemy fire, and they got shredded, we had to watch that we weren't suddenly streaming light out into the darkness so that enemy aircraft could pick us up. Surrounding the intense flak barrage would be hundreds of searchlights. Some of these were radar predicted. When an aircraft was caught, it was speedily enveloped by a huge cone of searchlights, and every available gun would fire at it. It would swerve and dive and climb like a moth in a flame, and all too often there would be a blinding flash as its bombs and fuel blew up in a massive explosion which few crews survived. At the same time, German night fighters buzzed overhead, their cannon at the ready, seeking revenge on those trying to destroy their homeland.

The section which follows is based on the entries in Stevie's log book, detailing each of the operational missions flown by Stevie and his crew. It testifies to the extraordinary courage and determination shown by them, and by all the young men of Bomber Command who volunteered to brave the horrors of the air battle over and over again, and succeeded in turning the tide of the War.

OPERATION 1: DUISBURG, 12 MAY, 1943

Stevie's first operational target was the city of Duisburg, located at the confluence of the Rhine and the Ruhr, the largest inland port in Europe, and home to important chemical, steel, and iron works. Stevie, his Flight Engineer, Eric Blanchard, and his Bomb Aimer Dickie Newcomb were detailed to fly with Acting Squadron Leader Ronald Edward Sidney Smith DFC in Lancaster ED827 DX-Z. They took off from RAF Scampton shortly before midnight, one of twenty Lancasters from 57 Squadron which joined an attacking force of 572 Halifaxes, Wellingtons, Stirlings, and Mosquitos. The Squadron records noted that this was *'believed to be the largest number flown by any four-engine squadron'.*

Stevie's first op was to leave a lasting impression on him. As was standard practice, he flew this op, known as a 'Second Dickie', as Second Pilot in a Lancaster with an experienced pilot and crew as an initiation into the grim realities of the air war:

> *I did my first and only op as Second Pilot. Squadron Leader Smith flew me, my Flight Engineer, Eric Blanchard, and my Bomb Aimer, Dickie Newcomb, to Duisburg. Smith was a nice chap who had very posh flying boots, always polished up very nicely. Long before we arrived at the target, the Ruhr flak batteries put up a huge barrage. 88mm heavy batteries blasted the air with massive explosions which rocked the aircraft, while lighter flak streamed up like flaming onions. The whole scene was lit up by searchlights which turned night into day. It was absolutely terrifying. When you reached the target, it looked just like a flaming street, and you could really feel the heat as you went over the fires. You had to turn up your oxygen, make sure the oxygen mask was working, and then make absolutely certain you were strapped in, because flak exploding nearby could cause the aircraft to drop 300-400 feet just like that. The density of the flak amazed me, but I was impressed by the calmness of the crew and the unflappable behaviour of my Bomb Aimer, who guided us to his first target and obtained a very good photograph. On return, it was sobering to learn that 34 of our aircraft had been shot down, including two from our Squadron. Several other aircraft had been badly damaged. With another twenty-nine trips ahead, I thought my survival chances were small.*

Eric Blanchard recorded his recollections of the Duisburg raid nearly sixty years later, in 2001:

It was now our turn to go on a real op, but first of all, we had to do a 'Second Dickie'. Ours was to be with Squadron Leader Smith, one of the Flight Commanders of 57 Squadron. What was quite unusual was that his own Flight Engineer must have been sick, so Sgt Stevens, my Pilot, and I went together. I was the Flight Engineer, and Sgt Stevens was under instruction from S/Ldr Smith. The Navigator, W/O Brown, was a Canadian, and when he came out of his compartment to see what was happening as we made our approach, we were all pointing to things. I remember someone saying, "Balloon barrage," but he said, "No, it's flak." We bombed the target, and as we started our home run, there was a scream from the Mid-Upper Gunner, Sgt Wood, "Ooooh, my lungs are collapsing." Smith dived down and lost height very quickly, and I could see the moon reflected on the Rhine. I was never to see it like that again. When we came out of the dive, the Mid-Upper Gunner said, "Sorry Skip, it was my Mae West." His life belt had inflated accidentally, and it had been crushing him in the turret.

S/Ldr Ronald Smith [Photograph: Gerald Smith, son of S/Ldr Smith]

At the time of the Duisburg raid, Squadron Leader Smith was on his second tour of operations. He completed it successfully, and was awarded a Bar to his DFC. The citation reads:

The King has been graciously pleased to approve the following awards in recognition of gallantry displayed in flying operations against the enemy.

Bar to Distinguished Flying Cross.

Act. S/Ldr R.E.S. Smith DFC RAFVR, No.57 Sqn – S/Ldr Smith, now on his second tour of operational duty, has completed a large number of sorties. These include nine attacks on targets in the Ruhr Valley, three attacks on Hamburg, and one on Peenemünde.

Squadron Leader Smith was subsequently transferred from 57 Squadron, but tragically he would lose his life on 9 September 1944, when the de Havilland Mosquito he was flying crashed on take-off at RAF Northolt.

Thirty-four aircraft were lost on the Duisburg raid (a loss rate of 5.9 per cent). Two of them were from 57 Squadron. Lancaster ED329, piloted by F/O Victor Wilson, was shot down by a German night fighter and crashed at Maasniel in southern Holland. F/O Wilson, F/O John Wallace, Sgt Samuel Laughlin, Sgt Richard Loverseed, Sgt Alexander Steele and Sgt Cecil Gerding all died in the crash. The sole survivor, Sgt P.G Kehl, the Bomb Aimer, was made a POW (Prisoner of War). Lancaster ED778 was shot down by German night fighters near Netterden in eastern Holland on its way to the target. The Pilot, F/Sgt G.B. Leach, and Navigator, F/Sgt N. Rees, were taken prisoner, but the rest of the crew, F/O Hugh McNeil, Sgt Thomas Gregory, Sgt Henry Sheehan, F/Sgt Milford Levins, and W/O Allan Home were all killed.

Another Lancaster of 57 Squadron had turned back because the Navigator had fallen sick, but the remaining seventeen reached Duisburg. Just able to make out the red Target Indicators (TIs) through the thick smoke rising from the fires started by the preceding wave of aircraft, they bombed from around 19,000 feet and returned safely to Scampton. This was the fourth raid carried out on Duisburg since the start of the Battle of the Ruhr. Stevie noted that the fires they started could be seen as far away as the Dutch coast. Photographs showed that the port area had been severely damaged, and the old town completely gutted. Four of the Thyssen steel works were severely damaged, as were the main railway station and the marshalling yards.

After the Duisburg raid, Stevie conducted more flight tests and training exercise with his crew:

From 13 to 23 May I flew by day and night, continuing to gain experience by practising bombing, gunnery, navigation, and instrument flying. The magnetic compass was 'swung', the bombsight levelled, and the gun turrets tested. The front gun turret had a faulty rotating servo joint which would spray the windscreen with a light oil, and on two occasions I had to land the aircraft at night peering through the small clear vision panel. This was a useful exercise, as there were later occasions when the windscreen became so thickly coated with ice that forward vision was negligible.

After carrying out these tests for performance, speed, fuel consumption, weaponry and instrument calibration, we did some practice bombing and gunnery. We spent some time correcting the P4 compass and getting the bombsight to work to the satisfaction of our Bomb Aimer Dickie Newcomb. George Martin almost lived in the gun turret, and we did occasional long bursts at a wreck just off the coast at Wainfleet, where we dropped several bombs. During our air test on 23 May, Dickie scored two direct hits at Wainfleet, and was happy with the group of bombs we dropped in a banked turn.

When Stevie and his crew joined 57 Squadron in May 1943, they found themselves sharing RAF Scampton with 617 Squadron, which would subsequently be known as 'the Dambusters'. 617 Squadron was in intensive training in preparation for Operation Chastise, the raid on the Eder, Möhne and Sorpe dams led by Wing Commander Guy Gibson which would become the stuff of legend. While Stevie was doing his practice tests in preparation for his second mission, he witnessed the aircraft taking off on the Dams raid:

On 16 May I was doing an air test. I was held back on the runway and had to wait for a 617 Squadron flight to take off. We had noticed the modified bomb bays on their aircraft earlier. They looked like huge dustbins mounted laterally.

Normally, a crowd of airmen and airwomen stood near the take-off point to wave the aircraft farewell and cheer them on their way, but this night no crowd gathered. Only a few duty airmen knew of the impending operation. I had no idea what was happening, nor did anyone else. The officer in charge of security, F/Lt Evans, had all the phone lines tapped. They were cut off at the first hint of a leak, letters were all censored, and if the aircrew of 617 said anything about their mission on the bus or anywhere else in public, they promptly got run in!

Just after I landed, one of the 617 aircraft followed. The pilot was very upset. He was flying so low over the sea that his bomb had struck the water and broken away. Much later, we heard some of the other aircraft returning. As we would soon discover, they had undertaken a raid that made history, and 617 Squadron would be known as the Dambusters.

The morning after the raid, my crew and I went to inspect the model of the Dams that had been made as a guide for the raid. It was an absolute masterpiece.

A 617 Squadron Lancaster taking off on the evening of 16 May 1943 from Scampton for the famous Dambuster Raid. Stevie witnessed it all as he waited in his own Lancaster for permission to take off for an air test.

H-'Harry', the Lancaster Stevie had witnessed return early, was piloted by F/O Geoff Rice, who had served with 57 Squadron before being transferred to 617. His target had been the Sorpe Dam, but he had misjudged his height and brushed the sea as he approached the coast of Holland. The bouncing bomb designed by Barnes Wallis had been torn away, and as Rice fought to gain height, water had poured down the fuselage to the rear of his aircraft, almost drowning the Rear Gunner, Flight Sergeant Stephen Burns. Aborting the mission, Rice returned to Scampton, and landed after managing to lower the undercarriage of his aircraft manually because of a hydraulic failure.

Like Stevie, Eric Blanchard remembered the night of the Dambusters raid well:

617 Squadron didn't do any operations, they just seemed to be practising taking off and landing. We hadn't yet done an operation ourselves, and I saw 617 aircraft coming around to take off in front of us. They looked strange, as they had bombs that looked like great big drums underneath. We went off on our practice trip to Wales, came back and went to bed. Then the next morning, a big low-loader lorry was outside collecting kit. That was always a bad sign, although we wouldn't have known — we were a bit 'green' as we hadn't yet done an op — but all the kit going on to the lorry belonged to the 617 crews who hadn't come back.

We were told we could go to the Intelligence Room and see what had happened, and there we saw the models of the Dams that had been used for the briefing, and some early pictures of the damage that had been done.

OPERATION 2: DORTMUND, 23 MAY, 1943

In the week after Operation Chastise, Bomber Command did not mount any significant operations, but on 23 May it launched its heaviest attack to date in the Battle of the Ruhr. A giant force of 826 Lancasters, Halifaxes, Wellingtons, and Stirlings guided by Mosquitos was detailed to attack Dortmund. Twenty-four aircraft from 57 Squadron were assigned to the raid, and the Squadron records noted, *'This was easily a record number of sorties for the squadron and is believed to be the biggest effort put out by a four-engine squadron'.* Stevie took off at 22:30 in his Lancaster E-'Easy'.

Fifty years later, on 23 May 1993, Stevie wrote an account of the Dortmund raid, his first action with his own crew: Sgt Ernie Howes (Navigator), Sgt Eric Blanchard (Flight Engineer), Sgt Dickie Newcomb (Bomb Aimer), Sgt Ken Brown (Wireless Operator), Sgt George Martin (Mid-Upper Gunner) and Sgt Bernie Townsend (Rear Gunner). The raid turned out to be a baptism of fire for Stevie and the crew of E-'Easy'.

There were twenty-four of us pilots at the Captains' briefing, so we knew it would be a big raid, and were told that this would be the largest operation since the previous year's 'Thousand Bomber Raid'. An hour before take-off, we went out to the aircraft and checked everything. We climbed to 20,000, feet. I let the automatic pilot fly for a bit, but whipped it out when I was caught in the slipstream of another aircraft I had not seen in the gloom. The navigation lights were extinguished as we crossed the English coast. There were several uncomfortable bumps caused by the slipstreams of other aircraft. I checked all the equipment again, and the Gunners tested the guns. Ernie, the Navigator, sounded calm and confident. Flak opened up over Holland, and an aircraft was coned by searchlights and shot down. We were in the sixth wave to bomb. The target looked like a string of brilliant jewels where fires were burning. I opened the bomb doors and flew steadily, obeying the Bomb Aimer's instructions. Flak was bursting all over the place. The Gunners started to shoot at an approaching fighter. He sheared off, and we released our bombs.

When Stevie completed his bombing run, he felt a wave of exhilaration:

As the bombs left the aircraft, I felt a moment of exhilaration. Two years earlier the Germans had dropped a bomb on my house, temporarily burying my parents and destroying all my belongings but for a school prize and a pair of Scout shorts. Now, I thought, I had paid the debt I owed.

But any thoughts of retribution were short-lived. '*After that, I had had my fill of hatred,*' Stevie remarked in an interview published in the *Eastern Daily Press* on 5 December 2013. As he turned for home, he was attacked for a second time by a German fighter:

I held the aircraft steady to get a good picture of the target, and closed the bomb doors. As I turned for home, the Gunners reported a fighter approaching from starboard. I turned steeply into him, George and Bernie both opened fire. He disappeared, and we flew home unharmed. Several aircraft landed before us, but at last I got the instruction to 'Pancake', and made a good landing on the grass. I went to debriefing feeling euphoric, and the next morning I went out early to look at the photograph. Slap bang on target.

The two attacks, by Junkers Ju88 and Messerschmitt Me109 fighter aircraft, did not inflict any serious damage, and Stevie and his crew returned safely to Scampton, landing at 04:05 on 24 May. Stevie noted laconically in his log book, '*Intercepted on run up and after bombing. Good show!*' Later he noted that the damage inflicted by the raid had been exceptionally concentrated and severe, and that the huge Hoechst steel works complex was put out of production for a lengthy period, with 48 buildings suffering hits.

This came at a high cost. Thirty-eight aircraft from the force sent to Dortmund failed to return (a loss rate of 4.6 per cent). Among them were two from 57 Squadron. F/O Ernest Chivers in Lancaster ED707 was shot down over the Island of Texel in north Holland, and was killed together with all the members of his crew: Sgt Philip Parkin, Sgt Thomas Bayles, Sgt Ivor Jervis, Sgt David Robb, Sgt William Rawnsley, and F/Sgt William Bestwick. Sergeant Alan Leslie, piloting Lancaster ED970, was intercepted over the North Sea at around 02:00 while homeward bound, and he, too, was shot down and killed with all his crew: Sgt Harry Kleiner, P/O John Morton, Sgt Peter Hemingway, Sgt Alexander Henderson, Sgt Peter Daly and Sgt Walter Bennett.

Four days after the Dortmund raid, Stevie and his crew were given nine days leave. The start of their leave coincided with the visit of King George VI to RAF Scampton on 27 May to congratulate 617 Squadron on the Dams Raid. Stevie was eager to begin his leave, and approached his CO, Wing Commander Hopcroft, for permission to absent himself from the parade in honour of the King:

> *When the King came to congratulate 617 Squadron, our Squadron was included in the parade. We were all preparing for it, and I went to see Wing Commander Hopcroft and asked, "I should be going on leave tomorrow, Sir. Would you mind if I don't go on this parade?"*
>
> *He said, "Not at all, you go and enjoy yourself. B-- off out of here, find the nearest pub, and go and get effing plastered. When you're well and truly p--ssed, find a wicked woman and sh--g yourself silly. You'll feel better for that when you start your leave!"*
>
> *I replied, "Are you suggesting, Sir, that I go early, get piddled out of my mind, get VD, then start my leave?"*
>
> *He looked at me and said, "Well, Stevens, you've got to grow up sometime!"*
>
> *Hopcroft was a splendid leader, good to the point of brutality. He backed his aircrew up to the limit, but if they did step out of line, he would tear them off a ferocious strip, and his language would have made a hardened Billingsgate fish porter blush.*

Stevie stayed long enough to watch the parade, and saw Hopcroft make a typically noisy intervention as 57 Squadron were marching out to greet the King and Queen:

> *I saw the King and Queen come in just as I was leaving. They passed the office where Hopcroft was, and he screamed out right across the parade ground at Squadron Leader Avis, who was one of our Flight Commanders, "AVIS, AVIS, SWING YOUR EFFING ARMS!" Hopcroft was like that, he really lost his temper sometimes. It was the only time I ever saw anyone shout like that at a senior officer on parade.*

The King inspecting ground crew on 27 May at Scampton in front of Hopcroft's 'Frederick III' ED989. His previous 'Frederick II' (seen earlier in this book) had been shot down three days earlier.

Wing Commander Frederick Campbell Hopcroft DFC, who had commanded 57 Squadron since 23 September 1942, had a cartoon image of himself painted on his Lancaster, F-'Freddie'. He was respected and admired by the men of 57 Squadron because he led from the front, and flew on raids that were likely to be dangerous. He also made a point of driving around in his car to check with each pilot going on ops before take-off that everything was in order. In October 1943 he was awarded a DSO in recognition of his courage and leadership qualities. His citation reads:

W/Cdr F.C. Hopcroft D.F.C. R.A.F. No 57 Sqn. W/Cdr Hopcroft has rendered valuable service since the commencement of hostilities. W/Cdr Hopcroft has undertaken very many sorties, involving attacks on a wide range of important targets. In July 1943 he flew the leading aircraft of a bomber force which attacked a switching and transformer station in North Italy. In spite of opposition from the ground defence, the target was subjected to a determined attack from low level.

Stevie recalled:

I think Hopcroft retired and ran a pig farm. He was always the first back from a raid. He told us in no uncertain terms that it was against regulations to dive down and gather speed to get home, and that he would severely reprimand anyone who did. I think he ignored that regulation himself, and that was why he would always be home first. I remember him once asking me:

"Stevens! What height did you fly on your return trip?"

"22-23,000 feet, Sir."

"I'll chuck you off the Squadron if you do any more effing low flying!"

OPERATION 3: DÜSSELDORF, 11 JUNE, 1943

When he returned from leave, Stevie resumed operational flying and took part in a massive raid on Düsseldorf, in which twenty-three aircraft from 57 Squadron joined an attacking force of 760 aircraft.

Dickie Newcomb was diagnosed with tonsillitis and declared unfit to fly. In cases of sickness, it was standard practice in Bomber Command for replacements to be drafted in from a crew not on operational duty. Sergeant I.H. Lambdin stood in as Bomb Aimer. Stevie took off at 22:37. Two aircraft from 57 Squadron had to return early: P/O P.H.F. Hawkins with the rear turret unserviceable in Lancaster ED616 and F/Sgt T.G.L. Irwin in Lancaster ED994 with engine failure. All the remaining aircraft, including

Stevie's, reached the target. The fires caused by the raid were of such intensity that they could be seen on the return journey from the Dutch coast.

Thirty-eight aircraft failed to return (a loss rate of 4.9 per cent), but none of them were from 57 Squadron, and Stevie landed safely at Scampton at 03:56. His log book notes that they were attacked by a Junkers Ju88 night fighter, but that no serious damage was sustained. To be attacked by a Ju88 and survive required coolness and skill on the part of the pilot and the gunners, whose job it was to provide a running commentary on the position of the fighter to enable the pilot to take evasive action and at the same time try to give the gunners a field of fire. The tactic most commonly employed by the Ju88 was to try to fly underneath a Lancaster and rake it from close range. The odds were stacked in favour of the fighter, which was equipped with cannon, whereas the Lancaster was equipped only with much lighter Browning machine guns. As Stevie put it:

Three 20mm cannons were fitted in the nose of the fighter. Each cannon fired at the rate of 520 rounds a minute, and these rounds were fed to the cannon in sequences of three. The first round was a thin-cased high explosive shell containing Hexogen Aluminium; the second round was an explosive armour-piercing shell with a heavy steel point; and the third shell was an incendiary which burned for nearly a second at 2000-3000 degrees C.

The German night fighters were very good. They shot down a lot of people and adapted their techniques as the War progressed. I spoke to one German pilot after the War, wearing a Knight's Cross around his neck, who said he had been credited with shooting down more than a hundred of our bombers. He told me that once the German fighters had targeted an aircraft, they would follow it, line it up, and then fly underneath it, where they were invisible to the crew. When in position, they would fire with their upward guns into the petrol tank, bomb load and ammunition tanks, taking the crew completely unawares and giving them no chance. Knowing that the Lancs would all be flying close beside one another for safety in numbers, the Germans were often able to shoot down more than one aircraft in a single sortie.

Sergeant Lamdin, who replaced Dickie Newcomb as Stevie's Bomb Aimer on this trip, was shot down shortly afterwards, on 24/25 June, on a mission to Wuppertal. He managed to bail out and was taken prisoner, but the pilot, Sgt Stanley Fallows, and the rest of the crew were killed.

OPERATION 4: BOCHUM, 12 JUNE, 1943

There was to be no respite for Stevie. The following night, he was detailed to take part in the third attack mounted by Bomber Command on Bochum, just west of Dortmund.

Twenty-two Lancasters from 57 Squadron joined a force of 503 Lancasters, Halifaxes and Mosquitoes. Dickie Newcomb returned as the Bomb Aimer, and Sgt J.B. Hughes took over from Bernie Townsend as the Rear Gunner. Stevie took off at 22:51.

He and his crew completed their mission and returned to Scampton at 04:45. There was heavy cloud cover over Dortmund, and the target markers had been dropped short, so the raid was not considered a success.

One of the 24 aircraft lost on the raid (a loss rate of 4.8 per cent) was from 57 Squadron. Lancaster ED668, DX-Y, was shot down over the North Sea around 02:50, and the entire crew, Sgt Kenneth Dowding, Sgt Thomas Burgess, Sgt George Ayres, Sgt Walter Redman, Sgt Jack Hyam, Sgt Stanley Tuck and F/Sgt Clifford Challenger, were lost without trace. Four other Lancasters from 57 Squadron had to return early. W/Cdr Hopcroft and Sgt 'Jos' Josling both suffered oxygen failure; S/Ldr Leland had intercom failure; and Sgt. J. Parker had a rear turret malfunction.

OPERATION 5: OBERHAUSEN, 14 JUNE, 1943

The Battle of the Ruhr was unrelenting in its intensity, and Stevie undertook his third operation in just four days in what must have been a mentally and physically exhausting period.

On the night of 14/15 June, eleven aircraft from 57 Squadron joined an attacking force of 186 other aircraft to attack the city of Oberhausen, a key producer of iron and steel in the northwest of the Ruhr. Stevie took off at 22:31 in Lancaster ED931, which had been assigned to him for this raid. Sergeant Maynard Burston again replaced Dickie Newcomb as Bomb Aimer, and Bernie Townsend returned as Rear Gunner.

Three of the 57 Squadron aircraft had to turn back because of technical malfunction. P/O R.H. Wilson in Lancaster W4797 lost his starboard inner engine; F/Lt W.E. Roberts in ED779 had problems with brake pressure; and Sgt P.J. Piggin suffered oxygen failure in W4358. All the other aircraft reached the target, but they encountered heavy night fighter presence.

Stevie was intercepted by both Ju88 and Me109 fighters, but managed to take evasive action, and his Mid-Upper Gunner George Martin claimed to have hit one of the attacking aircraft. Stevie landed safely at 03:42, with no significant damage to his own aircraft.

A total of 17 aircraft failed to return from this raid (a very high loss rate of 8.6 per cent), and though all 57 Squadron aircraft made it back to base, one was badly shot up. Sgt Bert Moores, a friend of Stevie's who was, like Stevie, on his fifth operation with the Squadron as a pilot, was attacked on the approach to the target by a Ju88 fighter. His Lancaster, DX-M 'Minnie the Moocher', took incoming fire which riddled the fuselage with holes, damaging the radio and navigational equipment; and a cannon shell exploded in the rear turret which killed the Rear Gunner, Sergeant Reginald Haynes. Bert Moores had pressed on and completed his mission, managing to land his badly damaged aircraft despite a burst tyre.

Stevie recalled this incident vividly:

> *A pilot I knew quite well, Bert Moores, came back one night, and his Rear Gunner had been shot to pieces. In fact, his head had been blown off. The next morning, Bert Moores watched while the remains of his Rear Gunner were washed from the rear turret, and went straight back to operational flying. In due course, he was awarded a DFC for pressing on with the raid despite losing his Gunner and sustaining severe damage to his aircraft.*

Bert Moores was promoted to Pilot Officer, and awarded a DFC in November 1943. The citation referred to the bravery he had displayed on the Oberhausen raid:

> *This officer has completed a large number of sorties, including attacks on such strongly defended targets as Berlin, Hamburg and industrial centres in the Ruhr. He has displayed great skill and determination throughout, and his efforts have been worthy of the highest praise. On one occasion his aircraft sustained extensive damage when attacked by a fighter. In spite of this, P/O Moores skilfully out-manoeuvred the attacker and afterwards flew his damaged aircraft to base. His tenacity was highly commendable.*

The wrecked FN20 rear turret of Lancaster ED413, DX-M flown by Bert Moores. The rear gunner was killed instantly.

OPERATION 6: COLOGNE, 16 JUNE, 1943

Back in his own Lancaster, E-'Easy', Stevie was among nine aircraft from 57 Squadron which formed part of a force of 202 aircraft detailed to attack Cologne, a key industrial target for Bomber Command. This was the first of three raids Stevie would make on Cologne in the space of three weeks. Sgt Burston again replaced Dickie Newcomb as the Bomb Aimer, and Sgt E.W. 'Wally' Bark deputised for George Martin as the Mid-Upper Gunner. Wally Bark was an experienced Gunner who formed part of the crew of an American pilot, Sgt Jack Russell, who was on detachment to the RAF. Jack Russell had joined 57 Squadron on 5 March 1943, and Stevie remembered him *'appearing in his American uniform, smoking a briar pipe, and saying that he was being paid more than the CO.'* Stevie took off at 22:16, and E-'Easy' was one of only four aircraft from 57 Squadron to reach the target. Stevie noted that only half of the aircraft detailed to make the attack claimed to have completed their mission successfully.

The weather hampered this particular raid. Severe icing conditions crippled much of the bomber force, less than half of which managed to reach the target, which was obscured by 9/10ths cloud cover. S/Ldr Smith, with whom Stevie had flown as Second Pilot on his first op in May, suffered electrical failure in EE193 and F/Lt W.E. Roberts suffered oxygen failure in ED779; both were forced to return. Sgt G.N. Parker in ED943, Sgt E.T. Hodgkinson in LM322 and F/O P. Whittam in EE197 all had iced-up turrets, and they, too, returned early.

Fourteen aircraft were lost (a loss rate of 6.6 per cent), but none of these were from 57 Squadron, and Stevie and his crew landed safely at 03:50.

After returning from this raid, Stevie was debriefed by Air Vice Marshal Sir Ralph Cochrane, AOC 5 Group, Bomber Command. Impressed by the fact that Stevie was one of only four pilots from the Squadron to have reached the target, Cochrane recommended him for a commission.

This was the second occasion on which Sgt Maynard Burston replaced Dickie Newcomb as Bomb Aimer in Stevie's crew. Just a few days later, on 21 June, he went on a raid to Krefeld in a Lancaster piloted by Sgt G. Kitson which was brought down near Boxtel in Holland. There were no survivors. Sgt Burston lies in the General Cemetery at Eindhoven.

American Jack Russell with his crew; L-R; Jack Lazenby, Jack Russell, Richard Wright, John Dow, Nick Golden, Ron Marston and Wally Bark. Wally Bark flew with Stevie as a replacement gunner on this raid.

OPERATION 7: KREFELD, 21 JUNE, 1943

The city of Krefeld, the largest producer of specialist alloy steels in Germany and a key manufacturer of textiles, was to be Stevie's own next target, and his last for the month of June. A large bomber force of 705 aircraft was assembled for the raid, thirteen of them from 57 Squadron. Stevie, again in his trusted E-'Easy', took off at 23:20. Sgt Arthur Matthews came in as Bomb Aimer for Dickie Newcomb, and Sgt V.R. Hawking replaced Sgt Bark as the Mid-Upper Gunner. Hawking was a member of the crew of P/O Keith Ryrie, who had joined 57 Squadron at much the same time as Stevie. Stevie remembered Keith Ryrie as *'a slim, red-headed Scot'*. He finished his tour of operations soon after Stevie, and, like Stevie, was awarded an immediate DFC. His citation appeared together with Stevie's in the *London Gazette* on 23 November 1943.

This proved to be a hazardous mission. Sgt Matthews, the replacement Bomb Aimer, lost his nerve when they reached the target, and Stevie was obliged to do his bombing run three times. This was an extremely dangerous manoeuvre, as it meant turning back into the bomber stream and being exposed for a lengthy period to attacks by German night-fighters:

> *We got to the target, and Sgt Matthews, the substitute Bomb Aimer, started saying, "Left, left, left," then he just stopped. I said "Bomb Aimer?" No response, so I repeated, "Bomb Aimer?". Nothing again, so I said, "Bomb Aimer, for goodness' sake give me some directions!" He still didn't respond, so I had to go around again, which is a really dangerous thing to do, as all the other aircraft are coming towards you at the point where you turn. I told him to get his finger out, and that I didn't just want him to chuck the bombs away, but get them off on the target. We went around again, and once more he started giving me directions, then began stuttering. I said to him if he did that once more, and I had to go around again, I would shoot him and have him chucked out of the aircraft! I had never had to say anything like that before, but it was incredibly dangerous for all of us. Poor old Matthews, I didn't fly with him again, and I never saw him after that.*

Fortunate not to have been attacked during his three bombing runs, when he would have had to hold course and been unable to take evasive action, Stevie landed back at Scampton at 04:00. Nearly half of the centre of Krefeld had been burnt out, and it was also reported that a number of industrial production sites had been so severely damaged that they would be unable to operate for six months.

The clear, moonlit conditions over the target were ideal for the bombers; but they also favoured the German night fighters, and there were heavy casualties, with 44 aircraft failing to return (a loss rate of 6.2 per cent), including one Lancaster from 57 Squadron. Sgt George Kitson and his crew in Lancaster W4377 were shot down at 02:39 and crashed north of Boxtel in Holland. Sgt Kitson, Sgt George Hull, Sgt Arthur Pain, Sgt Louis Ray, Sgt Henry Alexander, Sgt George Robinson and Sgt Maynard Burston, who had flown with Stevie just a few days before as his replacement Bomb Aimer on the missions to Oberhausen and Cologne, were all killed. Another aircraft from 57 Squadron suffered damage: Sgt P.J. Piggin, flying Lancaster ED698, was attacked by a night-fighter as he approached the target. His rear turret was put out of action, so he released his bomb load on flak positions before turning back to base.

As for Sgt Matthews, he evidently recovered his nerve. He was commissioned and went on to serve with 630 Squadron. On 23/24 November 1943, he took part in an attack on Berlin in a Lancaster piloted by P/O Joseph Howe. Matthews, Howe and the rest of the crew were lost without trace, and are commemorated on the Runnymede Memorial.

In an intense series of operations carried out in June 1943, 57 Squadron had sent a total of a hundred and fifty Lancasters on 11 missions. Eighteen Lancasters were forced to return early because of poor weather, illness, and mechanical or technical failures, while four had never returned at all.

Stevie and his crew were given a further period of leave, and it would be almost two weeks before they returned to operational duties.

When he arrived at the railway station at Grantham to start his leave, Stevie chanced across a fellow trainee from War Eagle Field:

We were at Grantham Station, and I happened to see C.V.L.R. Hulbert, who had trained with me at War Eagle Field in California. Though it was absolutely pouring with rain, he was sitting outside on the steps of the station. I went up to him and said, "Hello, I haven't seen you since our American days, what's happened to you?"

He said, "Steve, I'm sorry, but I've just got a premonition."

"Well, go and spend a penny and get rid of it," I replied.

He said, "No, I really don't think I'm going to survive another month." I could tell that he was quite serious.

I said, "Well, don't worry, we all feel like that sometimes."

He wasn't crying, but he was utterly miserable. He said, "No, I just feel desperate, Steve. I'm sure I'm going to get killed."

I took him to a pub and we had a couple of pints, but when we came out, he said, "I don't feel any better, I'm still sure I'm going to die shortly." We said our goodbyes, and sure enough, a week or so later, he was killed, just as he had feared. He took off from his airfield at Dunholme Lodge, and was shot down on his return journey by a night fighter. At War Eagle Field he had been a happy, charming man who enjoyed parties and socialising, but when I saw him again, he was certain that the figure of death was on him, and he was really struggling to hold himself together. It was a tragic loss of a splendid chap.

CVLR Hulbert at War Eagle Field in 1942

Sergeant Charles Vernon Leslie Hulbert flew his one and only operational sortie with 44 Squadron, which was based at Dunholme Lodge, on the night of 28 June 1943, just a few days after his meeting with Stevie. His was one of twelve aircraft from the Squadron detailed to raid Cologne. It was shot down over Nuenen, near Eindhoven in Holland, by a German night fighter, and Hulbert and his entire crew were killed. Hulbert was just 21. He is buried in Eindhoven with the members of his crew: Sgt Dennis Lewis, Sgt Joshua Sykes, Sgt Arthur Tooth, Sgt George Denney, Sgt Thomas Jones and F/Sgt Patrick Galligan.

OPERATION 8: COLOGNE, 3 JULY, 1943

When Stevie returned from leave, he was detailed to make his second attack on Cologne. The regular crew of E-'Easy' were all back in place, with Dickie Newcomb returning as Bomb Aimer, and George Martin as Mid-Upper Gunner. Six hundred and fifty-three aircraft took part in the attack, including twenty from 57 Squadron. Stevie and his crew took off at 22:57, reached the target, and returned safely at 04:50 after what he described in his log book as an *'Uneventful trip'*. Twenty industrial complexes were reported as having been destroyed, with fires still visible as far as the French coast.

On this raid, the Luftwaffe employed a new defensive tactic known as *Wilde Sau* ('Wild Boar'). German pilots flying at pre-arranged altitudes to avoid their own anti-aircraft fire were ordered to engage British bombers illuminated by searchlight batteries. The Luftwaffe shot down thirty British aircraft (a loss rate of 4.6 per cent), twelve of them using the *Wilde Sau* tactic. No aircraft from 57 Squadron were lost, but F/Sgt H.S Gifford, flying Lancaster ED757, was forced to land at RAF Waterbeach, just north of Cambridge because of engine problems; P/O Eric Hodgkinson returned early after his Lancaster ED941 collided with another aircraft just off the coast of Lowestoft, and Sgt Joseph Howe in ED758 aborted the mission after compass failure.

Shortly after Stevie returned from this raid, he was granted an emergency commission and promoted to Pilot Officer. This was on the recommendation of Air Vice Marshal Sir Ralph Cochrane, AOC 5 Group, on his return from his first raid on Cologne on 16 June.

Stevie with his mother in June 1943, shortly before he was commissioned. This is the only photograph of him in his Flight Sergeant's uniform.

OPERATION 9: COLOGNE, 8 JULY, 1943

After a few short night flying and bombing practices on 5 and 7 July, Stevie undertook his third mission to Cologne. With his crew unchanged, and flying in E-'Easy', he formed part of an attacking force of two hundred and eighty-two Lancasters and six Mosquitos. The western area of the city was now the target, the eastern area having been bombed on the previous raid five days earlier.

If Stevie's previous trip to Cologne had been uneventful, this turned out to be anything but:

> *On 8 July 1943, we were briefed to bomb Cologne. The weather was expected to be unsettled, and the main force was composed entirely of Lancasters. The target was cloud covered, but the sky marking was good. We saw a small cluster of red target indicators and bombed them, then set course for home. Suddenly a loud crash shook the aircraft; there was a smell of cordite and dust, and a great deal of noise. I called each of the crew in turn. The Gunners did not reply. I asked the Wireless Operator, Ken Brown, to see if he could find out what had happened to them. He went back, and I lost contact with him. After a while I asked the Bomb Aimer, Dickie Newcomb, to see if he could find out what was going on. He, too, disappeared and lost contact.*
>
> *I was beginning to feel a bit lonely in the cockpit, and the screaming draught and creaking noises did not help, but the aircraft had settled down and was handling well, with the engines steady. Eric Blanchard seemed happy with the fuel and thought the flying control rods were running smoothly, so I asked him to see if he could find out what was happening in the rear of the aircraft. He took a full oxygen bottle and our last feeble torch, and made his way to the rear, leaving me and Ernie Howes, our Navigator, feeling isolated in the front of the aircraft. Ernie was trying to ignore the excitement around him as he concentrated on his calculations, which were made more difficult because none of our navigational equipment was working. Using 'Dead Reckoning' to plot his Mercator chart, he was trying to estimate our course for home and write up his Navigation log.*
>
> *After what seemed an age, the intercom sprang to life. "Engineer to Skipper, I've pulled the Bomb Aimer up the fuselage and am going back for the Wireless Op." Heavy breathing and gasps were heard, and then nothing. Another series of gasps as the microphone woke up again. "I've got the Wireless Op on the bed, and both of them on oxygen. Bit of a shambles at the back. I'll go back and see what I can sort out."*

Ernie Howes was looking out of the front windscreen trying to find a landmark, and my eyes were covering every part of the sky searching for fighters and gazing below for flak. The microphone came on again. "Skipper from Engineer, I have plugged the Mid-Upper Gunner into the oxygen, but I can't get the Rear Gunner to help himself. I'm coming back."

My instincts were to dive down to a level where the air was less cold, but light flak caused me to think again. I was not sure of the strength of the fuselage, and wanted to keep sufficient height to bail out or fly home.

Eric Blanchard came back and told me what had happened. Only those who know how cramped and awkward the rear of the Lancaster is will be able to appreciate his efforts. He had struggled in the dark and extreme cold trying to rescue four members of the crew. He was clad in his flying gear and relying on a bottle of oxygen to breathe. He had discovered a large hole caused by flak under the mid-upper gun turret. Dickie Newcomb had made his way to the rear and found the Wireless Op Ken Brown in a heap on the floor. Ken's leg had gone through the weakened part of the fuselage, and

A view inside a Lancaster from the mid-upper turret position, looking forward to the cockpit area. (A) is an inspection window through to the bomb-bay and beyond that is the raised floor which is the roof of the bomb-bay. (B) is the main spar which has to be climbed over to get to (C) the cockpit area. Difficult enough to clamber through on the ground but even more challenging at night, in the air and in full flying gear.

been trapped by the slipstream. Dickie Newcomb had tried to free Ken's leg, but his oxygen supply had failed, and he had lost consciousness. Eric had pulled Dickie along the fuselage and plugged him into the oxygen supply, then returned to rescue Ken Brown. He had manoeuvred Ken's trapped leg back through the fuselage, managed to get him to the rest bed, and given him oxygen. He then went back to get George Martin and brought him round by plugging him into the oxygen supply. Finally, he went all the way back down the plane to help the Rear Gunner, Bernie Townsend, but Bernie was rigid in his turret, very cold, and struggling to breathe, and Eric was unable to move him.

Stevie landed E-'Easy' and his shaken crew at Scampton at 04:42:

We lost height as soon as we safely could, flew back to Scampton, landed, and taxied to the dispersal. An ambulance arrived and collected Ken Brown, and it was discovered that he had a frostbitten foot. I got out of the aircraft feeling tired and drained. Bernie Townsend's face was ghastly, and his hands were trembling so much that he had to make several attempts to light his cigarette. He could not control his lips when he did get the cigarette between them. Was he packing up? George Martin had a slight sheen on his face, and there were patches where the sweat had frozen under his helmet. Dickie Newcomb looked pale and drawn, but managed to say he was alright. The Navigator, Ernie Howes, put down his flight bag containing his charts and equipment, smoked quietly, then said, "That was a bit fraught." It certainly was! He had shown great skill in getting us back to base with no navigational aids working.

During debriefing, Eric Blanchard helped me to fill in Form 700, on which we set down our account of the raid and also reported damage. When we finished, he lit his briar pipe and looked no more concerned than if we had just done a practice flight. He had been moving around in our dark, damaged, bitterly cold aircraft on an oxygen bottle, giving First Aid to four injured and unconscious crew mates at great risk to himself, and yet, as always, he exuded an air of calm confidence. As for me, I offered a prayer of thanks for safely escaping a dangerous situation and for having completed one more op. Could our experience and luck hold out to complete a tour?

Tongue in cheek, Stevie noted in his log book *'Quiet Trip! W/O Frostbitten Foot'*.

Stevie and the crew of E-'Easy' were not alone in encountering trouble on the Cologne raid. Sgt Hilary Lewis and the crew of ED947, DX-G, were shot down over Belgium, near Evergem, just north of Ghent. Before the Lancaster crashed, it jettisoned its bombs near the village of Oosteeklo, and the crew had managed to bail out. Sgt Lewis, Sgt John Twigg, Sgt John

Flight Engineer Sgt Eric Blanchard, May 1943

Seeles, Sgt William Bailey, Sgt Joseph Hodgson, Sgt James Stevenson and Sgt Howard Dewar were all captured and taken prisoner. F/Sgt G.A. Parker's Lancaster ED616 was damaged by flak, and Lancaster ED779, piloted by F/Lt J.M. Greig, was attacked several times by a night-fighter over the target. His Mid-Upper Gunner, F/Sgt Joseph Nutt, was seriously wounded, and F/Lt Greig made an emergency landing at RAF Manston in an attempt to save his life. The Squadron records reported, *'This desperate attempt was in vain, however, as F/Sgt Nutt died the following day.'* He was just 22 years old.

OPERATION 10: GELSENKIRCHEN, 9 JULY, 1943

There was to be no respite. The day after being shot up over Cologne, Stevie was detailed to attack Gelsenkirchen, just northwest of Essen. The flak damage on E-'Easy' had been swiftly patched up, and F/O R.E. Gibbons was drafted in as the Wireless Operator to replace Ken Brown, who was in hospital being treated for hypothermia and frostbite, while Sgt H.E. Morris replaced Bernie Townsend as the Rear Gunner.

Four hundred and eighteen aircraft attacked Gelsenkirchen, with eleven Lancasters from 57 Squadron taking part in the raid. Stevie took off from Scampton at 22:20 and returned safely at 05:30. No aircraft from 57 Squadron were lost, but P/O Bill McCrea was forced to return early in ED944 with engine failure. All the others reached the target, but heavy cloud cover made accurate bombing difficult. The markers were inaccurate and the bombing extremely scattered, resulting in only light damage to the target. The returning crews reported seeing large explosions and fires through occasional gaps in the cloud, but the raid was deemed unsuccessful. Twelve aircraft were lost in total (a loss rate of 2.9 per cent), none from 57 Squadron, but Stevie noted in his log book that they had encountered *'intense flak'*, and later described it as so heavy that *'we could have taxied on it'*.

OPERATION 11: TURIN, 12 JULY, 1943

After ten successive missions over Germany, Stevie's eleventh operation took him to Italy. Allied troops had begun the invasion of Sicily on 10 July, and Stevie would recall later:

I was the Captain of one of a force of two hundred and ninety-five Lancasters which was to undertake the longest operational flight in history. Our mission was to attack the factories in Turin, incite a little more disaffection towards Mussolini, and help the troops invading through Sicily.

Stevie and his crew flew in Lancaster ED944, with Bernie Townsend returning as Rear Gunner. Sgt J.F. Helmore, who normally flew in the crew of Stevie's friend 'Jos' Josling, stood in as the Wireless Operator for Ken Brown, who was still in hospital. Fifteen aircraft from 57 Squadron joined a force of 295 Lancasters from 1, 5 and 8 Groups, with Stevie taking off from Scampton at 22:03.

The operation turned out to be an extreme test of endurance, as it took more than ten hours to reach Turin and return to England. This was a raid that would remain indelibly etched in Stevie's memory:

I was at the controls going over the Alps. There was black cloud, it was very bumpy, and I could hardly see the inboard propellers. We were going through a fierce storm, with beautiful Catherine wheels and great jagged flashes of white-blue lightning. I remember pointing out something to Eric Blanchard, and I was quite surprised to find a spark about a foot long shooting from my fingertip.

We were tossed about like corks in a rough sea, with fire flashes sparking over the windscreen, and haloes surrounding the propellers so that I could see the outboard engines again. The aircraft was flung over 200 feet downwards, with the altimeter unwinding in spite of climbing revs and boost. The peaks of the mountains seemed very close, but there was a sudden lift, and we were flung 100 feet upwards. There were crashes on the side of the fuselage. Flak? No, not here! What then? After a while, I realised that ice forming on the propellers was being flung off into the side of the fuselage.

The engine revs fluctuated. If they cut, we were finished. There were several more loud crashes and bangs, and another blinding flash of lightning. The compass was circling wearily, but thank God, the gyro and gyro-compass were still working, and the engines seemed to be steady again. My back, arms, and legs were aching from the effort to control the aircraft, but we were not yet near the target, and we had another 1,000 miles to fly before we returned to base. A noise came through from the Wireless Op to say that his set had been struck by lightning and his trailing aerial had disappeared. We were being tossed about like a small cork in a tropical storm, and I had to wrestle with the flying controls to keep what stability I could.

Eric Blanchard impressed me with his total sangfroid. He was sitting on the floor absorbed in his work in spite of the extreme turbulence and the overpowering noise. I asked him what he was doing. He just said, "Just checking the fuel consumption, Skipper," in a voice as steady as it would have been had we been circling the airfield on a calm afternoon. Luckily the weather cleared as we approached the target, and Turin was bombed.

After the attack, Stevie and his crew had the difficult and dangerous task of making their way home on very limited fuel reserves, and with their radio not functioning. As it was high summer, and the nights were short, they had been routed over Switzerland and France to the Bay of Biscay, then back up the Atlantic coast to avoid German fighters. When they reached the English coast, they were unsure of their position because of heavy cloud cover, and Stevie was preparing to bail out. Then, suddenly and unexpectedly, there was a break in the cloud, Stevie put the nose down, and discovered that they had fetched up, as if by a miracle, directly over the remote RAF station at Davidstow Moor in Cornwall:

It was a long time to be strapped in the seat, but it wasn't difficult keeping awake or alert as you are always scared something might come up behind you. Our outward journey had been about 700 miles, but our homeward trip was more than 1,300 miles and the tanks were nearly dry. Instead of the clear weather for which we had hoped, low cloud covered the coast, and we could only see small unidentifiable inlets through patches of cloud. I told my crew to be prepared to bail out if the engines coughed again without further instruction from me. By an incredible stroke of luck or, more likely, by the power of prayer, a hole suddenly appeared in the cloud, revealing an airfield below. I lowered the wheels and flaps, dropped thankfully through that hole, and landed at an airfield I didn't know existed until that moment. It was Davidstow Moor, built high on Bodmin Moor, with Brown Willy, the highest point, almost on the landing circuit. I had been strapped in my seat for 10 hours, 10 minutes, and I was mightily relieved to land.

The return leg from Turin also left a vivid impression on Eric Blanchard:

That was an unforgettable raid. As we had to come home in daylight, we were briefed to head back over the south of France, keeping the Pyrenees on the port side, and then fly up the Atlantic coast. We were told to drop down almost to sea level, which was quite a dangerous thing to do, then to start climbing as we approached Brittany, where we were promised fighter protection. We did this, but we didn't see any fighters.

When we reached the English Channel, at about 10-12,000 feet, the Gee (Radio Navigation System) wasn't working, so the Navigator and the Bomb Aimer had their maps out trying to locate our position. They thought we'd passed over Torquay because they had caught sight of a balloon barrage.

Being a Devonian, I was familiar with that part of the world; I told them it was Plymouth that had the balloon barrage, not Torquay, but they didn't take any notice of me. They turned to port, and looking out I saw Dartmoor Prison. I had been there, though not as a customer, and I knew what It looked like. Then suddenly, George Martin, the Mid-Upper Gunner, screamed in his French accent, "THERE'S A MOUNTAIN, THERE'S A MOUNTAIN". It turned out to be Brown Willy, the highest peak in Cornwall, which was very close to the RAF station at Davidstow Moor, where we were lucky enough to be able to land.

Although Stevie had been promoted to Pilot Officer on 4 July, he had not had time to change his uniform, and he was still wearing his Sergeant's stripes when he landed. RAF Davidstow Moor was at that time home to a Polish squadron attached to Coastal Command, and the Poles found it very difficult to believe that a Lancaster could be piloted by anyone who was not an officer:

A Pole came up and said, "Where is your officer?"

I said, "We don't have one."

He said, "Well, who runs the aircraft?"

I replied, "I do!"

"Are you sure you haven't got an officer with you?"

"Yes, I'm sure."

"Well we don't do that in Poland."

I said, "This isn't bloody Poland, it's the RAF!"

But he rang up to check that I really was the captain of the aircraft before he would provide me with any fuel.

The aircraft was refuelled, and after a short rest, Stevie and his crew returned to base at Scampton. In Eric Blanchard's words:

We had a little sleep, refuelled, and took off. As my pilot had been born and bred in Torrington, we passed over Torrington into Wales, then North East to Scampton, where we landed.

Only six of the Squadron's aircraft managed to return direct to Scampton. These aircraft had been spotted by a Mosquito escort over the English Channel and were shepherded home via Land's End. Five of the other Lancasters returning from the Turin raid had been forced to make emergency landings because of navigational problems and shortage of fuel. F/Sgt

A 57 Squadron Lancaster warming up its engines at Scampton

G.A. Parker landed at Farnborough in ED616; F/Sgt Irwin flying W4822 and Sgt Bert Moores in ED777 both landed at RAF St Eval in Cornwall; and F/O J.H. Pratt in ED758 touched down at RAF Portreath in Cornwall. Sgt L.F. Scott in ED989 and F/O P. Levy in W4353 took a shorter route to safety because engine problems made the return leg to England impossible, and landed with their crews in North Africa.

Stevie's log book noted *'10/10 cloud to target'*, but the aircraft that did eventually reach Turin found that visibility was good. They completed their bombing runs, and reported large explosions and concentrated fires. The Squadron records noted, *'It is considered that this was an outstandingly successful operation both in its planning and its execution.'*

A total of thirteen aircraft were lost on the Turin raid (a loss rate of 3.4 per cent), including that of Wing Commander John Nettleton of 44 Squadron, who had been awarded the VC for leading an attack on a U-boat engine plant in Augsburg in April 1942. His VC citation noted:

S/Ldr Nettleton was the leader of one of two formations of six Lancaster heavy bombers detailed to deliver a low-level attack in daylight on the diesel engine factory at Augsburg in Southern Germany on April 17th, 1942. The enterprise was daring, the target of high military importance. To reach it and get back, some 1,000 miles had to be flown over hostile territory. Soon after crossing into enemy territory his formation was engaged by 25 to 30 fighters. A running fight ensued. His rear guns went out of action. One by one the aircraft of his formation were shot down until in the end only his own and one other remained. The fighters were shaken off, but the target was still far distant. There was formidable resistance to be faced.

John Nettleton VC

With great spirit and almost defenceless, he held his two remaining aircraft on their perilous course and after a long and arduous flight, mostly at only 50 feet above the ground, he brought them to Augsburg. Here anti-aircraft fire of great intensity and accuracy was encountered. The two aircraft came low over the roof tops. Though fired at from point blank range, they stayed the course to drop their bombs true on the target. The second aircraft, hit by flak, burst into flames and crash-landed. The leading aircraft, though riddled with holes, flew safely back to base, the only one of the six to return.

S/Ldr Nettleton, who has successfully undertaken many other hazardous operations, displayed unflinching determination as well as leadership and valour of the highest order.

It so happened that Stevie knew Sgt Seager, who went on the Turin raid as Nettleton's Navigator.

Strangely enough I had asked Seager if he would care to be my Navigator when we were at OTU, but he had already agreed to fly with F/Lt Shorthouse. Nettleton had "borrowed" him for that fatal flight.

But it was the loss of a friend and fellow pilot from 57 Squadron which was to affect Stevie most deeply. 20-year-old F/Sgt Johnny Pickett from New Zealand failed to return from the raid. His Lancaster ED861 and its entire crew, Sgt Gordon Grew, Sgt Cecil Still, F/Sgt William Doran, Sgt George Haywood, Sgt John Carpenter and Sgt Ernest Goldstraw were lost without trace. On the way back to England, Stevie had made contact with a Lancaster flying on three engines, and he always wondered whether this was Johnny Pickett's aircraft:

I could not contact him by radio, but I asked my Wireless Op if he could contact him in Morse Code using the Aldis Lamp from the astrodome. This he did. I asked him to send a message to see if he needed help. The reply came back, "Don't worry we are saving petrol!" We replied, "Good Luck," and that was the last we saw of them.

Stevie and Johnny Pickett had done the heavy bomber conversion course at Spitalgate together, joined 57 Squadron within a few days of each other, and flown on many of the same operations. Stevie would never forget him. Many years later, he noted:

His was the only loss I recorded in my log book. He came from New Zealand. He converted to twin engine-aircraft with me at Spitalgate (Grantham), went on to OTU and Lancaster conversion, and was posted to 57 Squadron a few days after me. His broad forehead, blue eyes, narrowing face and ever ready smile impressed themselves for ever on me. His crew had complete confidence in him. After briefing for a raid, he and I would make for the bathrooms and soak lazily for about half an hour, shouting and occasionally singing through the adjoining walls. We never spoke of the forthcoming raid, but I suspect we both remembered the words of a Medical Officer who reminded us that wounds were not so easily infected if the entrance was clean. It is Johnny's spirit which reminds me how lucky I am to be alive, to greet each day with a feeling of gratitude, and to enjoy that extra pint so enormously.

Service Flying Training School, Grantham 1942. Stevie is middle row, 4th from the left. Johnny Pickett is standing on his right.

When Stevie landed at Scampton after returning from Davidstow Moor, he went for tea in the Sergeants' Mess:

> *An elderly Signals Flight Sergeant came up to me and gave me a hug, and said "Thank God you've come back, boy. I thought you'd got the chop." When I looked at him, I saw there were tears in his eyes. He told me that my great friend F/Sgt Johnny Pickett RNZAF had not returned. I spoke to his corporal engine fitter later. He said that the whole ground crew liked Johnny, and that several of them had shed a tear when he did not return.*

The names of Stevie's friend Johnny Pickett and his crew can be seen at the RAF Memorial at Runnymede. They are commemorated along with more than twenty thousand other aircrew who died on active service with the RAF and have no known grave.

OPERATION 12: HAMBURG, 24 JULY, 1943

On 24 July Bomber Command launched Operation Gomorrah, a concentrated campaign of attacks on Hamburg, Germany's second largest city. The assault, the heaviest yet mounted on any target in Germany, continued for eight days and seven nights.

It had been twelve days since the attack on Turin, and during that period Stevie had flown just a single air test in E-'Easy'. He and his crew were assigned Lancaster ED920, DX-A, and F/O Gibbons, who had flown with Stevie on the Gelsenkirchen raid, replaced Sgt Helmore as the Wireless Operator. Seventeen aircraft from 57 Squadron formed part of a massive force of 791 Lancasters, Wellingtons, Stirlings and Halifaxes detailed for the attack.

Stevie took off from Scampton at 23:06, and when he landed at 04:10, he noted in his log book that it had been a *'Good Trip'*. The squadron reports suggest that flak was moderate, but they attributed the relatively low loss of aircraft on that particular night (twelve in total, 1.5 per cent of the force), to the use for the first time of a tactic codenamed 'Window'.

The bombers were ordered to drop packets containing thin pieces of aluminium glued to paper strips designed to swamp the German radar screens. One bundle was dropped every minute through the flare chute using a stopwatch, and the result was that the German radar-guided master searchlights wandered aimlessly across the sky, the anti-aircraft guns could not fix on a target, and the night fighters failed to locate the bomber stream.

Eric Blanchard would later describe the use of Window on that raid:

> *That night we were to use a device to make it difficult for the enemy to pinpoint our aircraft accurately. The code name for this new device was 'Window'. The idea was to release strips of aluminium glued to paper in sufficient quantity to confuse the enemy radar. During briefing it was decided that the Flight Engineers, who were detailed to release Window, would wear the heavy protective Taylor suits worn by Rear Gunners. Though I did not have my suit plugged into the electrical circuit, it was bulky and uncomfortable, and I found it difficult to perform my normal cockpit duties.*
>
> *The Navigator had been briefed that when a stipulated latitude and longitude had been reached, he should report to the pilot, and the Flight Engineer*

A cloud of glittering Window goes down through the bomber stream

would be told to couple up to a portable oxygen bottle which would last fifteen minutes. Then, with his torch, he would climb over the main spar, drop down into the hold of the aircraft, and plug into the oxygen point near the flare chute, through which the packets of Window were to be thrown. It was a dark and an awkward place, with the Mid-Upper Gunner's turret directly above it turning frequently as he scanned the sky. Luckily, we were not taking any violent evasive action. The Bomb Aimer had been issued with a stop watch and gave the order "Window" to me to release the packets at intervals of one minute as we approached the target.

When we reached the target, I looked out of one of the small portholes in the side of the aircraft and could see flak bursting, and there was a red glow in the sky. Soon after, the Bomb Aimer undertook his normal task, and we were on the bombing run. Now the bomb doors were open, I could look out of the small circular port hole along the full 33ft length of the bomb bay, and there, just in front of me, was the Cookie, the 4,000lb bomb, together with another 10,000lbs of incendiary bombs. It was petrifying being so close to the Cookie, but the most horrifying sight was the target area. It was just a vast expanse of red. There was no doubt that the target was on fire. When the Bomb Aimer said the magic words, "Bombs gone", and the bomb doors closed, I was very relieved to get back into the cockpit and undo part of the Taylor suit to get more comfortable.

The following day it was reported that the enemy radar operators had been confused. Window had been a great success; twelve aircraft were missing out of 791 despatched. Later someone had the bright idea to cut a slot in the step leading down to the Bomb Aimer and Window could be dispensed from there, with no more dressing up in a Taylor suit.

Stevie, too, later put into writing his own recollections of the first use of Window on the Hamburg raid:

Window consisted of rectangular strips of black paper backed with aluminium foil, which produced an echo on the German radar screens comparable to that caused by an aircraft. The first raid to use Window was the one on Hamburg on 24 July. It was top secret, and we knew nothing of it until just beforehand. Initially, Window was thrust down flare chutes in bundles at one-minute intervals and much of it flew back into the aircraft. The Bomb Aimer and the Flight Engineer shared this task, and Eric Blanchard reminded me that over the target, he was lying in the fuselage, immediately behind the bomb bay, throwing Window out through a port hole. You can imagine his feelings, being virtually perched over the bomb bay looking through the bombs down onto the target, hoping the bombs would drop before the flak came up through the bomb bay. A terrifying experience for him!

OPERATION 13: ESSEN, 25 JULY, 1943

On the night following the bombing of Hamburg, Stevie was detailed to attack the industrial city of Essen. The intention had been to target Hamburg again, but it was decided that the smoke from the fires, which continued to rage unchecked, would make accurate bombing impossible. 705 aircraft were instead routed to Essen, their primary target being the Krupps Works, a key producer of steel and armaments. This would be the last attack on Essen during the Battle of the Ruhr. Stevie was again assigned Lancaster ED920 for this raid, and his crew remained unchanged, with F/O Gibbons again standing in as the Wireless Operator while Ken Brown was being treated in hospital. This was to be F/O Gibbons's third and final sortie as Stevie's Wireless Operator. He normally formed part of the crew of P/O Raymond Grimwood DFC, who managed to complete his tour of operations, and was posted to No. 17 OTU as a Flying Instructor on 1 August.

Shortly after he returned from the Essen raid, Stevie was asked to record a detailed account of it. He made a voice recording on wire which was subsequently transferred to reel-to-reel tape, then to cassette, and finally to CD. It is remarkable for its descriptive clarity and command of detail; it is also of surprisingly good quality, and apart from the introductory paragraph, which was added later, the voice is that of Stevie, then aged 21 and the Captain of a Lancaster bomber, in a brief period of respite between operations. The difficulty and dangers of flying on night raids are vividly evoked, and the recording, which is readily accessible on the internet, offers its own unique and very personal tribute to the courage and heroism of the young aircrew of Bomber Command:

From the beginning of March 1943 until the end of July, British bombers raided targets situated on the Ruhr. These raids resulted in the destruction of 872 of our aircraft over Germany and the loss of 6,000 aircrew. Additionally, 2,126 heavy bombers were severely damaged, or crash-landed in England.

This is the story of one Lancaster Bomber taking part in one raid on 25 July 1943. Scampton airfield is just north of Lincoln and on this particular day aircraft of A, B and C Flights of No.57 Squadron are dispersed over the airfield. During the day they have been thoroughly tested – guns, ammunition, bomb sights, compasses, engines, wirelesses, oxygen supplies, petrol and oil have all been carefully inspected. Tractors have drawn long lines of trolleys to the bombers. Each trailer carries one or more bombs, and each bomb has been carefully hoisted into its correct position in the bomb bay. Buses now travel from aircraft to aircraft, and at each a crew is dropped off.

There are seven members in my crew. I am the Pilot and captain of the aircraft, and with me are my Navigator, Bomb Aimer, Wireless Operator, Flight Engineer, Mid-Upper Gunner and Rear Gunner. Each of us is clad for our own particular job and each carries a bulky parachute. My clothing consists of clean silk and wool underwear. Clean, because a bullet or a piece of shrapnel may plaster my clothing into a wound. The cleaner therefore the better. A yellow shirt open at the neck with a silk scarf inside. I wear a yellow shirt as I may be shot down over enemy territory and an Air Force blue shirt would be conspicuous and attract attention if I were to try to escape. I do not wear a tie in case I have to crash-land in the sea. The collar and tie might shrink and cause discomfort if it didn't actually strangle me.

Around my neck is a loose loop of string which has two plastic discs on it. Each bears my name, number, Air Force rank and blood group. If I am killed, one will be buried with my body, and the other sent to England. If I am seriously wounded and need a blood transfusion the doctor will know which group of blood to put into me. I am wearing battledress, and the blouse of the battledress has many pockets. In one of these I have a small escape outfit, in another, currency of the countries over which I shall be flying. The contents of the escape outfit are interesting, and all would be useful to help me escape if I were to parachute out — we call it 'bailing out' — over enemy territory.

I have a pair of sheepskin-lined, black flying boots. In the leg of one is concealed a knife so that I could cut the pieces covering my legs away from the lower part and change my flying boots into shoes. Again, this would be a help if I were to attempt to escape. Over the top of my battledress I wear a light, windproof flying suit. I have a heavier one, too, but should only wear it if the cockpit heating system broke down. Over my flying suit is strapped a bright yellow buoyancy jacket which we call a Mae West. By pulling a lever I could blow up this jacket so that I should be able to float for some time if I came down into the sea. Over the Mae West is a parachute harness to which I could clip my parachute if I needed it. I also have a soft leather flying helmet with combined oxygen mask and microphone and a pair of goggles. These goggles are secured to the top of the helmet and I should only pull them over my eyes if the windscreen were shattered or the aircraft caught fire. I also wear long gauntlet gloves and the object of having long gauntlet gloves is to protect my wrists if the aircraft catches fire.

The Engineer, Wireless Operator and Navigator are similarly dressed. The Mid-Upper Gunner and Rear Gunners are much more heavily dressed. They wear huge electrically heated flying suits with electrically heated socks and gloves. Their turrets are not heated, and they will be working in temperatures far below freezing for hours tonight.

We enter the aircraft and check everything in it with great care. The Navigator sets out his charts and equipment; the Gunners, Engineer and Wireless Operator make sure they have everything in order. We stow away our carrier pigeons too. I notice a tiny spot on the windscreen and get it cleaned off. I could easily imagine that spot to be an enemy aircraft later in the night, and I don't want to take unnecessary avoiding action from imaginary aircraft.

Having checked everything, we get out of the aircraft again for a last stretching of limbs. A senior officer and a doctor come around for a last-minute check and then we go back into the aircraft. I adjust the seat and rudder pedals and make sure my equipment is comfortable, then I fasten my safety belt tightly, clip on my face mask and switch on the oxygen. I call up each of the crew in turn to make sure they are comfortable and then tell my Flight Engineer we are ready to start up the engines.

The cockpit is about twenty feet above the ground, so the Engineer has to signal the ground crew below with a light. Each of the four Rolls Royce engines bursts into life, the instruments quiver, and the needles move on them. The Gunners rotate their turrets, and each crew member again reports that all is well. I flash a light and the huge chocks holding the wheels are tugged away. I release the brakes and the aircraft, about thirty tons of it, taxis slowly under my control. I taxi steadily, I have 11,600 pounds of bombs, very nearly five tons, and thousands of rounds of ammunition as well as 1,850 gallons of petrol on board.

At the point where we turn onto the runway, we stop. The green light flashes from the caravan showing that I am the next to take off. We do not use the wireless to talk to the controller, or the Germans would hear us. Well, I suppose the Germans wouldn't literally hear us, but a number of transmissions would give them a warning that something was happening our side of the Channel, and we want to take the Germans by surprise if we possibly can.

I turn onto the runway, making sure that the aircraft is pointing right down the middle. Then I say to the Engineer, "Flaps 20, Engineer." He replies, "Flaps 20, Skipper", and moves a lever. I then say, "Crew, prepare for take-off" and slowly open the throttles whilst keeping the brakes applied. I release the brakes and we speed down the darkening runway. As the tail rises the aircraft swings slightly, and this I immediately correct with the use of rudder and throttle. The speed builds up, I ease the control column back gently, and we climb, ponderously at first.

"Wheels up, Engineer."

"Wheels up, Skipper."

Green lights in front of me change to red and then the red lights go out showing the wheels are now tucked up.

"Flaps up, Engineer."

"Flaps up, Skipper."

The Engineer moves a handle, and the wing flaps rise.

"Plus 9, 28, 50, Engineer."

"Plus 9, 28, 50, Skipper."

The deafening roar of the Merlin engines, each of which has been producing about 1,390 horsepower, dies down a little as the aircraft settles into a steady climb. The Navigator then says, "Navigator to Skipper, Course Zero Nine Two."

I move the controls, turning the aircraft gently until the compass reads 092. "On Course Zero Nine Two, Navigator."

Then all is quiet except for the steady beat of engines. No one will use his microphone now, except to pass a message. When a microphone is switched on, there is a noise which makes every crew member even more alert.

Tonight, we are going to bomb the Krupps Works at Essen, but first we have to climb over England to a height of 20,000 feet. In fact, I have to be over Sheringham at 20,000 feet at 22:02 hours to set course for Essen. At 21:50 I say to the Navigator, "Skipper to Navigator, height now at 20,300 feet," and to the Engineer, "Cruising revs and boost." The engines again alter their note, I lower the nose of the aircraft slightly to gain a little speed and lose a little height, and at 21:59 the Bomb Aimer, who is sitting at the guns in the front of the aircraft, says, "Coastline ahead — it could be Sheringham." The Navigator gives a correction of course, and we head over the sea to Holland and Germany.

Every member of the crew is now very alert. The Navigator and Wireless Operator are in lightproof compartments and cannot see out, and every other crew member has an area of sky to watch, and this he will watch most intently. There are no lights other than those now used by the Navigator and the Wireless Operator inside the aircraft. Only the luminous pointers on our instruments show what is happening and where we are going. We are very aware that at any moment a fighter may come up from the dark shadow beneath the aircraft, pull up its nose, and spray our underside with cannon-shell and incendiary bullets. One burst on our bomb load and petrol tanks must mean immediate death for us. To allow the Rear Gunner to see as far underneath as possible, I bank the aircraft from side to side so that he can swing his turret and look underneath the aircraft. We have found that however much the perspex turret is polished, it still hinders visibility, so a large panel has been taken out. This gives the gunner a clear look, but it also means he is bitterly cold.

When we are about five miles from the coast, I give the instruction, "Gunners, test guns." The Rear Gunner fires first and leaves his microphone switched on so that the crew can hear the heartening noise of four Browning guns firing simultaneously. The Mid-Upper then fires his twin machine guns and the Bomb Aimer the front guns. Every fifth bullet is tracer, so that a red stream seems to pour from each gun into space.

The Rear Gunner reports, "Rear guns OK, Skipper." The Mid-Upper Gunner reports, "My port gun is misfiring." He strips it down in the dark without using a light and then he says, "Mid-Upper to Skipper, the port gun has breech block trouble, and I cannot repair it." I don't like this and say, "Skipper to Mid-Upper, any suggestions?" A pause while the Mid-Upper Gunner thinks, then he says, "Could I change it for one of the front-guns?" I reply, "How long will that take?" He replies, "About ten minutes, I think."

The decision is now mine. I think the chances of using the front guns are slight tonight as we are flying high. If we were flying low, we should need our front guns for strafing. On the other hand, if I immobilise the front and mid-upper turrets for ten minutes, this could be fatal if we were attacked. Again, German night fighters are more likely to be met after we cross the enemy coast than at this particular point. I therefore instruct the Bomb Aimer to dismount one gun from the front turret and the Mid-Upper Gunner to dismount the faulty gun from his turret. The Wireless Operator gives the Mid-Upper a hand. Before he can move, of course, he has to plug into an oxygen bottle. The Mid-Upper dismantles his gun. The Wireless Operator sits in the mid-upper turret keeping watch while the mid-turret gun is taken to the front turret. The Mid-Upper Gunner passes his gun to the Engineer, who passes it to the Bomb Aimer. The Bomb Aimer puts this gun in the front-turret and passes the good gun from his turret back to the mid-upper turret. Still working in the dark, the Mid-Upper Gunner and the Wireless Operator between them assemble the gun in the mid-upper turret. We're relieved to hear the microphone click and the Mid-Upper Gunner say, "Guns remounted. Permission to test?" I say, "Test gun, and look out for fires". The Mid-Upper fires, both guns work well, and we breathe a sigh of relief. Very few minutes have in fact passed since the fault was first discovered, but it seems quite a long time to me. Minutes later the Bomb Aimer calls, "Enemy coast ahead." He has seen the coastline of Holland.

I would like to digress now to tell you what has been happening on the German side. As soon as our aircraft have reached 15 to 20,000 feet, the German radar operators have been watching them. At first, they have picked them up on equipment known as 'Freya'. This equipment has a range of about ninety miles and can give the bearing and distance of an aircraft, but not its height. As our bombers approach the enemy coast, a second group of radar instruments takes over. These are known as 'Würzburgs'. They have a range of about 45 miles and can give height, speed and bearings of aircraft very quickly. This information is given to German night fighters and flak regiments. Now the German squadrons of night fighters warm up their engines and check fuel and ammunition. Searchlight operators and flak batteries stand by. The battle is about to begin!

Back in my aircraft, the enemy coast has been crossed. We see some searchlights probing in our direction and see some bursts of anti-aircraft fire. Usually, we take little action about flak unless we can hear it crack or smell it. We have to get to a target on time, and we don't want to dart about all over the sky unless there is real danger.

A single searchlight picks up an aircraft on our starboard side. Within a second or two a huge number of searchlights illuminate this aircraft, and gunfire flashes around it as it twists and turns in an effort to escape. We know that every gun in the area is directed at this aircraft. At first it seems it may escape but suddenly there is a brilliant flash, a red glow and a ball of smoke, and we know that at least seven of our men have been blown to pieces. The searchlights flicker again and catch another aircraft.

Suddenly a series of flashes ahead makes me jump. I realise a fighter, quite invisible until that moment, has tried a head-on shot at us with cannon and machine guns. He speeds by overhead, narrowly missing my aircraft. This happens so quickly I cannot report it. The Gunners have seen the flash and the Mid-Upper shoots at the aircraft, but it has gone away, disappeared. We see flashes of tracer as other fighters shoot at other bombers, and then the sky seems empty, and we drone on.

As we approach the Ruhr valley, we see searchlights ahead of us, thousands of them apparently, and among the searchlights, huge numbers of angry red flashes of bursting shells appear, leaving behind dark mushrooms of smoke. I know that before long I shall have to fly my aircraft through those searchlights and through the gunfire to get to the target. I check each needle on every instrument carefully and ask the Engineer to switch to the fullest tanks. The Navigator gives the wind speed and direction to the Bomb Aimer, who sets it on his bomb sight. I turn up the oxygen so that we have a maximum supply. The Rear Gunner cracks the ice which is forming on the inside of his oxygen tube. The Wireless Operator has been tuning into the wavelengths used by German night fighters. If he hears a German voice, he pushes a key and blasts out the noise of our engines and the wind blowing past them. This, we hope, will upset the wireless communication between the German night fighters and their ground control.

Now we are among the searchlights, anti-aircraft gunfire bursts on each side, night fighters blast in, firing at bombers, and bombers shoot back. Our bomber suddenly lurches and drops several hundred feet as a shell bursts nearby. If you could see the Navigator at this moment you would find him rescuing his instruments from mid-air. So far, we've not been hit, and only had one small attack.

Suddenly, a string of red and green markers burn brilliantly on the ground. These are target indicators dropped by Mosquito bombers flying much higher than we are. I say to the Bomb Aimer, "Aim for the red target indicator." At this point the target disappears under the nose. The Bomb Aimer, lying in the noise, sees through a transparent panel all the target area set out in front of him. He lines the red target indicator up in his bomb sight and operates a switch to fuse the bombs. He knows I hate to open the bomb doors too soon as this makes the aircraft less manoeuvrable. As the target appears, he gives me instructions, "Left, left, right, right, steady, steady, steady, left, left, steady, steady." Then he says, "Bomb doors." I move a lever and say, "Bomb doors open."

"Steady, steady, steady, steady," says his voice, and I concentrate on holding the aircraft level and exactly on course. This is a most trying time. If a fighter comes in, we cannot take avoiding action now.

An explosion rocks us, an aircraft nearby has blown up! "Right, right, right, steady, steady, steady" says the Bomb Aimer, and I put every mental and physical effort into carrying out his orders. Suddenly I feel the aircraft lift and know our bombs are dropping. Then comes the voice of the Bomb Aimer, "Bombs gone." He strains his eyes to see the results. With the bombs, we drop a three-million-candle-power photo flash which burns dazzlingly, enabling a camera we have in the aircraft to take photographs of our bombing.

I fly straight and level for another thousand years, only thirty seconds or so as we measure time now, while the camera records its evidence. Then I open the throttles and the lighter aircraft bounds away. We set course for home knowing that between us and England there are still fighters, anti-aircraft guns and searchlights, and our task is not yet over. However, this time we bombed on the first run. On one occasion we had to fly over the target three times to ensure a hit, and even after this period of time I still get goose pimples at the thought of that one. [The reference is to the Krefeld operation of 21 June 1943, when Sgt Arthur Matthews, Stevie's replacement

Bomb Aimer lost his nerve, and Stevie was forced to do his bombing run three times.]

As we settle down on course for home, the air seems suddenly empty. The target glows behind us, and we still find an odd searchlight flicking in our direction, but nothing else disturbs us. The earth is black beneath, stars wink above, and I see the Pole Star clearly, nearly on the starboard wing tip. We drone on, still banking, so that the gunners can look underneath.

Suddenly, we're galvanised again. A microphone clicks. "Tail to Skipper, fighter, fighter, port quarter down, range 600, port, port, go!" I push on the rudder, turn the ailerons, put the nose down, open the throttle and transmit to the gunner, "Diving port." I dive for the dark part of the sky, and as I'm going down port, the gunners aim for the upper starboard side of the fighter. The fighter blasts a frightening burst of cannon and machine gun fire, some of which I can feel hitting my aircraft. A stream of red and yellow fire passes me, and I seem to be in the middle of it. The Mid-Upper Gunner says, "Fighter's broken to starboard up," and I bring the aircraft back onto its course for home. The German fighter pilot is a persistent fellow however, and again I hear, "Fighter, fighter, starboard down, range three hundred." This time I say, "Corkscrewing." The gunner says, "Starboard, go!" and I am surprised how calm our voices are.

I say, "Corkscrewing down, starboard." The gunners now aim about the fighter's port wing and fire long bursts. I don't want to be driven too low, so next I say, "Changing," and the gunners then aim their guns point blank at the approaching fighter. Then I hear, "Hit, hit, hit!" The guns continue to hammer, and then stop. "Look Skipper, he's hit, port down. He's burning." I look and see a red glow in the sky and a yellow flash, and I find my voice saying, "Switch off your microphones, keep searching."

The Navigator gives me a change of course, and says, "Dutch coast nineteen minutes." We fly on, every minute seeming like an hour. Looking out towards the wing tip I see a mist breaking over the wing. The engine temperature on the starboard engine is rising slightly, and I suspect the coolant is leaking. I ask the Engineer to keep a careful eye on the radiator temperature of the starboard outer engine.

We continue to fly, and once more on our left we see this terrible picture of an aircraft suddenly being coned and then shot down. Then the enemy coast passes beneath us, and we are over the sea. The engines feel rough and laboured and we gently lose height to 10,000 feet.

Suddenly the Engineer says, "Fire, starboard outer," and I see the engine glowing red. He cuts off the petrol while I haul back on the throttle. We wait until the propeller starts to windmill, and then he pushes the feather button. The propeller blades turn until they are facing fore and aft and the engine stops. Then the Engineer pushes the fire extinguisher button; I find myself saying, "Skipper to crew, engine fire starboard outer, prepare to parachute." The Navigator quickly gives our position to the Wireless Operator, who is ready to send an SOS. If that fire takes hold, the wing may burn through in twenty seconds. During that time, the Wireless Operator will give our position and clamp his key so that air-sea-rescue vessels know where to look for us. However, the fire dies, blanketed by foam from the extinguisher, and we fly on, still banking, still watching, still searching.

Getting near the coast of England, we switch on our IFF (Identification Friend or Foe). This identifies us on the radar screen as friendly. We load a special cartridge in the Very pistol and fire it as we cross the coast to make certain none of our own anti-aircraft gunners shoot at us. Then we fly to our own airfield.

As I near the airfield, I switch on my radio and call, "Hello Heron, Lounger Easy, over." A friendly, warm girl's voice comes back, "Lounger Easy from Heron, Pancake". I lower the wheels and flaps, line up with the runway lights, and land. The Lancaster lands easily on three engines — a tribute to its designers. Then the crew goes to a room to fill in forms about the flight and tell the intelligence officers about the trip. People bring us mugs of hot coffee and, those who feel like it, eat breakfast. Two other crews saw a battle going on in the positions which we describe, and they confirm that a German fighter appeared to have been shot down, so we go happily to bed. Only twenty-six aircraft are missing from this operation, and tomorrow night we may be flying again.

During the debriefing, Stevie's account of the attack by the German fighter was confirmed by other members of 57 Squadron returning from the raid, and Stevie noted in his logbook, '*FW190 shot down in flames, RT Aerial shot away*'. His Mid-Upper Gunner George Martin was credited with the kill.

Twenty-six aircraft failed to return from the Essen raid (a loss rate of 3.7 per cent), but as Stevie's recording makes clear, none of the aircraft from 57 Squadron were lost, though three had to return early because of engine and mechanical failure. As F/Lt Tony Gobbie was coming in to land, his port outer engine caught fire, and his undercarriage collapsed on touch down, but fortunately he and his crew were unharmed.

OPERATION 14: HAMBURG, 27 JULY, 1943

Hours after making his wire recording of the Essen raid, Stevie was detailed to attack Hamburg for the second time in the space of three days. He was reunited with his Lancaster E-'Easy', and Ken Brown, having been discharged from hospital, returned as Wireless Op.

Stevie's was one of eighteen aircraft from 57 Squadron which joined a huge force of 787 Lancasters, Halifaxes, Wellingtons and Stirlings. The attack wreaked the most terrible devastation. The weather was unusually dry and warm, and the concentrated and relentless bombing created winds of up to 150 mph, temperatures in excess of 800 degrees Celsius, and a huge firestorm which reached altitudes of more than 1,000 feet. More than eight square miles of the city were incinerated; asphalt streets burst into flame, and fuel oil from damaged and destroyed ships, barges, and storage tanks spilled into the water of the canals and harbour, causing them to ignite as well. The damage was so severe that Hamburg never returned to full production for the remainder of the War.

Seventeen aircraft were lost on the raid (a loss rate of 2.2 per cent), but all of those from 57 Squadron returned safely. Stevie took off at 23:06 and landed at 04:10 at RAF Dunholme Lodge. When he returned to Scampton later in the day, he noted in his log book: *'Quiet Trip'*.

57 Squadron took part in a third raid on Hamburg two days later, on 29 July 1943, when nineteen Lancasters joined a force of more than seven hundred bombers. The day before, on 28 July 1943, Wing Commander Walter Haskell DFC had succeeded Wing Commander Hopcroft as the CO of 57 Squadron. He lost no time in putting himself in the front line, joining Squadron Leader Malcolm Crocker and his crew in the attack.

Stevie and his crew were given nine days' leave, and did not take part in this raid, but two of his friends failed to return from it. F/Sgt Geoffrey Parker, on what was his seventh operation, was hit by flak and crashed near Fuhlsbüttel north of Hamburg. He and all of the crew on his Lancaster ED616, DX-B were killed. Stevie would later describe him as *'a pilot for whom every trip was sheer horror. He had not been terribly happy and had seemed scared. It seemed like he had to force himself to fly, and he was sadly blown up by flak over Hamburg. He was just 22.'* F/Sgt Ernest Allwright, who was also just 22, was shot down by a German fighter at Tostedt in ED931, DX-C, just south of Hamburg. Stevie rated him highly, describing him as *'dapper and always giving the appearance of bright efficiency. The sort, I thought, who was bound to survive. I was wrong. He was shot down by a fighter on his 21st op over Hamburg.'* Ernest Allwright and his crew were all killed, except for the Navigator, F/O B.G. Kennedy, who was captured and taken prisoner.

Bill 'Paddy' McCrea

A pilot in 57 Squadron who was a friend of Stevie's, Bill McCrae, noted in his memoir *A Chequer-Board of Nights* that 57 Squadron had been poorly briefed for this raid, and given the wrong time to arrive over the target. When the Squadron's Lancasters reached Hamburg, the main force had already gone:

> *Everyone was on the way home. Everyone, that is, except for the poor unfortunates from 57 Squadron who were over the city on their own.*

Bill McCrae managed to complete his bombing run and fly clear without incident;

> *but one of our colleagues was not so lucky. I watched as a bomber just ahead and slightly below was subjected to a series of attacks from a fighter. It burst into flames and soon commenced its fiery spiral into the earth below.*

The bomber in question was the Lancaster flown by F/Sgt Allwright. The briefing error had left the aircraft of 57 Squadron vulnerable to attack, and cost Allwright and most of his crew their lives.

Bill McCrea, who witnessed F/Sgt Allwright's last flight, was born in County Donegal and joined the RAFVR in 1941. Known to his friends in Bomber Command as 'Paddy', he was posted to 57 Squadron as a pilot in February 1943, and he and Stevie took part in many of the same operations:

'I was in A Flight,' Stevie recalled, *'while he was in B Flight, but we often flew on the same missions, and we got to talk to each other quite a lot.'*

By a strange chance, Bill McCrea was posted to Hamburg after the War in 1951. In his memoir, he describes driving through the ruins left by the bombing raids in which he had taken part:

> *My drive among the ruins was a sobering experience; I had been responsible in part for this destruction. Stories were filtering through about the effects of the firestorm following the second raid, and some officers on the Intelligence Staff had seen German newsreels that left nothing to the imagination. Of course, it had been horrible, but I felt that the Germans were largely to blame. After all, they had started it — on Rotterdam, on Coventry, on London — and when the time came for retribution, they made no attempt to evacuate their women and children, hoping perhaps that their continued presence in towns and cities might be a human shield against attack.*

The devastation of Hamburg is sometimes cited to discredit the strategy of area bombing and question both its morality and its effectiveness. But as Robert Tombs points out in his book *The English and Their History*, '*Bombing did work. It was inhuman and effective, devastating the economy, diverting crucial resources, and destroying German morale.*' It also needs to be remembered that many of the aircrew of Bomber Command had experienced at first hand the mass bombing of British cities in 1940 and 1941. Stevie liked to say that the Blitz proved to be a highly effective recruiting sergeant for the RAF. In the course of the War, as Robert Tombs notes, '*60,000 civilians were killed, half of them in London; perhaps 250,000 were injured and 2 million made homeless. In central London, 90 per cent of houses suffered some damage, and in the whole country 250,000 were destroyed, and 4 million were damaged; 20 per cent of schools and hospitals were damaged.*'

It is also worth pointing out that in 1943, the 'Final Solution', Hitler's policy of exterminating the Jews of Europe, was being implemented with ruthless efficiency. The German historian Volker Ullrich notes in his book *Hitler: Downfall 1939-45*, that after the bombing of Hamburg, the city's inhabitants were compensated with furniture and clothes looted from Dutch Jews gassed in the concentration camps at Sobibor and Auschwitz.

Some fifty years later, the Mayor of Hamburg, Henning Voscherau, asked in a commemorative speech, '*If the Allies had not had the courage and determination to answer Nazi violence with violence in order to stop the Germans running amok, would liberation, renewal, a democratic future have been possible?*'

There could only be one answer to Mayor Voscherau's question: Germany itself had to be liberated from Hitler before it could renounce his policy of aggression and mass murder and take its place among the Western democracies.

OPERATION 15: MANNHEIM, 9 AUGUST, 1943

Between 3 and 8 August, 57 Squadron flew no operations because of adverse weather conditions. At the end of his leave, Stevie returned to Scampton, and was detailed to attack Mannheim, another key strategic target on account of its industrial and oil refining plant. Sixteen aircraft from 57 Squadron formed part of a force of 457 aircraft. Nine were lost (a loss rate of 2 per cent), none from 57 Squadron, but the Squadron's newly appointed CO, W/Cdr Ralph Haskell DFC, was forced to return to base because the rear turret of his Lancaster was unserviceable. The remaining aircraft all attacked the target and returned safely. Dense cloud over the target resulted in widely scattered bombing, but considerable damage was done.

Stevie took off at 23:22 in E-'Easy' with his regular crew and landed at 05:21 after what he described in his log book as a *'quiet trip'*.

OPERATION 16: NUREMBERG, 10 AUGUST, 1943

The next night, Stevie and the crew of E-'Easy' were detailed to attack Nuremberg, and they took off from Scampton at 22:13. Seventeen Lancasters from 57 Squadron formed part of a force of 653 aircraft. 57 Squadron's new CO, W/Cdr, Ralph Haskell, again had to return early because of a problem with his rear turret; S/Ldr Smith, with whom Stevie had flown on his first mission, was also forced to return early; and F/O Pete Whittam in Lancaster EE197, DX-Y was forced to do an emergency landing at RAF Wing in Buckinghamshire.

Sixteen aircraft were lost on this raid (a loss rate of 2.5 per cent), including one Lancaster from 57 Squadron. The Pilot, F/Lt Robert Wilson, Second Pilot F/O Robert Radcliffe, Sgt George Pettefar, Sgt Aaron Burns, Sgt Raymond Garment, Sgt Alan Floyd, Sgt Gordon Major and Sgt John Broadbent were all killed when their Lancaster, ED992 DX-O, crashed near the village of Rummelsberg, just east of Nuremberg. They are buried in the Commonwealth War Graves Cemetery at Durnbach near Tegernsee, south of Munich.

Stevie reached the target and completed his bombing run successfully, but E-Easy was hit by flak as he turned for home. Unsure of the extent of the damage, he decided to make an emergency landing when he was back over England:

We got hit by flak and the aircraft was wobbling about a bit because a wing tip had been damaged. When we got back over friendly shores, I decided to make an emergency landing. Looking down, I saw the lights of an airfield underneath, and was able to make out the whole of the runway. I didn't know which airfield it was, but I made an emergency 'Darkie' call, giving my call sign and asking for permission to make an emergency landing. The station I had seen was RAF Aldermaston. The Americans were running it at that time, and they had never had a 'Darkie' call before.*

(*the 'Darkie' or 'Darky' system involved each airfield having an operator listening out on the allocated Darkie frequency. Being very short range, whichever airfield picked up the Darkie call could hopefully then guide the aircraft in for a safe landing.)

OPERATION 17: MILAN, 12 AUGUST, 1943

Stevie's next raid took him back to Italy, this time to Milan. The Italian armies in Russia and North Africa had been defeated; there was widespread acceptance in Italy that the War had been lost, and Mussolini had been dismissed from office by King Vittorio Emanuele. The planners in Bomber Command knew that Italian air defences were weak, and Milan was targeted to convey to the new Italian government under Marshal Badoglio the message that it should break with Hitler. In the event, Badoglio did sign an armistice with the Allies not long afterwards, in September.

Stevie's crew for this raid remained unchanged, but as the flak damage to E-Easy was still being repaired, he was allocated Lancaster JA896. Eighteen Lancasters from 57 Squadron joined a large force of 504 bombers which inflicted heavy damage on the main railway terminal and the Alfa Romeo motor works. Just three aircraft were lost none from 57 Squadron. Sgt H. Gifford in Lancaster W4358, DX-L was forced home early with a fire in his starboard outer engine, but all the other aircraft from 57 Squadron reached the target and returned safely.

Stevie took off from Scampton at 21:44, and landed back at 06:10. What he would remember best about this operation was seeing a profusion of lights as he flew over Switzerland which, because of its status as a neutral country, had no blackout in place.

OPERATION 18: MILAN, 14 AUGUST, 1943

After only a day's rest, Stevie was detailed to return to Milan. He was reunited with E-'Easy', the flak damage done to it during the Nuremberg raid having been repaired; but for the first time on his tour, Eric Blanchard had to stand down, and Sgt T. Davies replaced him as the Flight Engineer. Six aircraft from 57 Squadron formed part of a force of a 140 Lancasters from 1, 5 and 8 Groups on what turned out to be another long and tiring, but on this occasion trouble-free, mission. Only seven aircraft were lost, none of them from 57 Squadron. Stevie and his crew took off from Scampton at 21:27 and returned at 05:40 unscathed.

It would be just over a week before Stevie's next raid, and in the meantime, 57 Squadron would lose its newly appointed CO, Wing Commander Haskell. On 17 August, the Squadron was detailed to attack Peenemünde, where German scientists were developing the V2 rocket. Haskell had been in command of the Squadron for a mere three weeks, and he and his crew were lost without trace. It was assumed that they were shot down by a night fighter on their return from the target. Haskell's disappearance came as no surprise to Stevie and Bill McCrae, who thought that he appeared too stressed to survive. Stevie recalled that they *'had some serious doubts about some of the people on the Squadron, especially Haskell, the new CO. Paddy looked at me and said, "I don't think he's going to last, Steve," and I'd got that feeling myself. The CO took off to Hamburg, flying with another crew; on the next flight his aircraft went unserviceable, and on the one after that he had to make a forced landing. The next raid, on Peenemünde, he never returned from. I don't think he ever completed an attack, even though he was the CO.'* The mental and psychological stress of operational flying was immense, and command of a front-line squadron could take its toll even on a brave and experienced pilot like Haskell, who had already completed a tour of operations with 49 Squadron and been awarded a DFC. *'After a while,'* as Stevie put it, reflecting on his conversation with Bill McCrae, *'you were just betting how long the new pilots would last.'*

On 19 August Haskell was succeeded as the CO of 57 Squadron by W/Cdr Bill Fisher, an Australian from Perth who was commissioned before the War and had been awarded a DFC after his first tour of operations in November 1941, flying Hampdens with No. 49 Squadron. He would remain in charge of 57 Squadron until 15 April 1944.

OPERATION 19: BERLIN, 23 AUGUST, 1943

In August 1943 Harris launched the first phase of the Battle of Berlin. After the devastation wreaked on Hamburg, he was confident that mass attacks on the German capital would break German resistance and force Hitler to capitulate. *"It will cost us between 400 and 500 aircraft,"* he declared, *"it will cost Germany the War."* His confidence was misplaced. Although Bomber Command did inflict heavy damage on Berlin, it lost 492 aircraft, and more than 3,500 aircrew were killed or taken prisoner. The attacks had to be called off in March 1944 because the loss rate of 5.8 per cent was too high to be sustainable.

On 23 August, Stevie was detailed to attack Berlin. Eighteen Lancasters from 57 Squadron joined a force of 710 other Lancasters, Halifaxes and

57 Squadron Lancasters prepare for a night raid in the summer of 1943

Stirlings, with 17 Mosquitoes assigned to mark the targets. The raid was directed by a Master Bomber, Wing Commander Johnny Fauquier, who would later take command of 617 Squadron. His exceedingly dangerous task was to lead the bomber force and remain over the target for the entire duration of the raid, directing the successive waves of the attack by radio.

Stevie took off at 20:20 in E-'Easy', and landed back at base at 03:46. Eric Blanchard returned as Flight Engineer, but George Martin was replaced as Mid-Upper Gunner by Sgt Christopher Allen, who was borrowed from Bill McCrea's crew.

As the aircrew of Bomber Command were all too well aware, Berlin was the most dangerous target in Germany. It was ringed with a flak belt 40 miles wide and a searchlight band over 60 miles across, and defended by a heavy concentration of night fighters. Stevie later recalled:

> *We made our first trip to Berlin on 23 August, 1943 and took Sgt Allen as our Mid-Upper Gunner. He wrote in his own log book: 'Defences very active. Numerous searchlights over target. Very heavy flak en route. Night fighters plenteous and many combats seen. Rear Gunner passed out over target. Gee unserviceable shortly after leaving base. 1,300 tons of bombs reported dropped on city. Target well alight when we left it. 56 of our bombers missing.'*
>
> *My own log book only contains the very curt note 'Hit by flak', and I often wish I had written more. My own recollection is of flying through a massive warm front, through masses of thick, wet cloud which only slowly melted when we saw bits of Lüneburg Heath. Little could I imagine that this was the place on which the Germans would surrender two years later. Certainly, it was very busy; the flak belt seemed even deeper than that on the Ruhr, and there were plenty of fighters. I believe we came out near Rostock, and we saw some flak over the Frisian Islands on our return. Ernie, our Navigator, must have found it very difficult working out our course by dead reckoning, but at least we returned safely, unlike the poor chaps in the fifty-six aircraft which were shot down.*

None of the 56 aircraft which were lost (7.9 per cent of the total force) were from 57 Squadron. F/O J.H. Pratt returned early with technical difficulties, as did F/Sgt Parker. All the other aircraft from 57 Squadron bombed the target and returned safely to base, but the losses sustained by Bomber Command in this raid were higher in this raid than in any other raid on which Stevie flew.

The Berlin raid was also the last in which Bernie Townsend, Stevie's regular Rear Gunner, took part. Sgt Christopher Allen, George Martin's temporary replacement, noted in his log book that Bernie had passed out over the target. He told Stevie after they landed that Bernie had been opening fire randomly without seeing any enemy aircraft, and had clearly lost his nerve. Stevie later recalled:

Bernie Townsend crewed up with me as my Rear Gunner when I was flying Wellingtons at OTU. He was a nice chap who came from Australia. He did sixteen operational trips with me. After our ninth op to Cologne on 8 July, when we were badly damaged by flak and no contact could be made with him, he became increasingly quiet and withdrawn, and on several occasions, he froze in his turret, too frightened to speak or answer the intercom. I owed much to my Mid-Upper Gunner George Martin, who did his best to cover for him. I had tried to nurse him along, but he had reached a stage of paralysis, and this was his last operational flight with me.

Eric Blanchard also remembered that when they were hit by flak during the Cologne raid, Bernie Townsend had been so unnerved that he had been unable to function normally:

We didn't get any response from him and Skipper asked me to go back and find out what had happened and see if I could make contact. I went to the back of the aircraft and clipped into the intercom, and he was still there, he hadn't got blown away. We came to the conclusion that when we got to the target area, he had just pulled the plug on his intercom and wouldn't reply to us. He never really recovered, and in the end our Captain had no choice but to report this, and say we couldn't take him any longer.

Stevie, who liked Bernie Townsend, was determined not to see him shamed, so he approached his new CO, W/Cdr Bill Fisher, and asked him to stand Bernie down and give him a commission:

Greatly daring, I suggested to my CO that Townsend might be commissioned and so avoid being discharged and demoted as LMF (Lacking in Moral Fibre). The CO tore me off a mighty strip for being so bloody impertinent, but later the Intelligence Officer told me he thought things were moving.

Bernie Townsend was given a commission thanks to Stevie's intervention, and by November he had recovered sufficiently to resume flying as a Mid-Upper Gunner in the newly formed 630 Squadron. To return to front-line service in this way required courage and resilience of a high order.

OPERATION 20: NUREMBERG, 27 AUGUST, 1943

Stevie's next operation took him back to Nuremberg. Nineteen aircraft from 57 Squadron were detailed to join a huge force of 674 bombers for the raid. Stevie, flying in E-Easy, took off at 21:25. George Martin returned as Mid-Upper Gunner, and F/Lt Tony Wynyard, 57 Squadron's experienced and highly capable Gunnery Leader, who had been awarded a DFC in June 1943, replaced Bernie Townsend as Rear Gunner. Stevie had a high opinion of Tony Wynyard. *'He was a frightfully nice, well-spoken chap, whose address book was full of the names of women he had dated. He was as cool as a cucumber, and a very good Gunner. He'd say, "Oh yes, there's an enemy 109 coming in, I think it's an E, no, it's probably an F!" and he'd be doing his aircraft recognition over the intercom and firing his guns at the same time.'* Wynyard went on to complete a second tour, which included nine missions with No. 49 Squadron, where he was posted in July 1944, and in January 1945 he was awarded a Bar to his DFC.

He was soon to demonstrate his calmness and courage under fire. As E-'Easy' approached the target, it was attacked by a German FW 190 fighter, and with support from the Mid-Upper Gunner George Martin, Wynyard shot it down.

The raid itself went wrong; inaccurate marking meant that most of the attacking force missed their target and dropped their bombs on countryside to the south of Nuremberg. Thirty-three aircraft were lost (a loss rate of 4.9 per cent), including one from 57 Squadron. F/O Paul Levy, who had been stood down just before the Squadron's previous raid on Nuremberg on 10 August, was shot down by a German fighter near Zeckern, just north of Nuremberg. Only the Bomb Aimer, Sgt R. May, survived. F/O Levy, Sgt Walter Lynn, Sgt William MacKillop, Sgt William Thomas, Sgt John Perry and Sgt Thomas Crowther were all killed. They are buried in the Commonwealth War Graves Cemetery at Durnbach.

Another Lancaster from 57 Squadron had a narrow escape. P/O R. Hazelwood completed his bombing run, but returned with damage to his Lancaster ED827 DX-Z, and crashed during landing at 04:17, blocking the runway. This meant that the eleven remaining Lancasters could not land at Scampton, and had to be diverted to alternative stations. Stevie and his crew landed at RAF Swinderby, southwest of Lincoln.

Stevie was transported from Swinderby to Scampton because he was scheduled to go on another op the following night. He was in bed trying to catch up with his sleep when there was a knock at the door. The visitor was his friend and fellow 57 Squadron pilot 'Jos' Josling, who had been detailed to collect E-'Easy' and fly her back to Scampton:

I had just gone to bed and locked the front door when Sgt Josling knocked and said, "You're not flying tonight, Steve!".

"That's good news," I said.

He said, "Well, it's not all good news, Steve, I just pranged your aircraft!"

He was quite calm about it. The reason he had pranged E-'Easy' was that he hadn't checked the fuel. He'd taken off with almost empty tanks and opened the throttle; the two inboard engines had cut, and E-'Easy' had crash-landed in a field near Swinderby. Luckily, Josling had not been hurt, but the undercarriage had been severely damaged, and E-'Easy' was written off.

Faced with the prospect of having to continue his tour in unfamiliar aircraft, Stevie was very upset by the loss of E-'Easy': *'I knew that aircraft backwards, almost every trimmer. It was a very good aircraft, and I felt lost without her.'*

As for 'Jos' Josling, he completed his tour with 57 Squadron, and on 21 January 1944, he was awarded a DFC. But sadly, he did not survive the War. On 24 July 1944 while he was instructing at No. 1660 OTU at RAF Swinderby, a Short Stirling he was flying hit a tree during take-off and crashed while he was attempting an emergency landing at RAF Winthorpe. 'Jos' and all seven other men on board were killed. He was just 21.

Stevie was genuinely fond of 'Jos'. Looking back, he described him as:

A good pilot, and very lucky with his mishaps. He overstayed his leave when he got married, and was let off with the lightest of reprimands. When he wrote off my aircraft, we were so short of pilots that again he was only reprimanded, and he was commissioned shortly afterwards.

OPERATION 21: BERLIN, 31 AUGUST, 1943

On 28/29 August 1943, 57 Squadron relocated from Scampton to RAF East Kirkby in Lincolnshire, from where it would continue to operate until the end of the War. East Kirkby was still under construction when the Squadron arrived. It had nothing like the amenities of Scampton, and the move was not popular among the Squadron's aircrew. Bill McCrae described East Kirkby as *'primitive and functional: ten officers sleeping in a hut, outside washing facilities, and a walk through the mud to the Mess, which itself was devoid of any comfort.'* But unlike Scampton, East Kirkby did have concrete runways suitable for Lancasters and their heavy bomb loads.

By the time the Squadron moved to East Kirkby, Stevie, having completed twenty ops without a single early return, had acquired a reputation as a good pilot, and less experienced members of the Squadron referred to him as a 'gen man'. But it was an accolade with a sting in the tail:

> *I hadn't realised until later on that people coming into the Squadron on their first posting would keep an eye on a pilot who had done a good number of trips, and try to work out a pattern. I remember one filthy night when it was raining cats and dogs, and we were waiting for it to clear before we took off. Luckily that op was cancelled, but I needed a replacement Navigator, as Ernie Howes, my own Navigator, was feeling really unwell. He wasn't the sort to drop out, but he said he really didn't think he ought to be flying that night. I was offered a Navigator from another crew, but when I talked to him, he said: "I'm sorry, Sir, I can't fly with you." He explained that I had a reputation as a 'gen man'. When I asked him what on earth a 'gen man' was, he replied, "Well, it's a pilot who's good, but loses the blokes who fly with him." I pointed out that I'd never lost anyone, and that everyone who had flown with me had come back safe and sound. But he said, "Well, Sir, we know that all the substitutes you have taken have come back with you alright, but we also know that two or three trips later, when they weren't flying with you, a lot of them got shot down." I'd never heard the term 'gen man' before, and it seemed to me to be no more than superstition, but though I did my best to talk him round, this chap absolutely refused to fly with me. Fortunately, the raid was cancelled that night, and the next time round, Ernie Howes was well enough to fly.*

Superstition was in fact rife among the aircrew of Bomber Command. Stevie remembered another pilot *'who would never fly in a clean pullover. He always had a dirty pullover as he suspected that was his lucky top.'* And Stevie himself never agreed to having himself and his crew photographed because he had seen too many crews shot down after having their photograph taken. Otherwise, as a staunch Anglican, he trusted to the power of prayer, and on each mission, he took with him in his battle tunic a small leather-bound copy of the New Testament, marked at his favourite passage, John 14, 1-3:

> *Let not your heart be troubled: ye believe in God, believe also in me. In my Father's house are many mansions: if it were not so, I would have told you. I go to prepare a place for you. And if I go and prepare a place for you, I will come again, and receive you unto myself: that where I am, there ye may be also.*

Stevie would read these words at the funerals of family and friends, and when his own life was drawing to a close, he would quote it for the last time to his son, Adrian, saying: *"I still firmly believe that passage. We shall meet again."*

As E-'Easy' had been written off, Stevie was assigned Lancaster ED920 DX-A, with Sgt A.A. Smith (not to be confused with Sgt Johnnie Smith, who joined Stevie's crew later) replacing F/Lt Tony Wynyard as the Rear Gunner. Fourteen aircraft from 57 Squadron were detailed to join a force of 622 bombers to attack Berlin. The force suffered heavy losses, with 47 aircraft failing to return (a loss rate of 7 per cent), though none of them were from 57 Squadron. Intense fighter presence was reported, and the Germans adopted a new tactic of sending up aircraft detailed to drop flares to help the flak batteries and night fighters to target the bomber force. In the words of Bill McCrae:

> *Bright flares were being dropped on either side of the bomber stream, virtually turning night into day, and the fighters were flying along with the bombers looking for suitable targets. The flares kept appearing on either side of our planned route at least fifteen minutes ahead of our position. Apparently, the Germans were making an inspired guess at the route the bombers intended to take.*

For the first time since commencing his tour, Stevie did not reach the target. He took off at 20:50, but the oxygen supply in his Lancaster failed, so he was forced to make an early return to base, touching down at 22:39. Two other pilots from 57 Squadron, F/Lt Tony Gobbie in DV235, and F/O R.V. Munday flying JA910, were also forced to turn back early because of technical failures. Stevie noted in his log book with evident annoyance, '*First Boomerang*'.

By the end of August 1943, he had flown a total of 615 hours, and 57 Squadron had carried out twelve operations involving 179 Lancasters, four of which had been lost.

OPERATION 22: BERLIN, 3 SEPTEMBER, 1943

September started with a routine air test of ED920, following her oxygen failure on the previous sortie. On 3 September Stevie was again detailed to attack Berlin, but he was assigned a much older Mark I Lancaster, W7479, which he described disapprovingly as *'a clapped out old Lanc that wouldn't climb'*. F/Lt Tony Wynyard returned as Rear Gunner, and Sgt Wilson B. Yates joined the crew as Second Pilot for what would be his first operational flight or 'Second Dickie'.

Stevie's was one of fourteen aircraft from 57 Squadron with orders to join a bomber force of 315 Lancasters and four Mosquitos. He took off from East Kirkby at 19:45, but again, he was forced to make an early return, this time because of a string of serious mechanical failures. He landed back at East Kirkby at 22:32, and noted in his log book: *'Second Boomerang: PO engine U/S, MU Turret U/S, MU & BA heating U/S'*. With no port outer engine, no working mid-upper gun turret, and no heating for either the Mid-Upper Gunner or the Bomb Aimer, Stevie's only option was to abort the mission. In circumstances such as this, he noted:

> *There wasn't a serious inquiry because they could see if an engine was unserviceable or equipment not working. Sometimes people did get treated as LMF, but this happened very rarely, and generally, if you exercised your initiative, you were OK.*

The Squadron records noted that flak and fighter presence were intense on this raid, and that the searchlights had been highly effective. Twenty-two Lancasters were lost in all, including the aircraft piloted by F/Sgt William Grindley of 57 Squadron. It was shot down by a German fighter and crashed into the lake by the garrison town of Wünsdorf, just south of Berlin. The starboard wing and other parts of F/Sgt Grindley's Lancaster JA914, DX-O, were recovered and are now on display at the Museum of German Technology in Berlin. F/Sgt Grindley and his entire crew, Sgt Arthur Sutcliffe, Sgt James Carruthers, Sgt Henry Porteous, Sgt Albert Moore, Sgt Hugh Jones and F/Sgt David Livingstone were killed. Sgt Porteous, Sgt Sutcliffe and Sgt Jones are buried in the Berlin 1939-1945 War Cemetery; the rest of the crew are commemorated on the Runnymede Memorial.

OPERATION 23: MANNHEIM, 5 SEPTEMBER, 1943

Stevie's next target was Mannheim. He was assigned another Mark I Lancaster, W4948, and Sgt Yates was again detailed to accompany him as Second Pilot to gain operational experience.

Eleven Lancasters from 57 Squadron joined 605 Lancasters, Stirlings and Halifaxes for the raid. Stevie took off at 19:42 and reached the target. The attack was successful; clear skies enabled accurate marking, and extensive damage was done, with smoke reported as high up as 10,000ft. Stevie landed back at East Kirkby at 00:32 without incident, but three of the 57 Squadron pilots were forced to turn back: F/Sgt V. Evans suffered oxygen failure in ED944, P/O P.J. Piggin lost his starboard outer engine on ED777, and F/O F.L. Perrers lost his port outer engine flying W4822.

OPERATION 24: HANNOVER, 27 SEPTEMBER, 1943

It would be just over three weeks before Stevie would do another sortie. After carrying out a couple of short air and night flying tests on 24 and 25 September, he was briefed to attack Hannover, the site of a key railway intersection and of a large industrial complex which produced rubber, guns, and vehicles.

Stevie was at last given a permanent replacement aircraft which he would fly for the rest of his tour: JB311, DX-B. He was also joined by a new Rear Gunner: Sgt John George Lee Smith, who was just 18 years old. He would remain in Stevie's crew for the rest of his tour.

Thirteen aircraft from 57 Squadron joined a massive force of 678 bombers, which also included a small number of American B-17 Flying Fortresses. Stevie took off at 19:23. He and the other Lancasters from East Kirkby completed their mission, with the exception of F/Sgt V.D. Evans, piloting ED308, DX-O, who was forced back early with oxygen failure.

The operation was unsuccessful because strong winds caused the markers to drift off target, and it was reported that very little damage had been done. Thirty-eight aircraft were lost (a loss rate of 5.6 per cent), none from 57 Squadron, but severe weather forced the returning aircraft to divert to RAF Waterbeach in Cambridgeshire, where they rested and refuelled. Stevie and his crew returned to East Kirkby with the rest of the Squadron in the afternoon of 28 September.

The return to base was marked by tragedy. When P/O George Hargrave arrived back over East Kirkby in ED941, both his port engines cut. The aircraft crashed into a hill northeast of the airfield and burst into flames. The Bomb Aimer, Sgt J. S Whittle, Wireless Op, Sgt G. Huxtable and the Gunners, Sgt D. Hall and Sgt A.A Smith, who had flown with Stevie on the Berlin raid on 31 August, were pulled from the wreckage and survived. But George Hargrave, Sgt William Reeve, the Flight Engineer, and Sgt George Penny, the Navigator, lost their lives.

OPERATION 25: BOCHUM, 29 SEPTEMBER, 1943

Stevie's next target was the city of Bochum, located in the Ruhr Valley between Essen and Dortmund. Stevie and his crew were among fifteen Lancasters from 57 Squadron detailed to join a force of 352 Lancasters, Halifaxes and Mosquitos for the attack, but it was to be yet another aborted mission. Stevie took off at 18:11, with his aircraft and his crew unchanged, but an hour or so into the flight, Ernie Howes the Navigator reported feeling very sick, and Stevie was obliged to return, landing back at base at 21:08.

Stevie noted in his log book, *'Navigator too sick to cope, rest of crew peeved'*. But though the crew were disappointed not to be able to chalk up another operation, they had great respect for Ernie Howes. As Eric Blanchard put it, *'He was a stoic old boy (at 28 he was an old man compared to the rest of us), so we took his word for it.'*

Nine aircraft were lost on the raid (a loss rate of 2.6 per cent), among them one from 57 Squadron. Lancaster JA910 DX-H, piloted by P/O A.R. Wrangler, was shot down around 4km north of Raalte in Holland; but the entire crew managed to evacuate the aircraft, and P/O Wrangler, Sgt S.E Cornford, Sgt L. Barker, Sgt W.T. Curry, Sgt F.B. Raven, Sgt B.M. Quinn and Sgt R. Roberts became POWs.

Nine of the returning 57 Squadron Lancasters were diverted to other airfields because of bad weather and poor visibility over Lincolnshire, most of them landing at RAF Middleton St George in County Durham.

OPERATION 26: HAGEN, 1 OCTOBER, 1943

In September 1943, 57 Squadron had taken part in seven raids, and five of its Lancasters had failed to return. October began with a raid on Hagen, an industrial city on the south-eastern fringe of the Ruhr. Fourteen Lancasters from 57 Squadron were detailed to join a force of 243 Lancasters for the raid, with eight Mosquitos leading.

There was one change to Stevie's crew: F/Sgt Charles Neary, who formed part of the crew of F/Sgt V. Evans, was drafted in to replace Eric Blanchard as the Flight Engineer. Stevie took off in JB311 at 18:31 on what proved to be a relatively short and uneventful trip. No German fighters were encountered; flak was moderate; and despite low cloud cover over the target, the raid inflicted heavy damage.

Only two Lancasters were lost, and all the aircraft from 57 Squadron returned safely to base, with Stevie landing at East Kirkby at 23:51.

F/S Neary was subsequently transferred to No. 434 Squadron, and lost his life on 11 June 1944 on a raid to bomb railway facilities near Versailles in France.

57 Squadron Lancasters wait as dusk falls at Scampton in summer 1943

OPERATION 27: MUNICH, 2 OCTOBER, 1943

There was to be no rest for Stevie and his crew, as they were among fourteen Lancasters from 57 Squadron detailed to attack Munich the following night. Eric Blanchard returned as Flight Engineer, and Pilot Officer Walter Andrews RCAF was drafted in to replace George Martin as Mid-Upper Gunner.

Stevie took off from East Kirkby at 18:45, joining a force of two hundred and ninety-four Lancasters and two B-17 Flying Fortresses. Sgt W.B. Yates, who had flown as Second Pilot with Stevie, had to divert and land at RAF Waterbeach, and P/O W.M. Walton returned to East Kirkby with his 4,000lb 'cookie', which had failed to release, still in the bomb bay.

The crews found clear conditions over the target, but the markers were scattered, and much of the bombing was inaccurate. Squadron records reported intense and concentrated fires, and also noted strong night fighter presence and concentrated searchlight batteries. Stevie landed safely back at East Kirkby at 02:58.

Eight Lancasters were lost on the raid (a loss rate of 2.7 per cent), including one from 57 Squadron. DV235, piloted by P/O Robert Clements, was shot down by a German night fighter near Kirchheim unter Teck at 23:05. The entire crew: P/O Clements, F/Sgt James Wheatley, F/O Robert Burton, Sgt Herbert Hynds, Sgt Ronald Bishop, Sgt Ronald Large and Sgt John McGuirk were killed. They lie together in the War Cemetery at Durnbach in Bavaria.

P/O Walter Andrews, who stood in for George Martin as Stevie's Mid-Upper Gunner on this operation, was a Canadian. He normally formed part of the crew of Pilot Officer Keith McPhie DFC, RAAF. P/O McPhie, P/O Walter Andrews, and the entire crew of Lancaster JB311, DX-B (the same aircraft that had been assigned to Stevie for most of his operations from East Kirkby) were shot down and killed on a raid to Berlin on 28/29 January 1944.

OPERATION 28: STUTTGART/AMIENS, 7 OCTOBER, 1943

It was to be the third raid in the first week of October for Stevie and his crew, with George Martin returning as Mid-Upper Gunner. The target this time was Stuttgart in south-west Germany. It turned out to be an eventful trip.

Twenty aircraft from 57 Squadron joined a force of 343 Lancasters from 1, 3, 5 and 8 Groups, with Stevie taking off from East Kirkby at 20:11. But a succession of severe mechanical problems forced him to turn back and head for home. He was well on his way to the target when his aircraft's intercom and electrical heating systems failed, and the rear turret went out of action. He had no choice but to abort the mission, but he found himself without support in an aircraft with serious mechanical defects, and was highly vulnerable to attack.

As Stevie approached the French coast, searchlights lit up and began to scan the sky ahead. It turned out that they were close to the military airfield at Amiens, which had been commandeered by the Luftwaffe after the fall of France. As he was still carrying a full bomb load, Stevie decided to make an improvised attack, and when he landed at 03:08, he was commended for showing initiative:

> *It was very fortunate for me because Amiens was one of the French airfields which had been taken over by the Germans. It was an important Luftwaffe base; they had anti-aircraft guns there and searchlights, so it was quite a tough combination. I saw the searchlights coming up, so I flew over it, saw what was underneath, and dropped my bombs. We hit some enemy aircraft and blew up a hangar. It had all happened by accident, but it was counted as a trip because we did as much damage to the Germans by destroying the aircraft and the hangar as we would have done if we had reached the target.*

Numerous other aircraft from 57 Squadron failed to reach Stuttgart. The engines of P/O J. Howe's Lancaster ED758 overheated; F/Lt A. Dunn's hot and cold air supply failed in JA872; P/O W. Walton turned back because of severe icing to JB366, and Sgt A. Fearn lost his port outer engine on ED413.

The aircraft which reached the target encountered 10/10ths cloud cover, and the markers were reported to be as much as 4-5 miles apart, so that the bombing was scattered. Four aircraft were lost on the raid, none from 57 Squadron. No night fighters were encountered, and the German defences were rated very moderate.

OPERATION 29: HANNOVER, 8 OCTOBER, 1943

The target for Stevie's fourth operation in eight days was once again Hannover. Fifteen aircraft from 57 Squadron were detailed to join a force of five hundred and four Lancasters, Halifaxes, Wellingtons, and Mosquitos for the assault. Only fourteen aircraft actually took off from East Kirkby. Sgt Fearn was stood down, and P/O F. Smith in ED698 was forced home early because of engine problems.

Stevie took off with his regular crew at 22:40, and landed back at East Kirkby at 04:00 after a trouble-free sortie. The weather over the target had been clear, and both the marking and the bombing were accurate. Large fires were generated, and extensive damage was caused.

OPERATION 30: HANNOVER, 18 OCTOBER, 1943

After the Hannover raid, there was a ten-day gap in operations for the whole of 57 Squadron. The weather was persistently bad, and Stevie's only two flights during this period, on 13 and 16 October, were to do bombing practice.

When operational flying resumed on 18 October, Hannover was again the target on what would be Stevie's third and final trip there. His crew was unchanged, and his was among the twenty-one aircraft from 57 Squadron ordered to join a force of three hundred and sixty Lancasters for the raid. Two of the 57 Squadron aircraft were flown by aircrew from 207 Squadron based at RAF Spilsby, just east of East Kirkby.

Stevie took off at 17:12 and reached the target, but there was heavy cloud; the marking was inaccurate, and the raid was unsuccessful. Eighteen aircraft in total were lost (a loss rate of 5.0 per cent), but 57 Squadron suffered no losses, and Stevie made good time back to base, landing at 22:21.

The raid would go down in the annals of 57 Squadron because of an extraordinary act of individual courage. After completing its bombing run, Lancaster JB197, flown by F/Sgt W. Grimbly, was intercepted and attacked by a German Me109 fighter. F/Sgt Grimbly's aircraft sustained extensive damage; riddled with holes from both machine gun bullets and cannon

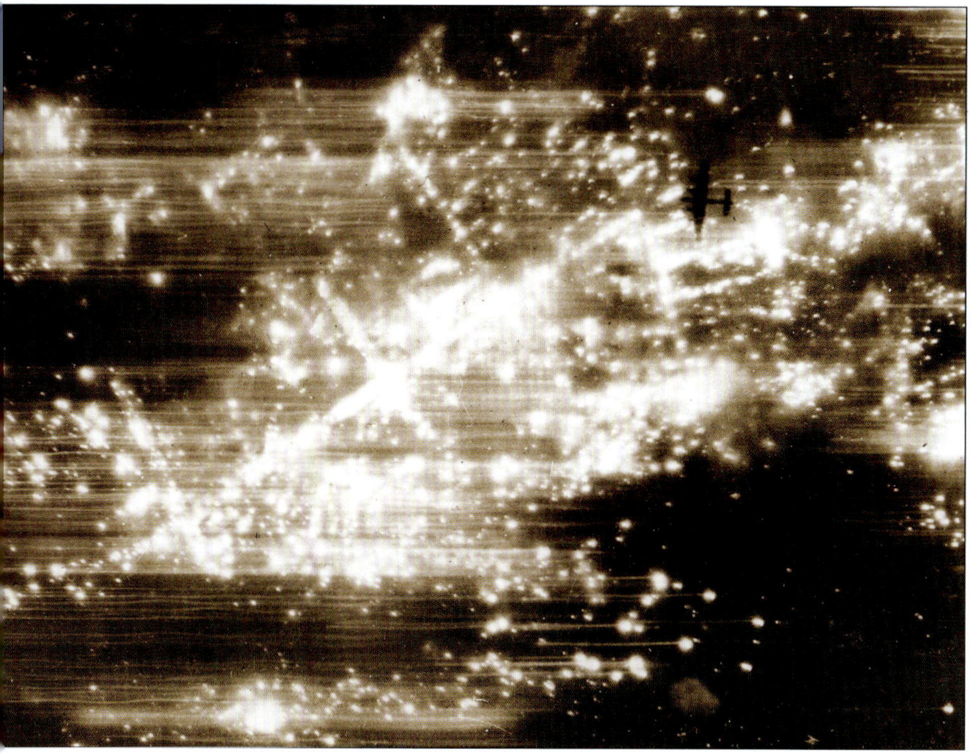

A Lancaster silhouetted over a burning Hannover in October 1943

shells, it lost its starboard outer engine, and a fuel tank was hit. The Mid-Upper Gunner, Sgt F.A. Fox, was shot in the foot, and the Rear Gunner, Sgt Arthur Humphrey Cowham, who was on his very first sortie, was also seriously wounded. Sgt Cowham, a Rhodesian who had joined 57 Squadron on 7 October, was blinded in one eye by a splinter from a cannon shell; a bullet had hit his shoulder, and his rear turret was wrecked. Despite this, he stayed at his post and managed to repel repeated attacks by German night fighters. He was awarded a CGM (Conspicuous Gallantry Medal), which was gazetted on 19 November 1943. The citation read:

> *One night in October 1943, this airman was the rear gunner of an aircraft detailed to attack Hannover. Shortly after the target had been bombed, the aircraft was engaged by a fighter and hit by a hail of bullets which caused much damage. Sgt Cowham was struck in the face and suffered a severe injury to one of his eyes. Although his turret was virtually wrecked, he fought on with great resolution and played a good part in driving off the attacker. Throughout the long journey home this brave gunner, although in*

intense pain and suffering from the loss of blood, refused to leave his post. Twice, subsequently, his accurate shooting prevented an enemy aircraft from closing in, while his skilful directions assisted his pilot to out-manoeuvre the enemy and fly clear. In harassing circumstances his gallant example greatly encouraged his comrades who were striving to bring the crippled bomber home. On this, his first sortie, Sgt Cowham displayed courage, fortitude and devotion to duty in keeping with the best traditions of the Royal Air Force.

OPERATION 31: LEIPZIG, 20 OCTOBER, 1943

This was Stevie's final operation, and it was to prove both eventful and hazardous. Nineteen aircraft from 57 Squadron formed part of a force of 358 Lancasters detailed to bomb Leipzig in eastern Germany. This was Bomber Command's first concentrated attack on Leipzig, a key railway intersection and home to prime industrial targets, among them aircraft factories producing Messerschmitt 109 fighter aircraft. Stevie, once again with his regular crew, took off at 17:25.

The weather was appalling: there were severe thunderstorms, and it was so cold that many of the aircraft experienced acute problems with icing. P/O D.A. Shewan in ED944 DX-I and F/Sgt H.S. Edwards in ED698 DX-R both had to return early because ice forming on their rear turrets put them out of service. Stevie would retain a vivid recollection of the appalling conditions he encountered:

If it is damp after the sun goes down, the aircraft has a layer of dampness on all the control surfaces at take-off. The normal fall in temperature when you go up is about three degrees for every thousand feet so that as the aircraft climbs and gains height, little blobs of ice form on it. This makes it unstable; the controls are affected, and they become a bit sluggish and unresponsive. On the trip to Leipzig, I got to the prescribed height and thought, 'it just doesn't feel right.' I was worried that I was getting some icing on the aircraft, so I moved the elevators and rudders, and they seemed alright. I asked Ken Brown, the Wireless Op, to get the Aldis lamp out and flash it along the wings to see if ice was forming. It was, and so I decided not to remain at that height. I asked Ernie Howes, the Navigator, to set another course which would allow us to join the main force later on. I could see a nice patch of grey in the sky, and I thought it would be warmer and less dangerous to fly down into it. Ernie was a very good Navigator, so he worked out a course for me, and we flew lower in order to avoid the hazard of icing.

Despite flying off course to avoid icing up, Stevie managed to link up with the main force and bomb the target. But he was still far from safety. On the return run to East Kirkby, his air speed indicator stopped working, and his port and starboard inner engines failed. Calmly and skilfully, he managed to make it back to base with only the two outer engines working, and touched down safely at 00:46.

A total of sixteen aircraft had been lost on the raid (a loss rate of 4.5 per cent). Two 57 Squadron Lancasters reported combats with night fighters, with F/Sgt A.Novick in JB315 DX-J suffering considerable damage to his aircraft. Lancaster JB234 DX-E, flown by P/O Frank Parker, was shot down and crashed into the River Elbe near Arneburg, killing him and his entire crew: Sgt Robert Chumley, F/O Peter Porteous, Sgt Cyril Harston, Sgt John O'Leary, F/Sgt John Read and Sgt Charles Wharton. All of them were laid to rest in the Berlin 1939-45 War Cemetery.

It so happened that Air Vice Marshal Sir Ralph Cochrane, AOC 5 Group, was visiting East Kirkby at the time of the Leipzig raid. He debriefed Stevie after he landed, and asked him how he had managed to deal with the icing caused by the adverse weather conditions. On the previous occasion Cochrane had debriefed Stevie, he had recommended him for a commission; this time, he recommended him for the award of an immediate DFC:

> *When I got down, Air Vice Marshal Cochrane was inspecting. He asked me how I'd managed to deal with the icing when so many other aircraft were getting trapped by it. The casualty rate had been higher than usual because of the temperature inversion, and sixteen aircraft hadn't returned, including one from our Squadron. I admitted that I had broken the flight plan, and used my own discretion as the aircraft was in danger. After hearing my report, Cochrane decided he'd decorate me!*
>
> The citation for Stevie's DFC, which was gazetted on 23 November 1943, reads:
>
> *This officer has displayed great skill and determination throughout his tour of operations. One night in October 1943, he piloted an aircraft detailed to attack Leipzig. On the outward flight violent electrical storms were encountered. Although the air speed indicator became useless and other equipment was rendered temporarily unserviceable, P/O Stevens went on to complete his mission. His persistence in the face of trying circumstances was most praiseworthy.*

Stevie had been in the front line for more than five months. After twenty-eight completed missions and three early returns caused by mechanical failure, W/Cdr Bill Fisher, Stevie's CO, and AVM Cochrane evidently decided that Stevie had done enough, and he was informed that he had completed his tour and was being stood down from operational flying. On 1 November 1943, Stevie noted in his log book in block capitals under Fisher's signature: *'END OF FIRST TOUR OF OPERATIONS'*.

Stevie wrote home to his parents to inform them he had successfully finished his tour, adding in a postscript that he had been recommended for a DFC:

> *Dear Mum and Dad,*
>
> *Just to tell you that at last I HAVE FINISHED the tour, and shall be home for 7 or 9 days leave on Saturday evening.*
>
> *That's all for now, but pretty good, don't you think?*
>
> *Sid*
>
> *P.S. Have been recommended for a DFC or something, but probably shall not hear about it for a couple of months.*

Stevie did not have to wait long for confirmation that he had been awarded an immediate DFC. On 6 November, he was sent a message signed by Sir Arthur Harris: *'My warmest congratulations on the award of your Distinguished Flying Cross.'*

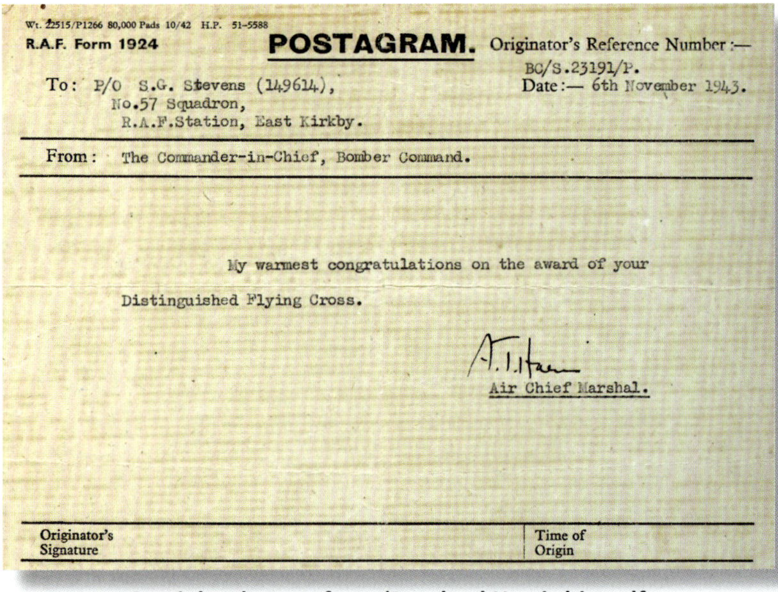

Wt. 22515/P1266 80,000 Pads 10/42 H.P. 51-5588
R.A.F. Form 1924

POSTAGRAM.

Originator's Reference Number :— BC/S.23191/P.
Date :— 6th November 1943.

To: P/O S.G. Stevens (149614),
No.57 Squadron,
R.A.F.Station, East Kirkby.

From: The Commander-in-Chief, Bomber Command.

My warmest congratulations on the award of your Distinguished Flying Cross.

A.T. Harris
Air Chief Marshal.

Originator's Signature | Time of Origin

Stevie's telegram from 'Bomber' Harris himself

On the following day, he received a telegram from W/Cdr Fisher, the CO of 57 Squadron.

Charges to pay
s. d.
RECEIVED
POST OFFICE
TELEGRAM
No.
OFFICE STAMP
7 NOV 1943
Prefix. Time handed in. Office of Origin and Service Instructions. Words.
98
From 198 3.54 NG/T OHMS 27
To
PO S J STEVENS 149614 16 OTU UPPERHEYFORD =
= HEARTIEST CONGRATULATIONS FROM OFFICER
COMMANDING OFFICERS AND MEN OF 57 TH SQUADRON
ON IMMEDIATE AWARD OF DFC STOP 57 TH SQUADRON
For free repetitic at office of delive 149614 16 OTU 57 57 NG/T or call, with this form If possible, the envelope
B or C
Wt. 45904. 100,000 Pads. 2/43. 51-4290. J. D. & Co. Ltd.

from his C/O

Fisher also wrote Stevie a letter:

Dear Stevens,

Confirming my congratulatory telegram on the Immediate Award to you of the Distinguished Flying Cross, I am appending below [an] extract from a signal received from Headquarters Bomber Command:

"HIS MAJESTY THE KING ON THE RECOMMENDATION OF THE AIR OFFICER COMMANDING IN CHIEF HAS APPROVED THE IMMEDIATE AWARD OF THE DISTINGUISHED FLYING CROSS TO PILOT OFFICER SIDNEY GEORGE STEVENS".

I wish to send my heartiest congratulations and those of all members of the Squadron.

Yours sincerely,

H. W. H. Fisher

Officer Commanding,
No.57 Squadron,
R.A.F. Station,
East Kirkby,
Lincs.

7th November, 1943.

Dear *Stevens*,

Confirming my congratulatory telegram on the Immediate Award to you of the Distinguished Flying Cross, I am appending below extract from a signal received from Headquarters Bomber Command:

"HIS MAJESTY THE KING ON THE RECOMMENDATION OF THE AIR OFFICER COMMANDING IN CHIEF HAS APPROVED THE IMMEDIATE AWARD OF THE DISTINGUISHED FLYING CROSS TO PILOT OFFICER SIDNEY GEORGE STEVENS".

I wish to send my heartiest congratulations and those of all members of the Squadron.

Yours *Sincerely*
[signature]

Wing Commander Commanding,
No.57 Squadron, R.A.F.

P/O S.G. Stevens,
No.16 O.T.U.,
R.A.F. Upper Heyford.

Fisher, who had been awarded a DFC himself in 1941, was not only a courageous pilot, but a CO concerned for the welfare of his men. Towards the end of September, shortly after he took command of 57 Squadron, he called Stevie's friend Bill McCrae into his office. In his book, Bill McCrae recounts the meeting as follows:

> *"I see you have been on the Squadron longer than anyone, Paddy," said Fisher. "You arrived early in February. What happened?" "Well, Sir, my eardrum was damaged when I was running up my engines before taking off for Wuppertal on 29 May, and I didn't fly on operations again until early July." "I've got some good news for you, Paddy," said the Wing Commander. "You've been here long enough. They are running short of instructors at Group and I have been asked to release a crew for instructional duties immediately. I've put your name forward. Go and tell your crew to collect their clearance chits. Your postings should come through in a day or two, and then you can go on leave. Well done. Thank you for doing such a good job."*

This was not favouritism, but a recognition on Fisher's part of the immense physical and psychological strain put on any pilot who had spent the best part of eight months on operations in the front line. In the event, Fisher's recommendation was overturned on the grounds that Bill McCrae had only completed twenty-six trips, and he went on to complete four more and do a full tour. His last trip was to Hannover on 18 October. Like Stevie, he was awarded an immediate DFC in recognition of the outstanding bravery and skill he had shown during his tour of operations. The citation, gazetted on 29 October 1943, reads:

> *This officer has completed many successful operations, including such targets as Berlin, Hamburg and many industrial centres in the Ruhr. He has displayed great skill and leadership and his efforts throughout have been featured by determination of a high standard. One night in September 1943, when returning from an attack on a target on the Ruhr, his aircraft was intercepted by a fighter. A prolonged combat ensued but coolly and skilfully P/O McCrae finally succeeded in out-manoeuvring his adversary. The bomber sustained much damage but this pilot flew it safely to base. He displayed great courage and resolution in trying circumstances.*

Bill McCrae continued to serve in the RAF after the War and retired in 1972 with the rank of Wing Commander. He was a fine amateur golfer with numerous trophies to his name, and helped Ireland to win the European Team Championship at the unlikely age of 44. On retiring from the RAF, he became Secretary of the Walton Heath Golf Club in Surrey, where he was instrumental in staging three European Open Championships as well the Ryder Cup. He and Stevie remained lifelong friends, meeting regularly at the annual reunions of the 57 Squadron Association at Woodhall Spa in Lincolnshire until Bill passed away in 2015. '*I liked him tremendously,*' Stevie noted in his diary, '*my son and his wife both went to his funeral, which I sadly couldn't make.*'

News of Stevie's DFC was quick to reach the local press. On 19 November 1943 the front page of the *Norwood News* carried the story, together with a photograph of Stevie, seen opposite:

Stevie took great pride in the fact that he lost none of the aircrew who flew with him during his tour. Ken Brown, his Wireless Op, survived the War and joined BOAC, where '*he did very well*'. Ernie Howes, his Navigator, was awarded a DFC in January 1944 on Stevie's recommendation, but Stevie lost touch with him. Eric Blanchard went on to complete a second tour with 57 Squadron as Engineer Leader, and was awarded a DFC in 1945. He and Stevie, fellow Devonians, remained firm friends. They met at Squadron reunions and whenever Stevie returned to Devon on holiday, sharing stories and drinks, reminiscing and laughing together, and telephoning each other regularly until Eric took his final flight on 31 October 2010, at the age of 88.

Stevie was devastated by Eric's passing, and composed a heartfelt tribute which was read out at his funeral:

> *On a glorious spring day, 67 years ago, Eric and I flew together in a Lancaster. It was my first solo flight and Eric's first on a Lancaster. We did a couple of landings to get used to the drill, then soared upwards through cotton wool cumulus cloud. We thoroughly enjoyed the view before returning to earth. We sat under the wing of the large aircraft and shared a cake which Eric's mother had cooked for his 21st birthday.*
>
> *During the next ten days we exercised by day and night, and then we were posted to join 57 Squadron at Scampton in Lincolnshire. We soon acquired a brand-new Lancaster and spent some time ironing out its teething troubles.*
>
> *We were taken for our first operational trip by Squadron Leader Smith and had our first experience of flying through heavy flak, illuminated by hundreds of searchlights. After that we flew on twenty-eight trips during the first four of which 134 of our aircraft were shot down, and by the end of our tour, 669 of our aircraft had been shot down over enemy territory.*
>
> *During these tense individual battles, Eric displayed calm unflappable skill, especially in dealing with an engine fire after a battle with a night*

EVEN MOTHER DOES NOT KNOW DETAILS

P/O Stevens' Work with Bomber Command

RAIDS ON GERMANY AND OCCUPIED TERRITORIES

SIDNEY STEVENS, elder son of Mr. and Mrs. G. W. Stevens, Belmont-road, South Norwood, always held an ambition to fly, and proof of his ambition being realised, and that he is no mean flyer, is given by the award to him of the Distinguished Flying Cross.

As a Pilot-Officer with Bomber Command, he has raided Hamburg, Nuremberg, Munich, Turin and has twice attacked Milan. One night, while over Essen, his aircraft "bagged" an enemy fighter.

His parents do not know why he has been decorated, and in a letter to them he mentioned, "I do not want any build-up in the newspapers. Just the bare statement that I have won the D.F.C. is enough."

Like many others, P.-O. Stevens trained for his "wings" in California, but had greater luck than some when he visited Hollywood. He met and chatted with Anna Neagle while at a party.

He is a native of Torrington, Devon, and an old boy of Henry Thornton School, Clapham. At one time he was Cubmaster of the Harrington-road pack, and has acted as a server at St. Luke's Church, Woodside.

His pre-Service effort took the form of A.R.P. duties at the Melfort-road Zone Post, in Thornton Heath. He was on duty there when his home in Macclesfield-road, South Norwood, was demolished by enemy action. He has now avenged this by his gallant service in the R.A.F.

P./O. SID STEVENS

Before volunteering at the age of 19—he first applied when only 18 but was turned down—he was an employee of the Croydon Borough Valuer's Office.

Next month he is to be married at Norwich. He is 22.

Norwood News **Article – Friday 19 November 1943**

fighter, and on another occasion rescuing four crew members who were suffering from anoxia, releasing the leg of one who had collapsed after his leg had gone through a hole made by flak in the floor of the fuselage.

Eric Blanchard in 1945, photographed after the award of his DFC

He was in the earliest raid to drop 'Window', which involved him lying on the floor of the aircraft and dropping quantities of metallic strips through the open bomb doors to confuse the enemy radar. He was also on the longest operational flight made by Bomber Command to Turin when shortage of fuel forced us to land at Davidstow Moor in Cornwall. This gives a small glimpse of Eric's early days in Bomber Command.

Not satisfied with that, he returned to 57 Squadron as Engineer Leader and completed a second tour. He was on the last raid of the War and bombed Hitler's retreat at the 'Eagle's Nest'. It was not surprising that he was awarded a richly deserved Distinguished Flying Cross. As fellow Devonians, Eric and I shared many air war battles and in peace, we expanded our friendship walking over the moors and by the sea. We also attended annual 57 Squadron reunions in Lincolnshire at Scampton and East Kirkby.

Our Squadron motto is 'Corpus non animum muto', meaning 'I change my body, not my spirit' Eric's body may change, but his spirit will be with his family and friends for ever. It is with inexpressibly deep sadness I say Farewell to a greatly respected, exceptionally brave and courageous Flight Engineer and long-time friend.

Tragically, Dickie Newcomb, George Martin, and Johnnie Smith did not live to see the end of the War. Just before Stevie's third operation to Düsseldorf on 11 June 1943, Dickie Newcomb had been taken ill and diagnosed with tonsillitis:

We had gone out to the aircraft to prepare when he complained of a headache and asked the Medical Officer, who was visiting the Flight Dispersal before take-off, for an aspirin. The MO took his temperature and told him he was not to fly. Dickie had developed tonsillitis. As a result, he missed the next five operations with me, and when I finished my tour, he still had several trips to complete. By this time, he was very experienced and was commissioned. He did his last trip with me to Leipzig on 20 October, when I finished my tour. On 18 November at 17:18 he took off for Berlin in a Lancaster flown by F/Lt Gobbie which crashed near Dresden. It should have been his last trip but one. All the crew except for Dickie and P/O Alf Gardner, the Navigator, survived and were taken prisoner. Dickie was lost without trace, and I was never able to find out what happened.

On 18 January 1945, Dickie Newcomb's aunt wrote to Stevie from her home in Ealing. She said that she and Dickie's father back in Chile had received no news of him, and they feared the worst:

Unfortunately, we have not received any news of Dick, as we so hoped might have been the case by now. But my brother Clive Newcomb in Chile was anxious that I should get in touch with you to thank you so very much for the nice letter you sent him some months ago. I know he wrote to you himself on 8 September, but the South American mails are so uncertain these days that he specially asked me to write to you. The letter you wrote I know gave him very great joy, and he told me how proud he was of all that Dick's friend said of him.

As you probably know, my nephew made his home with us here in London while he was in this country. He often spoke of you, and how happy he was in your crew, and I remember how upset he was when he got ill and had to change and do his last flights with another crew.

She added:

I am enclosing a snap of Dick, taken in our garden in the summer of 1943, which I think you might like to have. We like it because he is looking so very happy.

The photograph sent to Stevie by Dickie Newcomb's aunt, perhaps the last to be taken of him, shows Dickie in his Sergeant's uniform, sitting smiling and relaxed in a deckchair in her garden.

Dickie was the Bomb Aimer in a Lancaster piloted by F/Lt Tony Gobbie which took off from East Kirkby at 17:18 on 18 November 1943 to attack Berlin, and crashed at Bärnsdorf near Dresden. Tony Gobbie had trained in

The photograph of Dickie Newcomb taken in 1943 mentioned by his aunt in her letter to Stevie

America. He had completed his Advanced Flying Training at Maxwell Field, Montgomery, Alabama, and received his Wings on 5 August 1942, the same day as Stevie. But unlike Stevie, Tony Gobbie had been commissioned in the rank of Pilot Officer immediately after graduation. Tony and Stevie knew each other quite well. They had trained on the same OTUs at Spitalgate and Cottesmore, and been posted to 57 Squadron at the same time. Tony Gobbie was promoted to Acting Flight Lieutenant, and countersigned Stevie's log book in July, August, and September 1943 as his Flight Commander. By the time he took off for the Berlin raid, he had been awarded an immediate DFC, which was gazetted on 23 November 1943, a few days after his Lancaster was brought down. The citation reads:

> *F/Lt Gobbie has participated in very many sorties, including attacks on Berlin, Hamburg, Peenemünde and targets in the Ruhr. He has displayed skill, courage and determination, qualities which have earned him many successes. On recent occasions, against Leipzig and Kassel respectively, his efforts in the face of extremely adverse weather were worthy of the highest praise.*

He was evidently an experienced, brave and highly capable pilot, and W/Cdr Bill Fisher, the CO of 57 Squadron, held him in high regard. Tony Gobbie's daughter, Eve Janocko, kindly supplied a photograph of the letter W/Cdr Fisher wrote to Tony Gobbie's father on 19 November 1943, after he had failed to return from the Berlin raid:

F/Lt Antony Gobbie [Photograph: Eve Janocko, his daughter]

Dear Mr Gobbie,

It is with profound regret that I must now write and confirm my telegram informing you that your son, Flight Lieutenant Anthony F. Gobbie, is missing following operations on the night of 18/19 November, 1943.

He was the Captain of an aircraft detailed to take part in a raid against Germany, but as it is customary for radio silence to be maintained after take-off, it has not been possible to determine the cause of its failure to return.

Your son was an extremely capable Pilot of outstanding ability and had almost completed his first tour of operations. I held a very high opinion of him as a keen and determined Captain of Aircraft. He had carried out many successful sorties against the enemy with great courage and enthusiasm. He was the Captain of an excellent crew and I know he would do everything in his power to ensure their safety. There is, of course, every chance that they were able to abandon the aircraft and land safely in enemy territory and if, as we all sincerely hope, this proves to be the case, then news will ultimately reach you through the British Red Cross Society. We can only hope and pray that they are safe and I wish to extend to you my own personal sympathy and that of all members of my Squadron during the anxious time you will have waiting for news.

You will wish to know that I have arranged for his personal effects to be taken care of by the Committee of Adjustment Officer at this Station and they will be forwarded to you when circumstances permit.

Any further official information concerning the missing aircraft or crew will be sent to you by the Air Ministry, but if, as sometimes happens, you receive news from outside sources, I shall be most grateful if you will let me know.

In the event, Tony Gobbie survived the crash. He and four of his crew, Sgt Hemmings, F/O Scott, Sgt Pool, and F/Sgt Lamble managed to parachute from the plane. They were captured and interned at Stalag Luft 1, just outside the town of Barth in Western Pomerania, and liberated by the Red Army on 30 April 1945. Tony Gobbie emigrated to America in 1947, and settled in Florida. He married in 1953, and passed away on 26 December 1976 at the comparatively early age of 57. He never spoke to his children

Tony Gobbie's PoW Identification Card

in any detail about the crash, except to say that he had been shot down, and that when he bailed out of the stricken Lancaster, he had hit trees and sustained a back injury which caused him permanent pain. As he came down near Dresden, it is likely that the Germans were quick to arrive on the scene, and that neither he nor the surviving members of his crew, who must have been in a state of shock after the crash and in no position to investigate, knew for certain what had happened to Dickie Newcomb and F/O Gardner, the Navigator. The fact that their bodies were never found suggests that they were either killed or seriously wounded when their plane was shot down. The grim truth is that if they were trapped, and the aircraft exploded when it hit the ground, no trace of them would have been left. Their names are listed among those of the aircrew with no known graves who are commemorated at Runnymede.

Stevie's French Mid-Upper Gunner George Martin survived the four sorties he needed to complete his tour. In a letter dated 1 December 1943, Corporal Swinchatt, who was Stevie's engine fitter at Scampton and East Kirkby, wrote to him saying that George had been scheduled to fly with Tony Gobbie on the trip to Berlin which cost Dickie Newcomb his life:

> *George of Free French fame is still about [at East Kirkby], on his last trip. He should have gone with Gobbie, but went sick, and he's still here. It shook him a bit, though, especially when they started to sort his kit out, thinking he was in Germany. I don't think George ever panicked so much before!*

In the same letter, Corporal Swinchatt confirmed that Dickie Newcomb was missing: *'Yes, I'm afraid Dickie went down with Gobbie and crew, that was a shaky do. I only hope he is safe.'*

A few weeks later, George Martin was awarded a DFM on Stevie's recommendation. The citation, gazetted on 11 February 1944, read:

> *F/Sgt Martin has taken part in many sorties against strongly defended targets in Germany, including Berlin, Hamburg, Hannover and other towns in the Ruhr Valley. A most reliable Air Gunner, he has invariably displayed keenness, determination and cool courage. In June 1943, on the outward flight to Oberhausen, this airman damaged a Messerschmitt 110, and on the return flight a Junkers 88. In neither case were the enemy aircraft allowed to come close enough to open fire. On several occasions F/Sgt Martin's accurate fire has driven off enemy aircraft and, in the course of his tour of operational duty, he has destroyed one enemy fighter and damaged four others.*

By the time he was awarded his DFM, George Martin had been posted to the Training Unit at RAF Winthorpe as a Gunnery Instructor. He evidently made his mark there. Much later, Stevie would recall:

> *George had real presence. When he finished his first tour, he got posted on to Short Stirlings. He was sitting in the cockpit one day, and a pilot got in and made himself comfortable. They took off, and when they'd done a couple of landings, the pilot looked at him and said, "Can I go solo now, Sir?" He'd mistaken George for his instructor!*

George Martin himself wrote to Stevie from Winthorpe on 9 May 1944. He had hoped to remuster as a pilot; but, he reported, *'They won't take any more entries, so roll on the second tour, I am quite happy about it.'* He included in his letter this portrait of himself, which he inscribed, *'With my very best wishes to Steve — my skipper. George, MUG E-'Easy', Dortmund 25.5.43 — Leipzig, 20.10.43'.*

George Martin returned to East Kirkby to do a second tour with 57 Squadron, but sadly, he did not live to see it through. On 18 September 1944 the Lancaster in which he was flying, NG126, DX-L, piloted by F/O Robert Waugh, took part in an attack on Bremerhaven, and was brought down over the eastern outskirts at Schiffdorf. George Martin was killed along with F/O Waugh, Sgt Basil Cooper, Sgt Allan Rogers, Sgt Phillip

Photograph of George Martin wearing his DFM ribbon

Lunt, and Sgt Howard Shakespeare. The Wireless Operator, F/Sgt A.A. D'Oyley, was the sole survivor.

Like Dickie Newcomb, George Martin has no known resting place. He is, in Stevie's words, '*now just a name recorded in St Clement Danes Church and the RAF Memorial at Runnymede to those with no known grave. But I shall never forget him, and I am proud to have been his friend.*'

The third member of Stevie's operational crew who was lost without trace was Johnnie Smith. He was only 18 when he joined Stevie's crew as a Rear Gunner direct from training, and he flew with Stevie on his last sorties from East Kirkby:

> *Johnnie Smith joined me and did several trips with me. Small, quiet, pale, and keen, he learned quickly the splendid search talents taught him by George Martin. They complemented each other extremely well as Gunners.*

When Stevie finished his tour, Johnnie Smith transferred to 630 Squadron, which had been formed from and was based alongside 57 Squadron at East Kirkby:

> *On 23 November 1943 at 17:06 Johnnie took off for Berlin. F/O Joseph Howe was his pilot. The aircraft was lost without trace. Howe was beginning his tour as I was completing mine. I thought he was a steady and competent chap.*

Johnnie Smith formed a close relationship with George Martin, who became his mentor and held him in high regard. In the letter George wrote to Stevie on 9 May 1944, he told him that '*Johnnie went down on 23.11.43 on Berlin with F/O Howe. He has definitely been identified as killed by the Red Cross.*' George described Johnnie as '*the best Gunner I knew*', praise indeed from somebody so well qualified to judge. Saddened by Johnnie's tragically early death, he paid a visit to his parents in April 1944 during Easter Week talk to them in person about their son. He gave Stevie their address, asking him to write to them, and Stevie sent them a letter of condolence. Johnnie's father replied in a letter dated 20 June 1944, which brings home the suffering endured by the thousands of families whose sons fell on active service with Bomber Command. In a very real sense, it speaks for all of them; it is so moving in its expression of grief and pride that it deserves to be quoted in full:

> *Dear Skipper,*
>
> *I take the liberty of referring to you as above, as that is how Johnnie used to talk of you.*

My wife and I thank you very much indeed for your kind references to our boy, and who should know better than you what kind of man he was. He was heart and soul in his job; in fact, it was his life. We get a little consolation from the fact that he did what he set his heart on doing; and if he 'went out' doing it, he did it in the full knowledge of the risks entailed.

It is a terrible blow to us, as you may well imagine. He was a grand boy who was content in his home life and never at any time caused us a moment's trouble. He would, I am sure, have gone far in civil life. We miss him sadly, especially Mary, our daughter. They were never without each other. Both she and my wife are taking it wonderfully, but I tell you what I have told others. I cannot take it. I served four years in France during the last War, all front-line service, and had my pals killed at my side, and should be hard; but it is altogether different when it comes to your own.

We had a visit from F/Sgt George Martin in Easter Week. He was Mid-Upper Gunner with John. A French boy, I believe. He has the DFM, and said John should have had one, but evidently it was not to be. Had he come through this far, who knows, he may have earned one.

He had a very high opinion of you and was very sincere in his remarks about your capabilities. It was only rarely that he ever talked about the job, and we understood and did not press him.

My wife and daughter join me in wishing you continued good luck and a speedy end to this rotten business. But finish it this time. They stopped us last time, when we had them beaten.

Happy landings always,

Yours very sincerely,

J.H. Smith

On 30 April 1992, Stevie wrote in response to a request for information concerning the RAF Memorial at Runnymede:

An operational tour seemed like a series of thirty very testing examinations, requiring skill, intelligence and a grim determination to succeed. A momentary failure to concentrate and react swiftly usually resulted in death. During my operational flights between May and October 1943, 669 of our aircraft were shot down over enemy territory. Yet morale was invariably high. The friends of mine commemorated at Runnymede gave their lives so that the basic freedoms of speech, justice, and travel should not be eradicated. Whenever I vote at an election, drive my car, walk freely in the countryside or have a discussion over a pint in a pub, I am very aware that I enjoy those freedoms only because of the voluntary final sacrifice of my absent friends and so many others like them. Their struggle to defend our hard-won freedom must ever be remembered, and continued when necessary. The sites of the signing of Magna Carta and the Aircrew Memorial are in fitting and impressive juxtaposition. Long may they inspire future generations. The repressive tyranny of King John was infinitely lighter and much shorter than that which would have been imposed by Hitler and his minions.

For all his infectious sense of humour, Stevie had a deeply spiritual side which sustained him throughout his life, and without which he could not have survived his tour of operations. Shortly after returning from the raid on Krefeld on 21 June, he put into words the experience of inner withdrawal and illumination from which he drew the strength he needed to go into action. He called it *'The Sublime Moment'*:

THE SUBLIME MOMENT (Scampton Airfield 1943)

There are some moments which act on the memory like small lamps illuminating the mind with a force and brilliance in contrast to other periods which seem uneventful and ordinary.

After briefing, I knew the target for the night, and had my ritual bath, relaxing, then changing into clean underwear.

My brain had absorbed as much information about wind strengths and weather fronts, true tracks and approximate courses, enemy defence dispositions, emergency airfields, directions of approach to the target and possible variations of target illuminations as it could hold.

The last bellow of a distant Merlin engine spluttered and died. In an hour we should go to the crew room to kit up and get transport to our aircraft. For this short time, the airfield was at peace. I would leave my crew smoking, letter writing, or resting, to walk alone over the grass in front of the hangar.

This was the moment. Soon I shall be in my aircraft. Once airborne, I shall be totally alone, save for my crew, who are absolutely reliant on me. Only I can take them up and return them to earth safely. Unlike pilots flying by day, I shall see no one who can help, encourage, or advise me in an emergency.

A skylark twitters over the bomb dump. Why at dawn and dusk does it twitter there?

I hum, 'None but the lonely heart can share my sadness,' and think:

'The worldly hope men set their hearts upon

Turns ashes — or it prospers; and anon,

Like snow upon the desert's dusky face,

Lighting a little hour or two, is gone.'

A moment of quiet prayer: "God grant that I may never fail my crew and that I may ever fulfil the trust they place in me."

Time to breathe deeply of English air, put on the big, self-confident smile, and return to my crew. "The trip tonight? It will be a piece of cake!"

Stevie never forgot Dickie Newcomb, George Martin, Johnnie Smith, and Johnny Pickett. They remained vivid presences in his memory, and at times, especially on Remembrance Sundays during the two-minute silence, he seemed to sense them standing beside him. To be near Stevie on these occasions, wearing his medals and his Officer Pilot's tie, was to watch him withdraw into himself. Even in very old age, he would stiffen to attention and, lost in thought, commune with the friends who had disappeared without trace. There was a very real sense in which, for him, they had never died. His papers and diaries are interspersed with moving evocations of these moments he called sublime.

On Remembrance Sunday 1990, to quote just one example, he wrote:

From Battle of Britain Day on 15 September until Armistice Day, the sense of remembrance and regret seems especially sharpened. Ever with me are those members of my crew who started with training with me between November 1942 and April 1943 and who went on the first Operational flight with me to Dortmund on May 23rd, 1943. Dickie, George, then later little Smithy. Their spirits have not totally absented themselves. I have been much aware of them and others especially when walking in the grounds of Blickling Hall. They, Johnny Pickett, 'Jos' Josling, Bert Moores, and Johnny Leland have shared my uninhibited freedom as I have crunched through the autumnal leaves. My pint of beer has tasted especially good after the walk because I have, in spirit, shared it with them. I can accurately remember their faces and voices. Have their souls preserved the true brightness of youth? Will they recognise this 'old soul' when he arrives?

Stevie photographed in 1944 after completing his tour of operations. His strained face is in marked contrast to the one taken in May 1943.

OPERATIONAL TRAINING UNITS: INSTRUCTING ON WELLINGTON BOMBERS

Stevie was given just a week's leave after finishing his tour. Then, on 31 October, eleven days after his final raid on Leipzig, he was posted to No. 16 OTU (Operational Training Unit) at RAF Upper Heyford in Oxfordshire as Flying Instructor.

It was usual for those fortunate enough to complete a tour to be 'rested', and proven pilots with front-line experience like Stevie were urgently needed to train newly qualified pilots converting on to heavy bombers. In the autumn of 1943, 57 Squadron was being tapped for Instructors, and at least three of the pilots who completed their tours at the same time as Stevie were also posted to OTUs: Bill McCrae, Bert Moores, and 'Jos' Josling. Stevie and Bert Moores were both sent to Upper Heyford:

I was posted directly from 57 Squadron at East Kirkby, and so rapidly that I barely had time to say farewell to my crew, two of whom were killed within the following weeks. I was displeased at having been granted no end of tour break, and I had hoped to be posted to a Lancaster Conversion Unit. My only consolation was that Bert Moores was posted with me from 57 Squadron.

The reception given to Stevie and Bert Moores when they reported to Upper Heyford was far from warm, and left both of them feeling more than a little annoyed:

We were the first two pilots to be posted to Upper Heyford from recent operational flying, and we were not warmly greeted. The Adjutant, Heath-Bullock, told me I should have arrived much earlier, and asked me why it had taken me so long. He seemed rather disconcerted when I told him Butch Harris had asked me if I would mind doing a few trips to Hannover and Leipzig before coming to Upper Heyford. When I reported to the Flight Office, my Flight Commander looked at me and remarked, "They must be giving DFC's away these days." I suggested he should go to the stores and see if they would give him a spare. He was not best pleased!

Bert Moores was luckier. His Flight Commander did have a DFC, so I thought I would try and get a transfer to his flight on my return. Bert and I reported together to the Wing Commander who was the Chief Flying

Instructor. He asked us if we had flown Wellingtons before, and of course, we said "No". He told us we had better have a week to familiarise ourselves with them before we started instructing, so we saluted, left smartly, and helped ourselves to a week's leave.

On 7 November, after a couple of flights as Second Pilot, Stevie went solo on one of Upper Heyford's Wellingtons. Between 9 and 18 November, he was sent on a Group Instructors' Flying Course, and after that he began instructing on Wellingtons himself.

The Vickers-Armstrong Wellington Bomber, affectionately known as the 'Wimpy' (after the cartoon character J. Wellington Wimpy from the Popeye cartoon strip), played a key role in Stevie's career as a pilot. As his log book shows, he flew a total of some 635 hours in Wellingtons; he did 87 of those hours as a trainee pilot himself while converting on to heavy bombers between December 1942 and March 1943; and he accumulated a further 550 hours in Wellingtons as an Instructor between November 1943 and May 1947:

I spent most of my time from the end of 1943 onwards instructing on the 'Wimpy,' and I must say it was a bit of a disappointment after the Lancaster. However, as an introduction to heavy bomber techniques, it was outstanding. It was an amazing aircraft which flew at the beginning of the War, and was still fighting at the end. It also played a major part in training crews to fly the next generation of heavy bombers. I note from my own log book that after flying the old Wellington Mark 1c, I converted both to the Manchester and the Lancaster within a period of less than three weeks in April 1943, and then joined 57 Squadron at Scampton as an Operational Captain. Without the early Wimpy experience, such a rapid conversion would have been suicidal.

The twin-engine Wellington prototype K4049 was first flown at Brooklands in June 1936 by Vickers chief test pilot Captain Joseph 'Mutt' Summers, who had done the first flight in the prototype Spitfire K5054 just a few months earlier. The Wellington was ordered as a long-range medium bomber by the Air Ministry, and went into service in October 1938 with No. 9 Squadron based at RAF Mildenhall in Suffolk. At the outbreak of war in 1939, six Bomber Command Squadrons were operating with Wellingtons, but by May 1941, as production ramped up, Bomber Command had 21 Squadrons flying the Wimpy. 11,461 were built in total, and the Wellington saw service not only in Bomber Command, but in the Coastal, Transport, and Training Commands.

There are currently only two surviving Wellington Bombers, and neither is airworthy. Wellington MF628, originally built in 1942, and kept for many years in the Air Force Museum at Hendon, was moved in 2010 to the Michael Beetham Conservation Centre at RAF Cosford in Shropshire, where it is undergoing an extensive restoration programme. This was the aircraft used in the making of the 1955 film *The Dambusters,* in which Richard Todd plays the part of Guy Gibson.

Wellington N2980 (code letter 'R' for Robert) is a Mark 1a type which carried out 14 operations during 1939-40. It was forced to ditch in Loch Ness on 31 December 1940 after suffering engine failure during a training flight. Seven crew members on board survived, but the Rear Gunner, Sgt John Fensome, who was just 20, died. Young Fensome sadly failed to hear the pilot's initial instructions to bail out be immediately retracted, and his parachute failed to deploy. N2980 was located in 1976. It was recovered from Loch Ness in September 1985, and taken to the museum at Brooklands, where it has been on display ever since.

The Wellington may have lacked the glamour of the Lancaster, but Stevie developed a great affection and respect for it. In 2004, after viewing the remaining parts of a Wellington stored in the Lincolnshire Aviation Heritage Centre at East Kirkby, he noted nostalgically:

> *The Wellington has been allowed to fade into history almost without trace, yet it was the backbone of training for Bomber and Coastal Commands and the Desert and Middle East Air Force. It was a beautifully designed aircraft, and played a major part in our bombing campaigns. Wellington aircraft based at OTUs were often used to drop leaflets over occupied territory, and for some time I kept a sheet of toilet paper with Hitler's face on it! But Wellingtons also took part in the earliest daylight bombing raid. The Germans out-gunned the Wellington, however tightly it held formation to give its Gunners maximum fire power, and the resultant sacrifice of many brave aircrew revealed the impossibility of bombing by day. Wellingtons were the mainstay of No.3 Group based in East Anglia, and 57 Squadron flew them before it transferred to 5 Group and was equipped with Lancasters. Those of us privileged to fly the Lancaster admired the brave men who operated with us on Wellingtons. The last raid undertaken by the Wimpy in the European theatre was on Hannover in October 1943.*
>
> *In the early days of the War, magnetic mines were used to sink our merchant ships, and Wellingtons were equipped with large circular electro-magnets to counter these mines. The power for the magnets was produced by a Gipsy*

Six engine of the type used on elementary trainers such as the Tiger Moth. Wellingtons filled with early radar and Leigh Lights were also used to chase and sink U boats. It was the Wellington which dropped the first 4,000lb bomb (often referred to as the 'cookie'); and it was the Wellington that was used to test prototypes of the bouncing bomb invented by Barnes Wallis for the Dams raid. Wimps were even used to plot German radar frequencies according to R.V Jones, the scientist who did so much in the radar and intelligence war. They were also used as test beds for early jet engines and pressurised cabins, and in some early experiments, on airborne lifeboats.

Stevie was moved by his intimate knowledge of Wellingtons to set down a detailed reminiscence of the challenges and difficulties posed to the pilots who flew them. It is a piece of aviation history in its own right:

The unique geodetic structure of the Wellington allowed for excellent streamlining. It was only about 66% of the weight of other contemporary aircraft structures, and about twice as strong both in flexure and torsion.

The geodetic structure of the Wellington [Photograph: Ed Wilcock]

As for flying, the Wimpy could be flown solo, and I often did so. The controls were well grouped and adapted to many engine changes, but Wellingtons of all Marks had a tendency to raise their nose when flap was selected for landing. Taxiing could be quite a problem. On OTUs, take-off and landing were the major skills which needed to be acquired, and mastering them necessitated a lot of taxiing. The difficulty was that the brakes were powered by compressed air. The early BTH compressors took a long time to build the required air pressure, and if a pilot did not have sufficient air pressure, the aircraft could run away with him. Compressed air bottles were sometimes stored by the side of the perimeter track, and mechanical compressors were also provided at strategic points. In order to use them, the Instructor had to unstrap himself, open the lower hatch, climb down the ladder, walk around the propeller and plug the compressor into the starboard side of the aircraft. When the air pressure had reached the necessary level, he had to disconnect the compressor and take it to a safe distance from the perimeter track before he could climb back to his position. This could be quite a job, especially on a night of flying.

The elevator trim was connected to the flaps to give a nose-up correction when approaching to land, but it was insufficient in itself, so a lot of forward pressure had to be exerted on the stick to avoid a stall. This was the cause of many accidents, but it was only after the War that a modification was made to the elevator so that less heavy pressure was needed on the control column on the approach to land. An additional hazard was that the Wellington had marked swing while accelerating to take-off speed. This resulted in several accidents, especially when inexperienced pilots tried to take-off when the wind was blowing across the runway.

Mixture and hot and cold air controls were manually operated. With some engines, Weak Mixture was automatically engaged at +2 Boost. The clean lines of the Wimpy meant that it could be flown on a very weak mixture. In Weak Mixture, with boost cut back to -4 and revs down to 1,800, fuel consumption was about 68 gallons per hour; but in rich mixture, at +8 Boost and 2,000 RPM, consumption was about 320 gallons per hour.

For normal purposes, the wing tanks and two nacelle tanks held 750 gallons, but for the long range flying done by Coastal Command, the fuel load could be as much as 1,305 gallons. Fuel consumption was much affected by the skill of the pilot, but on Coastal Command and long-distance ferry flights, maximum range was obtained at about 145 knots.

About 120 knots minimum was required for single-engine flying. When used by Coastal Command as Torpedo and General Reconnaissance bombers, many Wellingtons were equipped with the old Mark VIII Pegasus engines. The loaded weight was 30,000lbs, range about 1,800 miles, and depth charge/torpedo load was 4,500lbs. With the later Mark XII Hercules engine, the loaded weight was 36,500lbs; range was just a little short of 1,400 miles, and the bomb load about 5,000lbs.

Speeds of course depended on the type of engine and the propeller fitted. For general instructional purposes the following rules were used:

Take off with 15 degrees of flap, about 90 knots.

Wheels-up, about 105 knots.

Flaps milked gently up at about 120 knots.

The aircraft tended to sink when flaps were raised, and usually this was not done until about 4-500 feet. The flap and undercarriage levers were identical in shape and adjacent. Raising the flaps in error caused several accidents.

On the downward leg, the undercarriage was lowered at about 125 knots and flaps lowered to about 20 degrees. Full flap was usually lowered in the funnels at about 600 feet. With full flap, speed could be reduced to 80 knots, but the engine was needed on approach. As with most heavy aircraft, including the Lancaster, the throttles had to be hauled back to avoid excessive float, especially on shorter runways.

In the early days, the pilot's control box also had a lever for discharging small flares. These were used for night landings on unlit grass airfields. When the Wimpy came into production, camera flashes to take pictures of the target had not been invented, and later models were fitted with a small chute on the starboard side of the fuselage through which a photo flash could be poked. Using this chute could be quite an exciting experience. The photo flash was a long cylinder. Attached to one end was a device like a small 5 bladed propeller, and the fuse was connected to a piece of wire in the roof. To drop the flash, an extension had to be slid from the chute and the flash loaded onto it. The flash was then pushed through the hole, the propeller unwound, and the flash exploded below the aircraft. Sometimes the flash stuck, and then the operator had to kick or push it out. If the flash exploded inside the aircraft, it made a great noise, and sometimes caused considerable damage.

From the beginning of WW2 until the end, the Wellington was involved in many critical phases of air warfare. In Europe, the Middle East, and the Mediterranean, where there was conflict, there was a Wellington. This splendid aircraft deserves our salute.

Stevie standing by a Wellington. The only photograph of him with a heavy bomber, taken by a pilot he was instructing.

Stevie began instructing on Wellingtons at Upper Heyford on 22 November 1943, doing Air Tests and exercises in Night Flying and Fighter Affiliation with both pilots and aircrew. During Fighter Affiliation exercises, Stevie will have demonstrated the 'corkscrew' manoeuvre, the technique of throwing a heavy aircraft into a series of diving climbs and turns to defend against attack by enemy fighters. Stevie's friend Bill McCrae explains in his book *A Chequer-Board of Nights* what 'corkscrewing' involved, and why the lives of aircrew depended on it:

> *Night fighters could be encountered at any time, and the best defence of all was without doubt the 'corkscrew'. A gentle dive to starboard was followed by a dive to port, then a climb to starboard and a climb to port. In theory, the manoeuvre was designed to make it difficult for the fighter to line up his sights before firing, but many pilots, of whom I was one, believed that if the fighter saw his intended target taking what looked like evasive action, he would decide not to attack and look for another bomber flying straight and level. There was no sentiment in the bomber war; it was every man for himself. Pilots were recommended to carry out the corkscrew manoeuvre every ten minutes or so, but this was not enough for me. On every one of my trips I corkscrewed continuously all the time I was over enemy territory, with the sole exception of the bombing run. Although some of the crew became airsick from the continuous movement, they were all supportive of my approach. They believed, as I did, that it was the best protection against fighter attack.*

Stevie's demonstrations of the 'corkscrew' manoeuvre were, of course, based on front-line battle experience: as his own wire description of the Essen raid on 25/26 July graphically illustrates, 'corkscrewing' had saved him and his crew, and given his Mid-Upper Gunner George Martin the field of fire that enabled him to shoot down the FW 190 night fighter that was attacking them.

Flying on OTUs may not have been as dangerous as operational flying, but it was far from hazard free, and training accidents and fatalities were all too common. During 1943 alone, accidents at No. 16 OTU resulted in the deaths of more than ninety aircrew. On 28 November, less than a week after Stevie had begun instructing, two Mark X Wellingtons (X3923 and HE904) on a training flight from Upper Heyford collided and crashed. Both were carrying instructors and trainees from the RAF and the RCAF, and thirteen of those on board were killed, leaving only one survivor, W/O Anthony Lowman, the trainee pilot of HE904, who was thrown from the aircraft and injured:

There was a tragic crash on the circuit when two aircraft, piloted by S/Ldr William Allison DFC and W/O Anthony Lowman, collided. Both aircraft were carrying instructors and pupils, and W/O Lowman was the sole survivor. The bodies of all the fatalities had been immolated in the crash, so that sandbags were needed to give weight to their coffins.

On 19 December Stevie's friend Bert Moores went to the funeral of the Canadians who had been killed in the collision (they are buried at Botley cemetery in Oxfordshire), while Stevie took W/O Lowman on a cross-country test to spare him the trauma of attending:

I took W/O Lowman for a night cross-country test on 19 December, the day of the funeral. On his next flight, on Christmas Eve, he had to make a landing away from base, at Castle Donnington. I picked up his aircraft from Castle Donington to take him and his crew back to Upper Heyford. His nerves were shot to pieces, and his white, shocked face before he covered it with his oxygen mask said it all! He certainly wasn't treated gently, but such thoughtless treatment after a prang was not uncommon.

Bert Moores was later to lose a pupil of his own while instructing at No. 16 OTU:

One of Bert Moores's pupils, who was to marry a local girl, crashed his aircraft and killed his crew whilst he was trying to show off by flying low over her house. Tragically, she found herself attending his funeral on what should have been their wedding day.

Stevie did not spend long at Upper Heyford. On 4 January 1944 he was promoted to the rank of Flying Officer, and then sent to No. 3 FIS (Flying Instructors School), at RAF Lulsgate Bottom (now Bristol Airport), where he flew the Airspeed Oxford, the twin-engine Advanced Trainer widely used by Bomber Command and many other Allied Air Forces. The cockpit of the Oxford was fitted with dual flying controls which could accommodate a Pilot and a Second Pilot or Navigator sitting alongside him. Stevie flew fifteen times as Second Pilot under instruction, and did nineteen solo flights, clocking up some 38 hours in total. His Second Pilot on many of these flights was none other than 'Jos' Josling, his friend from 57 Squadron who had pranged and written off Stevie's Lancaster E-'Easy' the previous August. 'Jos', like Stevie, was transferred to instructing duties after he finished his tour of operations.

When Stevie completed the course at Lulsgate Bottom on 8 February 1944, he was formally certified 'as a Flying Instructor awarded the Category Q (ME)', meaning that he was qualified to instruct on multi-engine aircraft. He was then posted to No. 16 OTU at RAF Barford St John, which had been the satellite airfield of RAF Upper Heyford since December 1942. Barford had been upgraded for use by heavy bombers; it had paved runways and was equipped for night flying. It was a smaller station than Upper Heyford, and more easy-going. Pip Beck, a WAAF radio telephone operator who was stationed at Barford at the same time as Stevie, describes in her book *A WAAF in Bomber Command* a party at a pub in Bloxham, the village just down the road from the camp, to which Stevie and the other Instructors were invited:

Drinks flowed, and there were sandwiches, and everyone was pleasantly happy. When the bar closed, the Wing Commander stationed himself behind the piano and produced his own supply of bottles, brought down from the Mess, and doled out drinks for us all. It was certainly true that Barford was a happy and relaxed station! Of course, it was understood that no advantage would be taken of such off-duty fraternising whilst any of us were on duty, which was probably why it was such a success. The party broke up at midnight, and we returned to camp tired but elated.

Such relaxation was necessary, and there was the occasional humorous interlude which raised a welcome smile. At one point, Stevie was informed by the CO at Barford that a detachment of Americans from the US Army Air force was due to arrive:

The CO told me that some Americans were being posted to Barford. Knowing that I'd trained in California, he asked me to welcome them and make them feel at home. An American duly appeared, wearing a superbly cut uniform. I thought he must be the CO, or at the very least a Colonel or some other high-ranking officer, so I politely went over and introduced myself. When I asked him if he was the CO, he said, "No, I'm the Dentist." He was with us for about three or four days, no other Americans showed up, and he was getting a bit bored. We suggested he might like to spend a few days in London while he was waiting, and told him that as soon as his own CO turned up, we'd let him know. Eventually the American CO did arrive, dressed like the dentist in a very expensive tailored uniform, but he had no men with him. We alerted the dentist, who came back and offered to show the CO around London while they were waiting for the rest of their detachment to arrive. I took them to Oxford, and they got on the train to

London. A couple of hours later, I got a call saying they were on their way back. I thought this was a little strange, but went to pick them up. It turned out that when the train pulled out of the station, the CO wanted the toilet. The dentist explained that that the toilets on English trains were located at the end of the coach, and told the CO to walk up the corridor and open the end door. Coaches were kept dark at night because of the blackout, so when the CO got to the end of the corridor, he opened what he thought was the door to the toilet, and stepped through it. The door he had actually opened was the exit door, so he had walked through it into thin air, and fallen out of the train. The train stopped and reversed, and the Guard went to investigate. The CO wasn't hurt, but his uniform was torn and filthy, and he was furious. When I got to the station, he and the dentist were shouting and swearing at each other, and the poor Guard was trying to calm them down, saying "Stop messing about, or I'll report you to the Station Master." When this story did the rounds, everyone except the two Americans found it highly amusing!

Such incidents apart, the day-to-day reality was that instructing at an OTU like Barford was demanding and difficult, and even experienced and highly capable pilots were at constant risk. One of Stevie's fellow instructors at Barford, Colin Wallace, an Australian attached to the Royal New Zealand Air Force, wrote to Stevie many years later with a vivid recollection of attempting a flapless landing:

One thing to be taught at Barford was a flapless landing. I tried it one day (with myself at the controls). I came in about ten miles from the runway, keeping her just above the stalling speed, and just above the scenery, and put her down right at the very edge of the runway. The bloody thing would not stop, I dare not use the brakes, and it only came to a halt at the very end of the runway. My first and last demo. I never tried it again, it was too dangerous.

Before being posted to Barford, Colin Wallace had completed a tour on Lancasters with 467 Squadron RAAF. By coincidence, he had gone on the same raid on Hannover as Stevie on 18 October 1943. While his aircraft was still over the target, having just dropped its bombs, a Ju88 night fighter made three attacks. The first two attacks were devastating. The Mid-Upper Gunner was hit in the eye and blinded. The rear gun turret was put out of action; the Rear Gunner's oxygen supply was cut off, and he passed out, leaving the aircraft virtually defenceless. When the fighter made its third and final attack, Colin put his stricken Lancaster into a steep 400 mph dive into the darkness. The fighter disappeared, but the Flight Engineer was hit in the stomach. To make matters worse, both port engines were on fire and out of action, and the aileron and rudder controls, which had been riddled with bullets, were barely functioning. Colin Wallace couldn't hold the aircraft straight with his right leg on the rudder pedal, but the Bomb Aimer was able to reach up and add his weight to it, so control was maintained, though with the utmost difficulty. Praying that he would not be attacked again, Colin ordered all superfluous and damaged equipment to be jettisoned. Nursing his two good engines, he managed to get back to England. Arriving over RAF Coltishall, he fired Very flares to signal that he was in distress, and after a delay, the flarepath lights were lit. Then, as Colin put down, he discovered that his starboard tyre had been hit and was as flat as a pancake. This caused a nasty ground loop, but he landed safely. His Mid-Upper Gunner and Flight Engineer were taken to hospital, and fortunately, they both survived. Colin was subsequently awarded a DFC for which the citation read:

> *Flight Sergeant Wallace is an extremely efficient captain and pilot. Through his tour of operations he has displayed great keenness and determination, which have earned him many successes. In a recent attack on Hannover, his aircraft sustained extensive damage, two of the crew were wounded in the engagement with an enemy fighter, but in spite of this, Flight Sergeant Wallace flew the bomber safely back to base. His example of devotion to duty has been highly commendable.*

Wallace's own log book for the raid read:

> *WHAT A NIGHT – AIRCRAFT ON FIRE, SHOT TO HELL, MID-UPPER GUNNER AND F/ENG BOTH WOUNDED – PRESSED ON REGARDLESS – JUST MADE ENGLISH COAST – MY BEAUTIFUL KITE ALL MESSED UP. 5 GONGS AWARDED.*

At Barford, he went out with Pip Beck, but was repatriated at short notice. Their romance was cut short, and he would later tell Stevie that he had always regretted not proposing to her before he was sent back.

Instructors like Colin Wallace and Stevie were all too well aware that the pilots they were training to fly Wellingtons would be responsible not only for themselves, but for the lives of their crews. Stevie noted in a piece he wrote entitled *'Instructing on Wellingtons'*:

> *Instructors were always careful before sending a pupil solo, but in the early stages of training, at least only the pilot and the aircraft were at risk. When a pilot arrived at a Wellington OTU, his role changed considerably because the lives of an entire crew (five or seven men) depended on him and him*

alone. As an OTU Instructor, you reached a time where you said to a trainee pilot, "Right, off you go." It's your judgment, and if you get it wrong, you can send an entire crew to their deaths. That did happen, and when it did, it was a dreadful experience.

On one occasion, Stevie did get it wrong, with terrible consequences. The memory of his misjudgement never left him, and caused him to suffer recurrent traumas. Long after he had left the RAF, he was driving to Devon with his wife and son to spend the Easter holiday in his old home town of Torrington, and stopped at Stonehenge in Wiltshire for a break:

I signalled a right turn, and was surprised to find I had touched the wrong control and activated the windscreen wiper. My fingers quickly located the traffic indicator, and I rectified the mistake: a trivial incident, yet one which affected me for the rest of the day. We ate sandwiches and drank tea from a thermos, and I walked to a gate to admire the view. A scene of perfect tranquillity. Suddenly my knees began to tremble, and a cold sweat formed on my forehead and under my armpits. I went rigid, and my mind focussed with awful clarity on a terrible accident that had happened while I was an OTU Instructor.

I had been instructing a Warrant Officer who had done a tour in Blenheims and then a second tour in Lancasters. I remember most distinctly saying to him, "Well done! There's nothing more I can teach you. Do three circuits and landings, then we'll chase up some bacon and eggs." The wheels switch and flap retracting switch on the Wellington are very similar and in close proximity to each other, so I impressed on him once more, "Be careful to choose the right switch, and remember to select Wheels Up just after you leave the runway."

I watched him go off. He started perfectly, straight down the flarepath. The aircraft lifted off, then paused for a little while with the engine still resounding, the wings came off, and it fell almost gently back down to earth. It hit a haystack, and the 4-500 gallons of petrol in the wing tanks ignited. The pilot had made an error similar to the one I had just made in my car: he had pulled the wrong lever, and raised the wing flaps instead of the wheels. He and four of the crew were reduced to ashes. The fire tender and ambulance raced over the airfield, and seeing a motorbike nearby, I jumped on it and went tearing off towards the blazing haystack. But I couldn't get anywhere near; it was so hot it was burning through my gloves, I just couldn't get any closer, and I watched him and the rest of the crew die horribly in an inferno. Only the Rear Gunner was pulled from the fuselage with terrible burns, and then part of the aircraft exploded and set light to the ambulance. Looking back on it, I probably did have some doubt about whether the pilot was ready to solo, but he seemed totally confident. I'd given him extra training, I'd explained the switches, and we'd also done a couple of dummy runs before he went ahead.

The vision passed, I took a deep breath, returned to the car, and had another cup of tea. By the time we were ready to resume our journey, I was relieved to find that my voice sounded normal and my hand was steady.

But the past was not yet done with Stevie. Yet another tragic accident he had witnessed at Barford was about to resurface in his memory. On Good Friday, the day after he arrived in Torrington, he went to church with his wife and his aunt:

The church bell was tolling, sonorous and heavily muffled — a tradition on the afternoon of Good Friday. We went to the service with my aunt. The Vicar talked in his sermon about the encounter between Jesus and his disciples on the road to Emmaus, then we sang the hymn 'O Sacred Head Sore Wounded'. I was thinking about the sermon and wondering how often I had sung that hymn in this church on Good Friday, when again my mind switched, just as it had at Stonehenge.

It was very late in the evening. I was about to taxi from Dispersal on a training flight when I saw F/O Morgan, one of my fellow Instructors, waving his arms and looking very agitated. I told my pupil to keep the engine running while I went to ask Morgan what was wrong. He bent over and vomited as I approached him, then told me what had happened. A Bomb Aimer he was about to take on a training flight had realised he might have forgotten to remove the fuses from his bombs. Morgan had opened the bomb doors and asked him to check. The Bomb Aimer had removed the fuses and turned towards the entrance hatch holding them in his hand. He had been so annoyed with himself that he had failed to notice the spinning propeller and walked straight into it. The blades had sliced off the top of his skull and killed him.

The Medical Officer, F/Lt Bebbington, and his Flight Sergeant came to collect his body. The following morning, when I went to the Sick Quarters, the Flight Sergeant was looking at five coffins. Apart from the Bomb Aimer, we had lost another four aircrew in a night crash. They had been immolated. From grim experience, the Flight Sergeant knew how to pack the charred remains to give a semblance of substance. Nearby, a WAAF Medical Corporal was sewing together the skull of the late Bomb Aimer with meticulous care and put a bandage on him so that he would appear "in a fair state" before his funeral. When she finished, he looked as if he were sleeping peacefully. The MO said, "Well done, Rosemary!" She murmured something like "Poor Boy," and as she turned, I could see tears on her cheeks. On parade, she would have looked quite unremarkable; but to me, at that moment, she was the embodiment of dedication and the glory of compassion.

Later, a train arrived at Banbury station. Two grieving men alighted with the other passengers. One was the Bomb Aimer's father, and the other the father of the pilot of the crashed aircraft. The pilot's father insisted on seeing his son, so we took him to the wreckage and showed him what was actually being buried. He broke down, completely overwhelmed. But when the Bomb Aimer's father went to look at his son, he was moved to find that, as a result of the WAAF Medical Corporal's ministrations, he seemed to be at peace, not disfigured, but recognisable and restored to wholeness.

When the hymn finished, we sat down, and I could do nothing to stop my tears flowing. O Sacred Head Sore Wounded, indeed! I remembered how Jesus's disciples had not recognized him on the road to Emmaus after his Resurrection. The torn, tortured body they had last seen had been transformed into spiritual perfection. The motto of 57 Squadron came to mind, 'Corpus non animum muto', 'I change my body, not my spirit'. My wife and my aunt thought I had succumbed to an excess of religiosity, and I did not dare explain my chain of thought to them in case I broke down completely.

But there were lighter moments at Barford, and there was one particular incident which Stevie would never tire of recounting, partly because it involved him in landing a Wellington at the RAF Training College at Cranwell — something that had apparently never been done before.

In August 1944 a huge Group Captain named Oliver was introduced to me, as he wanted to be instructed to fly heavy bombers. Not only was he built like a rugby forward, but he was decorated with a DSO and DFC. He said he would come to Barford the next morning. He made a spectacular arrival in a superb Spitfire powered by a massive engine and turning contra-rotating propellers.

I asked him if he had ever flown twin-engine aircraft. "NO!" Would he like me to take him up in an Anson? "NO!!!" We climbed into Wellington 809 and I flew him around, gave him general instructions, then gave him control. He found the controls heavy after flying fighters, and we tried some approaches to land. On each occasion, he made a perfect fighter approach, turning all the time so that, had he been in his super Spitfire, the engine would not have obscured his view of the runway. Unfortunately, this was far too steep for the poor old Wellington, and the flaps could not produce enough drag to slow the aircraft down for a landing. After several attempts, Gp Cpt Oliver was sweating a bit, and he suggested we go to RAF Warboys, which had a longer runway. We flew to Warboys, doing some gentle exercises on the way. We called up the airfield, and were given permission to land. We did two wide circuits on the approach, but still at too high a speed.

Gp Cpt Oliver was determined to make this landing, but he arrived a little high, and too fast over the runway. Although he hauled back on the throttles, the aircraft kept on floating and refused to stall to the ground. By this time, we were dangerously near the end of the runway, so I called, "I have control, Sir," and pushed the front wheels hard on the runway, still at flying speed. Using minimum brake, I turned the aircraft on to the taxi track and held it there until the tail came down. We were then able to slow down. As we approached the Control Tower, I looked from the cockpit and saw the Station Commander leaping up and down, showing every sign of incandescent rage.

I opened the lower hatch, put down the ladder, and politely allowed Gp Cpt Oliver to precede me, making sure he was wearing his posh cap. As soon as he touched the ground, an amazing change came over the fuming Station Commander. He gave a broad grin and said "Hello Ollie! I thought that was a spectacular landing! Let's go down to the Mess." I followed behind at a respectful distance. The Station Commander, Group Captain Hamish Mahaddie, was a highly decorated Scot, who had a DSO, a DFC and an AFC to his credit. He had risen from being a Halton 'Brat' to his present rank by bravery and having the luck to survive. RAF Warboys, where he was now the CO, was home to the Pathfinder Training Force Unit, which flew Mosquitos.

Group Captain Hamish Mahaddie

Gp Cpt Mahaddie ordered a pint of beer for himself and one for Gp Cpt Oliver, and asked if I would have one. When I hesitated and said that I was flying, he said "That was not a question, it was an order!" I thought a little lubrication would do no harm, so I had a pint. At that point, Squadron Leader Colin Campbell joined our group. In addition to the DFC he was wearing when I had last seen him as an OTU Instructor, he was now sporting a DSO, on which I congratulated him. He told me he was flying Mosquitos on ops, which was not nearly as dangerous as ops on Lancs had been, and probably less dangerous than instructing on Wimpys. Then he said he was just being posted to an Officers Advanced Training course at Cranwell, and asked if I could give him a lift.

I thought Cranwell might be too small an airfield to land a Wimpy, but my pupil Gp Cpt Oliver said I could show him the Short Landing Technique. He was backed by Mahaddie, so Colin Campbell went off to collect his bags while we finished lunch. We climbed into the aircraft and taxied to the take-off point, but a message from Flying Control said there was a runway change, and the reciprocal runway was to be used. I wondered whether someone in Flying Control was having a laugh, as this meant we had a long taxi to the other end of the runway, and I began to worry about the brake pressure. Wellingtons were designed for long range bombing, not long-range taxiing, and they were only fitted with small BTH air compressors to operate the brake and other systems. Later a larger Heywood compressor was fitted, but the compressed air storage was still limited, and even the Heywood would not provide a sufficient quantity of air pressure for prolonged taxiing.

My radio could not transmit to Cranwell, so I did a wide circuit and picked its larger landing field, which was used by Oxford twin-engine trainers. I made a low powered approach, and got a flashing green signal from the Duty Pilot. I landed, taking care to economize on the brakes, and using as little air pressure as possible. The aircraft slightly overran the airfield and edged on to a rugby pitch, on which a game had fortunately just ended.

Colin Campbell went down the ladder, and I handed him his bags. A mighty cheer went up from the rugby players on his arrival. He sent one of them up to Flying Control to report that I had a Group Captain on board who was on his way to an urgent conference. That was good thinking, as Flying Control was giving me a red signal to stop. As soon as the messenger arrived, the light changed to green, so I was able to take off. When we arrived back at Barford, Gp Cpt Oliver thanked me and went to his own superb Spitfire. He took off almost vertically, made a graceful slow roll, and rapidly disappeared.

I ran into Colin Campbell again some time afterwards, and he told me that our landing in a Wellington at Cranwell, almost within walking distance of the back gate, was thought to be unique! Some years later, I visited Cranwell and saw Gp Cpt Oliver's name on the Honours Board as an ex-Deputy Commandant. I was able to impress my guide by saying, "That chap was once one of my pupils!"

On 8 December 1944 Stevie was posted to No.11 OTU at RAF Oakley, the satellite station of RAF Westcott. He had grown attached to Barford, and was sorry to have to move, but it had been decided that Barford was to discontinue training on Wellingtons, and switch to training on Mosquitos.

Stevie's first impressions of Oakley, his new station, were distinctly unfavourable:

It was not impressive, and little had been done to provide decent living conditions or any amenities, although there was a warm Airmens' Club near the airfield. The Nissen huts were very damp and cold, and fuel was scarce. Generally, the heating was provided either by cylindrical and brick-lined 'Tortoise' stoves made of cast iron, or by small 'Rose' stoves, which had a rectangular top on which a kettle could be stood to boil water and provide hot drinks.

The food and accommodation were very poor, and the ground crews had to work in cold, wet and harsh conditions during the winter. It was not uncommon to see freezing and muddy RAF and WAAF mechanics climbing on the wings and fuselage of aircraft to service them, or balancing on flimsy scaffolding, wrestling with benumbed fingers with spark plugs and wiring. And the poor tyre checkers responsible for examining each tyre for wear, pressure, and creep before take-off had a bitterly cold and thankless task.

It was surprising that the aircraft were as serviceable as they were when one remembers the conditions under which they were serviced, and the continual demands made on the ground crew day and night when the weather was flyable. The fitters and engineers never got the recognition they deserved, except from us — the pilots and instructors, whose lives depended on their efforts.

But despite the heroic efforts of the ground crews, the Wellingtons used for training were aircraft that had done many hours and were deemed unfit for front-line service:

The aircraft were overworked; they showed signs of strain, and several accidents were due to structural failure. Cracks appeared in some main spars, and occasionally a wing fell off in flight. This happened to one of my own instructors at OTU, who was killed when a wing came off his aircraft. Detection of metal fatigue was crude, and many aircraft had labels warning that standard rate turns should not be exceeded. Engine failure was not uncommon, and on at least two occasions, I was forced to make landings on a single engine. A particular hazard at Oakley was that the main runway pointed directly at Brill Hill, close to the airfield, and if an engine failed to give full power, take-off could be a very dicey business.

But there were compensations. Large numbers of Australians and New Zealanders were posted to Oakley. Stevie was quick to warm to them, and learned to relish their individualism and lack of inhibition:

There was a high proportion of Australians and New Zealanders among both the Instructors and the trainee crews. They were splendidly individualistic characters, much given to raiding the local woods with axes and wedges to provide fuel (however green) for the fires. These activities were frowned upon by the Station Adjutant and the Wing Commander, but their control was limited.

I remember on one occasion the fire in the Officers' Mess would not burn, as it was full of green wood. The problem was overcome by 'finding' an old cylindrical vacuum cleaner, placing the tube in the blowing end, and supplying the fire with a mighty blast to keep it going. Two very large Australians had a party trick, which was to get under the full-size billiard table, lift it off the ground, and put it back again without damaging the cloth. One night, something went wrong, and a new game had to be invented because the cloth had become permanently creased. To liven things up, the New Zealanders would sometimes dance a haka, and finish it by spraying burning petrol on a portrait of HM the King.

The Station Commander, Group Captain Peter Stevens, kept a distant, but friendly eye on these happenings, although he would occasionally bear down heavily on anyone who went a bit too far!

The training programme at Oakley was a tough one:

Generally, the most experienced flying instructors were based at Oakley, but pupils did about two weeks preliminary training at the main base at Westcott before they were sent to us. By the time they reached us, they had formed into crews and attended lectures in their various specialisms, and the pilots had completed extensive cockpit drills. At Oakley, we did circuits and bumps with them by day and night, practice bombing, gunnery drills, single-engine flying and flapless landings. When they finished their training with us, the crews returned to Westcott to do day and night cross-country flying.

While Stevie was busy instructing at Oakley, the War with Nazi Germany he had joined the RAF to fight came to an end. He wrote across two pages of his log book in block capitals: 'UNCONDITIONAL SURRENDER OF THE ARMED FORCES OF THE THIRD REICH'.

By chance, on 8 May 1945, Stevie had an appointment at the Air Ministry in London, and caught a bus from his parents' home in South Norwood with his young cousin from Torrington, John Rew. When the bus reached the

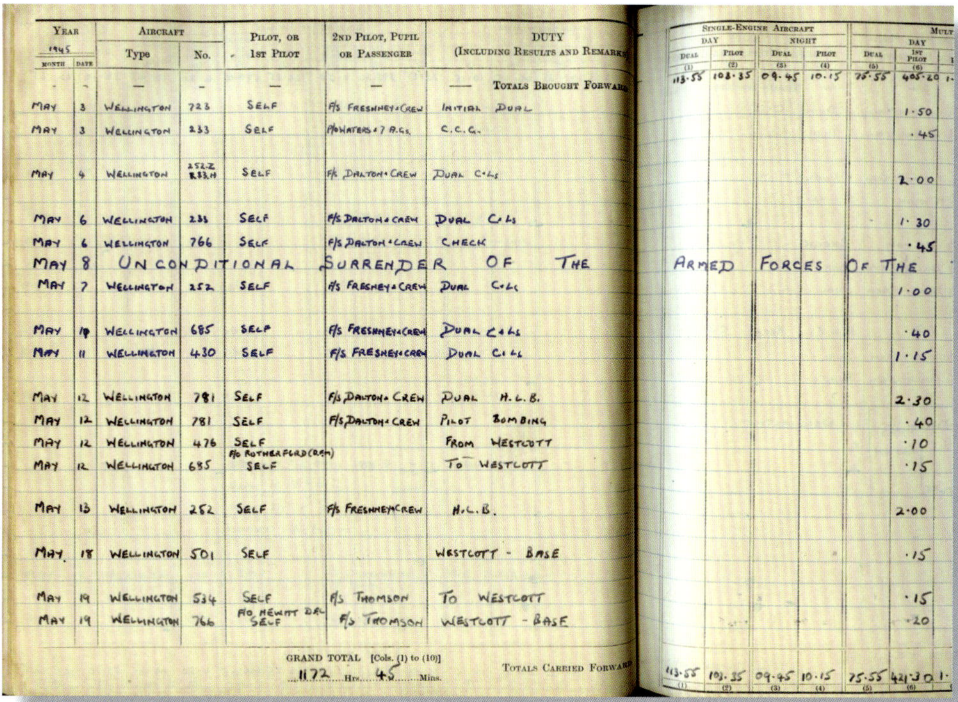

Stevie's log book with his entry recording the unconditional surrender of the armed forces of the Third Reich, 8 May 1945

Strand, it stopped. The driver got off, and said it was impossible for him to go any further because of the crowds gathering to celebrate VE (Victory in Europe) Day. Everybody left the bus, and Stevie, who was wearing uniform with his Wings and DFC ribbon, was mobbed. His cousin John Rew, a schoolboy at the time who would go on to have a successful career in the City of London Police Force, vividly remembers what happened next. Men came up to Stevie to shake his hand and thump him on the back, and women ran up laughing and crying to hug him and shower him with kisses. That evening, Stevie, John Rew and the rest of the family went into Croydon, where the lights were switched on for the first time since the start of the War, and there were more congratulations and celebrations in the streets.

The end of the War in Europe soon made itself felt at Oakley. 2 May 1945 saw the start of Operation Exodus, the massive airlift undertaken to repatriate the hundreds of thousands of Allied POWs who had been liberated from German internment camps. RAF and US Air Force bombers flew in relays to transport them back to England, and the first of those relays touched down at Oakley on 3 May, bringing three hundred men in a single day. By the end of May, 1787 ex-POWs had been brought to Oakley, and more than 350,000 were returned to England in all, with Bomber Command flying more than 3,500 sorties to collect them.

Stevie took no part in the air lift, but he made his mark as an Instructor. When he had completed the Instructors' course at Lulsgate Bottom, he had been categorised as 'B', or Average. But on 24 May he was retested at Oakley, and recategorized from 'B' to 'A2'. This was a real step up, and one that relatively few pilots achieved; as an 'A2' Instructor, Stevie had the authority to test and recategorize other instructors.

A month later, on 24 June, he made his last trip to the Ruhr, and his first by daylight, when he took eight trainee pilots and ground crew on a so-called 'Cook's Tour' to view Bonn, Aachen, Cologne, Duisburg, Düsseldorf and Essen from the air. He continued to instruct on Wellingtons at Oakley until it was deemed surplus to requirements and closed.

But the RAF had no intention of releasing him from active service. On 4 July, he was promoted to the rank of Flight Lieutenant, and on 2 August he was posted to No. 10 OTU at RAF Abingdon in Oxfordshire. On the other side of the world, on 6 and 9 August 1945, the US dropped atomic bombs on Hiroshima and Nagasaki. Japan surrendered unconditionally, and 15 August 1945, VJ (Victory in Japan) Day, marked the end of the Second World War.

Stevie did his last flight from Oakley on 25 July, and was given an extended leave before reporting to Abingdon, and it was not until 10 September that he resumed instructing on Wellingtons. On 30 October 1945, almost two years after being awarded his DFC, he was formally invested by King George VI at Buckingham Palace. There he ran into one of his fellow trainees from War Eagle Field, Colin 'Corny' Drew. He was an ex-London policeman who had failed the flying course, gone on to serve as a Bomb Aimer with No. 83 Pathfinder Squadron, and been awarded a DFC and Bar. Like Stevie, he was at Buckingham Palace to be invested:

> *At the Palace, I ran into 'Corny' Drew. He had been with me at War Eagle Field, and failed the pilots' course because he kept landing downwind. I said "Fancy us meeting up here, and getting our gongs together!" He told me that after he left War Eagle Field he had remustered as a Bomb Aimer, and that everyone in his crew had been awarded either a DFC or a DFM.*

Corny Drew at War Eagle Field wearing the 'Knothead' sign which reads: 'I ain't never careful' – his punishment for landing downwind.

Stevie found Buckingham Palace a great disappointment, and nothing like the story book place he had half expected:

> *I was expecting the inside of the Palace to be all polished and grand for royalty, but it was completely blacked out, and not very attractive. When we arrived, one of the officials came up to us and asked if we could bow as low as we could before the King, "because he gets very tired pinning on Decorations". I thought to myself, "He ought to try flying a Lancaster back from Berlin!" The King eventually reached me and asked me how many trips I had done, said "Very good," hung on my medal, and then moved on to the next chap.*
>
> *There was an orchestra sitting half way up the staircase, trying to play a bit from 'Chu Chin Chow', which didn't strike me as being particularly apt. Then they just opened the door and said goodbye, and that was it. The other thing I remember is that two Australians who were being decorated were trying to unscrew an ornament from the mantlepiece to keep as a souvenir. They tried their hardest, but they couldn't get it off, and that really made me laugh.*

Back at Abingdon, the memory of Johnny Pickett and of Dickie Newcomb, George Martin and Johnnie Smith returned with special poignancy on

Armistice Day 1945, which fell on 11 November, the day on which the First World War had ended:

> *On Armistice Day 1945 I was Duty Pilot at Abingdon, and I stood for the Two Minute Silence in the Control Tower. Johnny Pickett, smiling broadly, was first in my mind, followed by Dickie, George and Smithy. I remembered and still remember them, not only on Armistice Day, but on most other days.*

By the time he arrived at Abingdon, Stevie had evidently been earmarked for further promotion. Between 14 November and 12 December, he attended an intensive Junior Commanders Course at the Officers Advanced Training School. On his return, he found himself being called on to perform a wider variety of duties than ever before. As well as continuing to instruct, he acted as Wing Adjutant, Station Adjutant and Chief Ground Instructor, and he was also put in charge of Funeral Parties:

> *When I got back from the Officers Training School, I was considered an expert in Bull, and I was put on several Summaries of Investigation and Courts of Inquiry. I was also put in charge of Funeral Parties and had a Firing Squad all of my own. I always tried to get the funeral parties organized on Fridays, so that I could give the Firing Squad and myself a 48-hour leave. The high point was the funeral of Air Marshal Sir Bertine Sutton, one of whose claims to fame seems to have been that he gave Churchill a set of 'Honorary Wings'. I have never forgotten being in command of the huge escort (some 600 or so), and giving the order "Slow March" to half the top brass in the RAF. It seems to have passed off well enough, as I was invited for a sherry afterwards!*

(Air Marshal Sir Bertine Sutton MC, DSO had served with distinction in the RFC during the First World War, and rose to high rank during the interwar years. Between 1942 and 1945 he served as Member for Personnel on the Air Council. He retired from the RAF in 1945 in poor health, and passed away on 28 September 1946.)

Even when it came to instructing, things were changing. Stevie found himself having to deal not only with new trainees, but with returning senior officers who had been POWs. Some of these men were experienced pilots, but often they had spent years in internment camps; not only did they have no recent experience of flying, but in some cases, they were unfamiliar with the aircraft that had come into service. As an 'A2' Instructor with front line experience, Stevie was given the delicate task of refamiliarizing them with flying, and assessing their competence as pilots. Air Vice Marshal A.V.

Gray, AOC 91 Training Group, of which Abingdon formed part, hit on the idea of making things easier for Stevie by giving him enhanced status. On his instructions, Stevie was given the title 'Unit Master Pilot' (UMP). An indication of the privilege this conferred is that from December 1945 until his demobilisation in 1947, Stevie was able to certify the monthly flying totals he entered in his log book without the counter signature of a superior officer, signing himself as *'S.G. Stevens F/Lt, Unit Master Pilot'*.

It appears that Stevie was the only pilot in the RAF at the time to be given this title, and he took considerable pride in it:

> *Many of the returning officers who had been POWs were experienced pilots, but they had got rusty, and they often didn't know how to fly modern aircraft. AVM Gray decided to give me the job of reacquainting them with the basic elements of flying, so he ordered me to act as their Instructor, and gave me a new title, Unit Master Pilot. I took pilots who wanted to fly again and began training them from base, which usually worked very well. If they weren't sure of themselves, I would start them off on Oxfords and Ansons to get them used flying on twin-engine aircraft.*

But although some of the returning pilots reacted well to being retrained and assessed by the newly designated Unit Master Pilot, others resented his authority:

> *Some of them responded very well, but others were hopping mad! One chap I took up was a Squadron Leader who had been boasting in the Staff Room about what aircraft he had flown, and how he would do things differently on the station. He was ill-tempered and had a very short fuse, and when I took him up for the first time, he started waving impatiently at the ground crew to take the chocks away. I told him to slow down and give them time to do their job, but he just wouldn't listen. Although the engines had started, he stuck his hand out of the window, and got his gloves and fingers sliced by the propeller blades. I thought to myself, 'You deserved that, you idiot!' On another occasion when we were due to go up, he had got himself into such a state that he seemed to have forgotten how to fly altogether, so I had to suggest we stand down and try again another day. He just couldn't cope, and in the end, he was given a ground job. Even then, he went around boasting that he had a job for life, whereas I didn't!*
>
> *Another Squadron Leader I took up had spent a long time in India. He was always bragging about getting further promotion and using his authority to put up people he liked by a couple of ranks. He was so arrogant he thought that sharing the same transport with the lower ranks was beneath his dignity. One day a bus with some airmen on board came to take him*

Stevie pictured at Abingdon standing by an Avro Anson, 31 March, 1946. His younger brother Denzil, who was in the ATC at the time, is on the left.

to the Engineering Centre, and he kicked them all out, shouting "I'm not getting on this bus with you airmen, I'm not having that!" He was hopeless as a pilot. When I took him up for the first time, he made a total mess of starting the engines; he just couldn't get the aircraft going, so we had to empty the whole fuel system to start it up again. Eventually we did get up, and after we landed, I had to tell him that things weren't exactly looking promising when he couldn't even manage to start the engines for take-off. He started shouting and screaming at me, "Don't talk to me like that, I'm an effing Squadron Leader", and threatened that if I stayed in the Air Force, he would make sure I'd never get promoted!

But there were other ex-POWs Stevie met at Abingdon for whom he felt the greatest respect and admiration. One of them was Wing Commander Willis-Sandford, soon to be promoted to Group Captain and posted to RAF Swinderby as Station Commander. He had been interned by the Japanese at Palembang, Sumatra. In a report about his imprisonment submitted on 10 October 1946, he stated:

The Japanese did all within their power to humiliate, degrade and demoralise prisoners. They treated them as a source of coolie labour. The Japanese tried to impress upon us the 'fact' that Japanese soldiers were not afraid to die and never surrendered, and therefore prisoners were almost beneath contempt and so inferior that they must literally bow down even to the humblest representative of Dai Nippon. This attitude earned them our undying hatred.

Another former Japanese POW who made a deep impression on Stevie was W/Cdr Alan Groom, *'a tall, lanky Australian'*. Alan Groom had been posted to Far Eastern Command in 1940 and was among the 5,000 or so members of the RAF taken prisoner by the Japanese when they invaded Java in 1942. He ended up in the hands of the Kempeitai, the Japanese military police, and was tortured:

He told me how he been imprisoned with two other RAF officers. They were crammed together in a cell so tightly packed that nobody could sit. As people died, their bodies were thrown out, and eventually this made a little more space. When one of the officers with Groom cracked under the pressure and started raving, he was dragged out and stabbed to death. Groom was also forced to watch another RAF officer being held down and having his head sawn off with a blunt sword. Groom himself was thrown over the prison wall, made to bury bodies as they were tossed out to him, and fed with bags of rice attached to the bodies. After more than three years of living under unimaginably brutal conditions, he was summoned by the Japanese

Camp Commandant. He assumed he was about to be executed, but instead, the Commandant bowed to him, told him that Japan had surrendered, and informed him that, as the senior British officer, he was now in charge.

Java had formed part of the Dutch East Indies, and the situation there following the Japanese surrender was volatile and extremely dangerous. The Dutch wanted to regain control, but the Indonesian nationalist party led by Sukarno had declared independence. An Indian force under the command of Brigadier Mallaby was sent to accept the surrender of Japanese troops, and transport them to Japan. It was also mandated to maintain order in Java's principal cities, and release Dutch and Allied prisoners. When Mallaby reached Surabaya, he found himself heavily outnumbered by the Indonesian nationalists, and the few Dutch soldiers in the city were being tortured and murdered. Groom told Stevie that '*many of the hapless Dutch were crucified on doors or any convenient piece of timber, and if they moaned too much, their fittings were cut off and stuffed in their mouths*.' Mallaby himself was killed, but Groom, who had been seconded to his command, managed to secure the safe passage of many of the troops from the city. He had been imprisoned with some of the Indonesian nationalists who had taken over Surabaya. After the murder of Mallaby, he risked his life to negotiate the safe withdrawal of the Indian troops. For the courage and presence of mind he displayed in retrieving the situation and saving the lives of many men who might otherwise have been massacred, he was awarded a DSO on the recommendation of the Army. His citation reads:

During the period October 27th to October 31st, 1945, W/Cdr Groom was working with the 49th Indian Infantry Brigade at Surabaya, Java. Throughout this period the city was in the hands of an uncontrolled mob who, with Indonesian forces, launched continual and fanatical attacks against points held by detachments of Indian troops. The fighting was very bitter and lone men or small parties making their way to safety were butchered under circumstances of the utmost barbarity. British officers were dragged from their cars and murdered. W/Cdr Groom, in view of his personal knowledge of the Indonesian leaders, their language, and acquaintance with the freedom movement, volunteered to act as Liaison Officer. He completely ignored the extreme danger to his life, moving unarmed from area to area in which fighting was taking place and parleying with the frenzied mobs and their irresponsible leaders. W/Cdr Groom was threatened, abused and manhandled yet, despite fatigue, he continued unsparingly for 36 hours in his attempts to stop the attacks on our troops. By his efforts a number of engagements were brought to a close, and the movements of small bodies of troops to greater safety was successfully arranged. W/Cdr Groom afforded estimable help to the Brigade

Stevie with Alan Groom at Abingdon in 1946. Left to Right: S/Ldr Gibbs, F/Lt Pope, Stevie, W/Cdr Miller, W/Cdr Groom

Commander. By his sustained gallantry and resolution, he saved many lives and set an example that was an inspiration to all.

It was while he was flying with Stevie as Unit Master Pilot that Alan Groom told him about his time in Java:

Groom was a damn nice chap. Inevitably, he was affected by his experiences in Java, but he took to flying again like a fish to water, and he got back up on Wellingtons in no time at all, which was all he needed to keep his Wings. One day, he was my pupil at Abingdon, and the next day he had become the Chief Flying Instructor! He ranks in the top flight of the astonishingly brave men I met in the RAF.

Alan Groom was subsequently promoted to the rank of Group Captain and appointed to be Station Commander of RAF Waddington in 1952. Sadly, he was to lose his life in an accident in 1956, when a Vampire jet he was flying crashed in the Welsh Mountains.

Life in Abingdon also had its lighter moments. Air Vice Marshal Gray, who had invented the title Unit Master Pilot for Stevie's benefit, found out about the wire recording Stevie had made describing the Essen raid in 1943. He ordered Stevie to have it copied. He also put a jeep and an unlimited supply of petrol at Stevie's disposal so that he could visit local schools and Air Training Corps units and play the recording as a means of enhancing the profile of the RAF. Stevie took advantage of the jeep to tour the Oxfordshire countryside, taking some of his colleagues from Abingdon with him:

I was friendly with Jock Dow, a dark, thick-set Scot with rather curious false teeth. He was married to a small blonde WAAF who had projecting teeth, and I would take them to Henley and other beauty spots while I was making my visits to schools like Radley College and St Edward's in Oxford.

He also managed to fit in a few sailing lessons:

I also got on well with Flight Lieutenant George, a Gunner with a large grin rather like George Formby. He had got himself a comfortable niche organizing dinghy drill for aircrew. We had an airborne lifeboat complete with sails and two engines on the river at Abingdon, and we used to tow dinghies of the type stowed on aircraft upstream and cast them adrift. The aircrew practising on them were required to fly the kite connected to the aerial, set the sail, and try to stay afloat. Meanwhile, George would spend a couple of hours having fun sailing in the lifeboat before starting the motors and picking up the dinghies to tow them back to Abingdon. I went with him several times on these exercises and learned a bit about sailing. I particularly remember one afternoon we were sailing in a stiff breeze when we were taken unawares by a sudden gust of wind and capsized. The waterproof suits we were wearing proved to be very effective, and I emerged with the merest trickle of water down my neck.

Another Abingdon resident for whom Stevie had a particular affection was Squadron Leader 'Plum' Plumley, the Roman Catholic padre:

He had been a member of a strict order before the War and taken a vow of poverty. As chaplain, he was paid 12s. 6d a day, and any money he didn't spend he had to send to the Little Brothers at Walsingham. During his secondment to the RAF, Plum discovered the pleasures of smoking a pipe and imbibing the occasional drink. I could tell a hundred stories about him, but my favourite concerns a Methodist P/O who was getting married and decided to have his wedding reception in the Officers' Mess. On the day of the wedding, Plum dismissed the Corporal Barman and put on his jacket. He then took all the containers that had been carefully filled with soft drinks and strengthened them liberally with gin and sherry. When the teetotal guests arrived, Plum served them with generous helpings of his doctored and highly alcoholic concoction. The party got so lively that the wife of the Methodist padre climbed up a pyramid of chairs supported by cheering guests and wrote a very rude four-letter word in block capitals on the ceiling. The poor Methodist padre was posted the next day! I went to Walsingham to visit the Reverend Father some years after he was demobbed, only to be told by a very po-faced Abbot that he had volunteered for missionary work in China.

Stevie continued in his various roles at Abingdon until 29 October 1946, when he was posted to No. 17 OTU at RAF Silverstone in Northamptonshire, now the site of the motor racing circuit and home of the British Formula One Grand Prix. His stay there was brief. On 12 November 1946, 17 OTU was moved to RAF Swinderby in Lincolnshire. It remained there, but on 1 April 1947, it was renamed, and became No. 201 Crew Training Unit (CTU). Throughout his time at Swinderby, Stevie retained the title of Unit Master Pilot, and enjoyed cordial relations with the CO, Group Captain Wills-Sandford, whom he had got to know while they were both stationed at Abingdon. On 1 February 1947, Stevie was presented with a Certificate of Good Service signed by Air Marshal Sir Robert Saundby, who was then the Commander-in-Chief of Bomber Command.

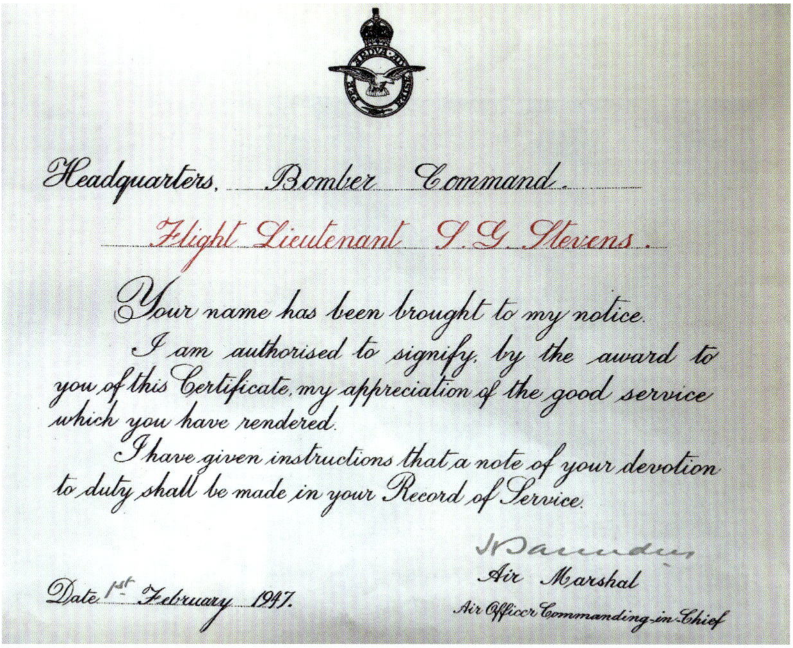

Headquarters, Bomber Command.

Flight Lieutenant S. G. Stevens.

Your name has been brought to my notice.

I am authorised to signify, by the award to you of this Certificate, my appreciation of the good service which you have rendered.

I have given instructions that a note of your devotion to duty shall be made in your Record of Service.

Air Marshal

Air Officer Commanding-in-Chief

Date 1st February 1947.

Certificate of Good Service

In May 1947, Stevie flew Wellingtons for what would be the last time. He had spent some 500 hours instructing on them, and clocked up 1,276 flying hours in total since he had started training at Carlisle in October 1941. He was released from service on 11 June 1947, and formally demobbed on 14 August 1947. But a condition was attached to his release: that he was to remain in the RAF Volunteer Reserve. On 31 October 1947 he relinquished his commission, but retained the rank of Flight Lieutenant when not on service. He was immediately granted a new commission as a Flying Officer for five years in the General Duties Branch of the Reconstituted RAFVR.

He reported for Annual Flying Training each year from 1948 until 1953, but his days on heavy bombers were over. Mostly, he flew either Tiger Moths or Chipmunks on what were essentially refresher courses, but at the time of the Korean War in 1950, he did his Annual Training on attachment to No. 511 Squadron Transport Command, flying Hastings transport aircraft. In 1951 he was notified that he might be called up as a Flying Instructor for the duration of the Korean emergency, and was asked to consider taking on a short service commission. But Stevie had experienced the human cost of war, and he was convinced that it should only ever be fought if there was no

Stevie at the time of the Korean war, seated at the front, second from left

alternative. Although he never doubted that the war against Hitler had been necessary, he was less certain about the war in Korea. He appealed against his recall, and heard nothing more of it.

On 11 November 1953, Stevie was awarded the Air Efficiency Award (AE) for meritorious service. He did his last flight in the RAFVR on 18 August 1955 at the controls of a Chipmunk, by which time he had accumulated 1,559 hours and 55 minutes flying time. But this was not the end of his Air Force career. In May 1954 he was commissioned in the Royal Auxiliary Air Force to serve in No. 3620 (County of Norfolk) Fighter Control Unit, and on 25 July 1956 he was granted a commission as Flight Lieutenant in the Secretarial (Intelligence) Branch of the Reconstituted RAFVR. He continued in this role until 24 July 1961, when his unit (No. 7016 Reserve Flight) was disbanded, and he finally left the RAF. In recognition of his twenty years of service, he received a well-earned Bar to his AE.

Stevie's wartime medals, including his Distinguished Flying Cross and his Air Efficiency Award with Bar

THE WAAF IN FLYING CONTROL: A BOMBER COMMAND ROMANCE

One key part of Stevie's wartime story remains to be told. In April 1943, while he was with No. 1654 Conversion Unit at Wigsley, he called up the Control Tower for permission to land, and was surprised to hear a woman's voice:

> *I was training in a Manchester at Wigsley, and as I was running low on fuel, I called up the airfield to get permission to land. I heard the clear, distinctive voice of a WAAF saying her call sign was 'Biddy', and giving me my instructions. I'd never heard a woman's voice transmitting landing instructions before, not even in America, so I was curious, and went up to Flying Control while the aircraft was being refuelled. There was a crowd of officers, which I thought was a bit unusual, but then I saw the reason! The centre of attention was the R/T (Radio Telephone) Operator who had given me my landing instructions. She was very glamorous, but she was surrounded by pilots she had known at Swinderby when they were on Hampdens. They were at Wigsley like me to convert on to Lancasters. There were too many of them for me to make any approach, and I was just a sprog, so I crept away.*

The glamorous young R/T Operator whose voice had so intrigued Stevie was Maureen Miller. Born in Norwich on 9 December 1919, she was the youngest of seven children. Her father, John Miller, was a professional soldier. He had served in the Royal Marines (*'the finest regiment of men in the world'*) from 1890 to 1913, spending many years in Africa. He had met Churchill as a young man during the Boer War. *'He was a toff,'* he used to say of Churchill, *'but he was tough and he knew men. When he became Prime Minister, I was sure we would see Hitler off.'* John Miller had a massive scar on his right forearm, the result of a wound he had sustained boarding a slaving dhow while his ship was on an anti-slavery patrol off Zanzibar. He had left the Marines in 1913 with the rank of Colour Sergeant, but was recalled in 1914. He served throughout the First World War, seeing action at Gallipoli, and by the time he left the Marines in 1918, he had been made a Warrant Officer in the Field for helping to foil a Zeppelin attack. He was called up again in 1939 at the age of 65 as the result of an administrative error. He was stood down a few weeks later, but immediately volunteered for the Home Guard and the Auxiliary Fire Service, and received a letter of commendation for the part he had played in fighting a serious fire in the Main Post Office in Norwich after a bombing raid. When the air raid sirens sounded, Maureen remembered, he would never rush to the nearby air raid shelter, but remain in his armchair in the sitting room, unruffled and smoking his pipe. He was a kind and generous man, but strict, and Maureen and her brothers and sisters grew up in a household where laughter was mixed with discipline.

Maureen aged 12 outside her parents' house in Norwich

Maureen was christened Maud, but as there were two other Maud Millers at the school she attended, she was asked if she would mind being called Maureen. Throughout her life, she was known to her family as Maud, but otherwise answered to the name of Maureen. She left school at 14, and got a job at Jarrold's printing works in Norwich as a copy-holder and proof-reader. This was a job normally done by older school leavers with a School Certificate, but Maureen was hard-working and naturally intelligent, and her lack of paper qualifications was no obstacle to her progress. She worked her way up through a variety of jobs, gaining recognition and promotion, and when the War broke out, she was Head Cashier and Advanced Booking Clerk at the Hippodrome Theatre in Norwich.

The Hippodrome had opened in 1903 as the Grand Opera House, but soon had to scale back its pretensions, and from 1904 it staged plays, musicals and variety acts. Archie Leach, better known as the Hollywood film star Cary Grant, made his stage debut in the Hippodrome in 1916 at the age of twelve, performing as an acrobat. By the time Maureen was working in the Hippodrome, it had become a cinema; but in 1942 it suffered heavy damage during a bombing raid, and did not reopen until 1948. It was forced to shut down for good in 1960, and in 1964 it was demolished and replaced by a multi-storey car park.

At the outbreak of War, Maureen was eager to do her bit, and her father, as a proud Royal Marine, encouraged her to volunteer for the Women's Royal Naval Service (WRNS), which had the recruiting slogan *'Free a Man for the Fleet'*. As luck would have it, she was deferred, and in July 1941 she was called up to join the Women's Auxiliary Air Force (WAAF). The WAAF had been established in June 1939 in anticipation of the outbreak of hostilities, and by the end of 1943 more than 180,000 young women had enlisted in it, most of them doing jobs that had previously been reserved for men. WAAFs were not allowed to serve in the front line, but they did a wide variety of essential jobs. Many were employed in catering, transport and administrative work; some were engaged in the interception of enemy communications, codes and ciphers; some were involved in Intelligence gathering, including the analysis of aerial photographs; and others performed vital support tasks in Operations Rooms across the network of RAF stations.

On 19 August 1941 Maureen reported to RAF Bridgnorth in Shropshire, a station which had no runways and which, by the time Maureen arrived, was used for training new WAAF recruits. She enlisted under her real name, Maud Miller, but continued to use the name Maureen, which she had come to prefer, and she would be known to everyone she served with in the RAF as Maureen Miller.

At Bridgnorth she was issued with her new RAF uniform and spent two weeks carrying out Basic Training or 'square-bashing'. But she also underwent an assessment process to determine what her role in the WAAF would be. Given the nature of the work she had been doing at the Hippodrome before she was called up, she had expected to be given a clerical job:

> *With my history as a book keeper, I thought I would be doing some sort of clerical work, and based on my experience, I expected to be a pay clerk. But in the interview, they kept me talking for a long time, and then said they had something different for me.*

That 'something different' came as a real surprise to Maureen: the assessment panel had decided to recommend her for training as a Radio Telephone (R/T) Operator in Flying Control — a position which had up till then been reserved exclusively for men. She was posted to RAF Waddington in Lincolnshire for training, together with two other WAAFs, Pip Beck and Lorna Cooper. Pip Beck, who became a lifelong friend, was later posted to RAF Oakley, and got to know Stevie while he was instructing on Wellingtons there. In her memoir *A WAAF in Bomber Command,* she recalled taking an immediate liking to Maureen. Describing her as *'tall, slender and attractive, with thick, honey-coloured hair and green eyes framed with long, black lashes',* she also noted Maureen's *'pleasant manner'* and *'air of gentle, though positive, self-possession.'*

Pip Beck

In September 1941 women R/T Operators were a novelty. Maureen, Lorna Cooper and Pip Beck were among the very first WAAFs to be posted to stations in 5 Group Bomber Command as R/T Operators, and RAF Waddington was totally unprepared for their arrival. In their papers they were described as 'RTOs', and it was assumed at first that this meant they were to be trained as Rail Transport Operators. When the confusion was cleared up, they were given a 48-hour leave to allow time for the necessary training arrangements to be put in place, and when they returned, they discovered that the male telephone operators working in Flying Control had been briefed to instruct them in R/T procedures. The training was intensive, and at first, Maureen found it daunting:

> *The first time I went into a Control Tower, I was absolutely petrified. I had never even been near an aircraft before, and I had never been away from home. We didn't travel in those days like young people travel today. I had never expected to leave Norfolk, and there I was in Lincolnshire helping to land aircraft!*

R/T Operators needed to have good voices, clear diction, and a calm and measured way of speaking. Their job was to transmit instructions from the Flying Control Officer or the Duty Pilot to aircraft preparing to take off and land, and clarity of speech and articulation were essential if pilots were to understand the instructions being sent to them. Maureen was blessed with a finely modulated speaking voice, but to put it to effective use, she had to learn how to work the TR9 radio sets with which Flying Control was equipped. She also had to familiarize herself with the 'procedure' used transmit and receive messages. In her own words:

> *The work was strictly controlled, everything being for the safety of the aircrews. Pilots under instruction were in touch with the Control Tower all the time, and my fellow R/T Operators and I, wearing earphones, were instructed by a Control Officer. Planes taking off on raids did not contact the Control Tower – it was only on their return that they would radio in. A log was kept of all the transmissions and calls received.*

> *Each aircraft had an identifying letter. After take-off, the letter was put on a board, and next to the letter, the pilot's name and rank. On return, the time of landing was put on the board. If the plane did not return it was left on the board, and rubbed off the next day. Many planes did not return.*

> *When the pilots came back, it was my job to land them, or tell them to circle in a stack. We would bring them down one by one in turn, unless one had been shot up and needed to land straight away. On return, the first plane to radio in was told to 'Pancake', using the station call sign. No names were ever used; the call sign for Wigsley, for instance, was 'Biddy', and Scampton was 'Heron'. The second aircraft to call in was told "Aerodrome one thousand," which meant he should circle at 1,000 feet. Subsequent arrivals were stacked at 500 feet intervals at different heights so that they landed in turn, avoiding confusion and collisions. If an aircraft radioed in that it was in trouble or had been badly damaged, the others were called collectively and asked to stand by. They were held in the air while the plane in difficulties was called in first.*

> *In between, we used to listen out for what we called 'Darkie' calls, now known as 'Mayday' calls. We obviously didn't get them every night, but*

Lincolnshire very often had bad mists and fogs, and sometimes a stray aircraft would call up and ask where he was. When that happened, you would go through the procedure of asking him where he came from and letting him know his position.

'Darkie' calls could be very exciting. If pilots were lost or disorientated, we had to talk them down safely. When this happened, it could be a very, very difficult job for the Control Officer, who might be on the balcony outside firing a Very pistol and communicating all the time on the R/T. I was on duty one night when the Control Officer was a Canadian. I remember that particularly because a pilot had made a 'Darkie' call, and it took ages for the poor chap to get down. I can't remember if he was running out of fuel, but he avoided a crash, and he was so grateful to us for getting him down safely that he came up into the Control Tower afterwards and thanked us. Moments like that made being an R/T Operator very satisfying and worthwhile.

All in all, it was a wonderful job, and I thoroughly enjoyed it. But I have never flown myself, and I never wanted to fly.

'All work and no play makes Jack a dull boy' was one of Maureen's favourite sayings, and hard as she worked while training as an R/T Operator, she also took every opportunity to play. She loved dancing, and Pip Beck remembered going with her to a dance in the Sergeants' Mess at Waddington. Drawing on her experience of working at the Norwich Hippodrome, Maureen demonstrated the benefits of using theatrical grease paint for lipstick and eye shadow; it was much cheaper than commercial make-up, she told Pip, and looked natural if it was applied with care. As soon as they entered the Mess, Maureen was invited to dance, and spent the rest of the evening with a succession of partners on the dance floor.

Maureen's Service Book shows that she qualified as an R/T Operator on 30 December 1941, and immediately afterwards she was posted from Waddington to RAF Swinderby, where No. 50 Squadron was operating with Handley Page Hampden bombers. On her first night on duty at Swinderby, she underwent a baptism of fire which she would never forget:

On my first night on duty at Swinderby, a Hampden took off and went up in flames. I felt sick and wanted to get out, and I went racing towards the stairs, but the Flying Control Officer pointed to my seat and said, "Miller! Your place is here, the lives of a lot of men depend on you." He told me to get back to my place, control my voice, and transmit his instructions to the aircraft that were stacking overhead. I went back, took a deep breath, and carried on with my job.

Maureen, second from the right, with her fellow WAAFs at RAF Swinderby in 1941

At Swinderby as at Waddington, life was not confined to the Control Tower, and there were off-duty periods during which Maureen could mix with pilots, aircrew and other WAAFs and let her hair down. There were dances and parties and regular trips into Lincoln for dinner, drinks or a film. But on one occasion, there was a much more unusual break from routine, and Maureen appeared on stage at a concert given by one of the popular dance bands of the time:

While I was working at Swinderby, one of the airmen was Joe Daniels, who had a band known as 'JD and His Hotshots'. He decided to put on a show, and chorus girls were needed. I was invited to take part; I thought about it, and did it!

In November 1942, No. 50 Squadron was transferred to RAF Skellingthorpe, west of Lincoln, and Maureen went with them. From Skellingthorpe she was posted to RAF Wigsley, and it was from the Control Tower at Wigsley on 13 April 1943 that she gave an incoming pilot the instruction to 'Pancake' which would change her life and his. The pilot was Stevie. It was the first time he had been addressed on R/T by a WAAF, and he had gone up to the Control Tower hoping to make a date with her. His hopes had been dashed, and when he was posted from Wigsley to Scampton to begin his tour, he never expected to see her again. But chance intervened. Maureen

In suitable attire for her appearance with 'JD and his Hotshots' at Swinderby

herself was transferred from Wigsley to Scampton a few days after Stevie, and again he heard her voice over the radio:

Soon after I arrived at Scampton, I was returning from a flying exercise and, to my surprise, I was given the order to 'Pancake' by the WAAF I had seen in the Control Tower at Wigsley. She was using the Scampton call sign 'Heron', but her voice was instantly recognisable. I went up to Flying Control and found out that she had been posted to Scampton. I was thrilled once again by those deep blue eyes and blonde hair, and this time, I did manage to ask her out. It took some courage to make the approach. As at Wigsley, she always seemed to be surrounded by a gaggle of officers while she was on duty in Flying Control, and I was still only a Sergeant — but operational aircraft captains are not so easily deflected from their target!

Maureen remembered Stevie coming up to the Control Tower, and formed a distinctly favourable impression of him:

I remember him coming in, but I don't recall why. I think it was purely curiosity. I remember while he was talking, thinking 'That young man would make a girl a very good husband'. But I honestly never ever dreamed then that he would be my husband!

Harold Brownlow Morgan 'Mickey' Martin would later become Air Marshal following a highly decorated career in the RAF

Maureen had got to know some of the pilots on the newly formed 617 Squadron before they arrived at Scampton, most notably Micky Martin. She had first met him while he was flying Hampdens with No. 50 Squadron at Swinderby and Skellingthorpe, and he had subsequently been posted to Wigsley, where he spent some months as an Instructor before being drafted to join 617 Squadron. They had struck up a friendship, and Maureen remembered his lucky mascot: a miniature koala bear given to him by his mother before he left Australia, which he always took with him while he was flying. He took part in the Dams raid, and would go on to become one of the most celebrated pilots in Bomber Command. By the end of the War he had been awarded a DSO and Bar, a DFC and two Bars, and an AFC. He stayed on in the RAF, and retired in 1974 as Air Marshal Sir Harold Martin.

Maureen in 1942 at RAF Wigsley

Stevie himself got to know Micky Martin and Guy Gibson slightly while they were training for the Dams raid, and he and his crew were preparing for their tour of operations:

> *I got to know several of the 617 types, and we envied them because they were enjoying their authorized low flying while our Squadron was flogging away on ops. But Micky Martin and Guy Gibson did buy me a beer on one 'stand down night'!*

Knowing that he had stiff competition for Maureen's attention, Stevie decided to wait for her to finish her shift so that he could talk to her alone. *'I went off duty one night and walked down the road,'* she recalled, *'and there was Stevie waiting on the path opposite.'* Their first meeting was soon interrupted. In Stevie's words:

> *When I met Maureen after duty at Flying Control, we had only walked a few hundred yards, when up drove Micky Martin and some of his crew and asked her if she would like a lift to Lincoln. I was a bit miffed, but to my surprise and relief, she refused, so we went to the Salvation Army canteen together and had tomato sandwiches and cups of tea. After that I walked her back to the Waafery, which was about two miles away at Welton.*

The Dams raid took place not long after this encounter. Maureen was on duty that night, and it was she who spoke over the R/T to Guy Gibson and the other 617 Squadron pilots who returned in the early hours of 17 May, and gave them their landing instructions. She had no idea that night that she was playing a part in the most celebrated operation that would ever be undertaken by Bomber Command, and that as she talked down Guy Gibson, Micky Martin and the rest of the Dambusters, she was rubbing shoulders with history:

I was posted to Scampton in May, I can't remember the exact date, but it was just a few days before the Dams raid. I never really knew where the planes were going each night. They used to take off when they were given the green light from a caravan at the end of the runway. As they took off, the pilot's name and the time of take-off were put on the board, but I never knew the target or anything like that. The only time I would speak to the pilot was on the way back when he called up. On the night of the Dambusters raid I was on shift from midnight until 8am, and as far as I was concerned, all I had done was talk down some aircraft which had come back from an op. It seemed to be nothing out of the ordinary, but I do remember that there was an unusually calm atmosphere. I'd had no idea of where the aircraft were going, the raid was 'Top Secret', and I knew nothing about it at all. It was only after I left the Control Tower at the end of my shift that I found an air of elation in the camp, excitement everywhere. It was later that I discovered I had talked down the Dambusters, some of whom, including Guy Gibson, I knew slightly.

She added, with the humility that typifies her and so many of the young men and women who served in Bomber Command: *'I don't really like talking about it because I was simply doing my job.'*

Maureen's friendship with Stevie developed into romance in the immediate aftermath of the Dambusters raid, during the weeks after Stevie began his tour:

'It was the person himself that attracted me,' Maureen would say later, *'the brave man who was doing a wonderful job going into battle every night. I wasn't the marrying kind. I didn't really want to get married. I was the youngest of seven, and had four older sisters, and I used to say I didn't want to be like them and spend my life with one person. Stevie first fell in love with my voice. The pilots returning from ops loved to hear my voice, and I loved to hear theirs.'*

Stevie would later put this last remark into context:

'Pancake' was the word every Bomber Pilot longed to hear over his radio. It was the final instruction to land after an aircraft had joined the airfield circuit and was approaching the runway. Pilots returning from raids eagerly awaited Maureen's voice to give them landing instructions. They were tired, often exhausted, some struggling with damaged aircraft, and hearing Maureen's calm voice saying 'Pancake' meant that the enemy and the elements had once more been vanquished, and English soil and a very warm welcome were within touching distance, only a few hundred feet below.

I was delighted and relieved to hear that particular voice on many occasions. It had transmitted 'Pancake' to me when I was learning to fly Manchesters and Lancasters at Wigsley, and now that same voice was giving the same eagerly anticipated instruction as I flew back from raids over Germany or Italy, leaving behind so many countries where people were subject to merciless tyranny.

Knowing the high casualty rates amongst Bomber crew, Stevie and Maureen agreed that they would not marry unless Stevie survived his tour:

As we were walking near the airfield one evening, I said to Maureen: "If I survive to the end of this year, we'll get married." It then started to rain like mad, so we took shelter in the porch of the church at Welton.

Maureen added, *'I think he said something like, "If I'm alive at the end of the year, we'll get married."*

On 12 July, while Stevie was preparing for the raid on Turin which would see him touch down at Davidstow Moor in Cornwall on his return, he visited Maureen in the WAAF Sick Quarters at Scampton:

Maureen had not been well, and had been admitted there for a few days. She and the Medical Officer and I sat in the bright sunshine on the grass outside and drank tea which the WAAF Medical Corporal had brought us. I told Maureen I was going on a long trip, and she was not to worry if I returned to base late. The War seemed a long way off. Only the sound of Merlin engines being run up on the other side of the airfield broke the peace and quiet.

Maureen at RAF Scampton in June 1943

Maureen was all too well aware of the dangers Stevie would be facing — on the Dambusters raid alone, eight Lancasters and 53 aircrew had been lost — but she had absolute confidence in his ability as a pilot, and a firm belief that his luck would hold. *'I still remember his plane did come in late. The Control Tower Officer was worried, but I said, "He'll be alright," and he was.'*

They were separated before Stevie completed his tour. At the end of August 1943 Stevie moved to East Kirkby with 57 Squadron, and Maureen was posted to RAF Dunhome Lodge, north of Lincoln.

While she was at Wigsley and Dunholme Lodge, Maureen kept an autograph book which offers a touching and very human insight into her life as an R/T Operator. The most eye-catching entry was made at Wigsley in November 1942 by one 'William A. Hindmarsh, AC1 rigger'. The page contains a cartoon of Maureen, looking very glamorous, speaking into her radio set at her desk in the Control Tower. Alongside it is a witty verse: *'Here's to the Lass / who causes the spark / to guide all our aircraft / home in the dark!'*

There is another verse in similar vein written by one 'S. J. Wood', dated 13 February 1943:

In dignified and queenly sate

Your TR-9 you operate.

With speech crisp, clear, articulate,

You're helping seal Herr Hitler's fate,

So "Good show, Maureen. Good show, mate."

Other entries, less concerned with Maureen's professional competence, were distinctly salacious:

Maureen had a little watch,

She tied it round her garter,

And when the boys asked her the time

She knew what they were after.

(Winnie, met Dunholme 12/10/43)

<u>*A Love Cake*</u>*: 2 ozs. Teasing; 2 ozs. Squeezing; 4 ozs. Kisses; 3 ozs. Love (Half Pint, Dunholme)*

Remember Maureen: None so chaste that can't be chased.

(Illegible signature, 25.4.43)

The apple of a man's eye grows on the loveliest of limbs

(Maurice H M Brown P/O)

Remember Maureen, "She who hesitates is last!!!"

(Sgt. Len B. Dansky)

But other entries, written by WAAFs who served with Maureen, are warm expressions of friendship and affection:

To Maureen, whose gay society and carefree companionship made the WAAFs a happier service for me. (Helen, Wigsley, January 1943)

May every leaf within this book,

From title page to end,

Recall to mind the form, the look,

The memory of a friend. (Best wishes always, Jessie Lee, RAF Dunholme)

HAPPINESS

Is to have enough for the day's needs with always some to spare for those who have not. It is to possess the love of friends and to have the knowledge that all is well with them. IT IS TO LIVE IN PEACE WITH ALL MEN.

HAPPINESS

Is to have the strength to face with courage all that the day may bring. It is to cherish the gift of laughter, to be quick to note all that is lovely and of good report.

HAPPINESS

Is to find out joy in the common things of life, for so will youth abide in our hearts till the end of our days.

(All the very best, Maureen, Jeannie, Dunholme, 1943.)

Time changes things in many ways,

But one thing changes never:

The memory of those happy days

When we were all together. *(W. Ballard, 20.11.43)*

On 20 October, some seven weeks after Maureen had been posted from Scampton to Dunholme Lodge, Stevie completed his tour, and he and Maureen lost no time in making arrangements for their wedding.

Shortly before the wedding, Stevie wrote to Corporal Swinchatt, his old engine fitter at Scampton, to tell him he was getting married. In the letter he wrote in reply, Corporal Swinchatt sent his congratulations, and offered Stevie some very pragmatic advice:

> *'Don't sleep under the bed on your wedding night, lay off the liquor. I can assure you it's not comfortable because I spent my own 'first night' there, and did my wife play hell! Cheerio, Old Pal, or should it be: I remain, Sir, Your Obedient Servant?, Cpl. Swinchatt.'*

He also congratulated Stevie on the award of his DFC:

> *'Glad to see you've got the DFC now, I bet that shook you! And I'm glad our meek efforts helped, that's going to cost you another pint at least when you come back to 57.'*

Stevie had taken W/Cdr Hopcroft's advice to get on good terms with his ground crew very much to heart, and he was firmly convinced that he would never have survived his tour without their unstinting and good-humoured efforts to maintain his aircraft and keep it in tiptop condition:

I owe my life to the splendidly dedicated ground crews. I can't praise them highly enough for their skill in maintaining our aircraft and keeping them airworthy. Things didn't stop when you left the aircraft. You had to fill in a form (700 it was called) and report the raid. Then you had to inspect the aircraft for any damage and see if it needed any repairs. Quite often, once the repairs were complete, you had to take it for an air test to satisfy yourself that the aircraft would take the strain of combat and that everything was working. The ground crews and engineers worked tirelessly around the clock and in all weathers to make sure our aircraft remained serviceable.

On 4 December 1943, Stevie and Maureen were married in St Matthew's Church in Thorpe Hamlet, Norwich:

'The wedding,' Stevie recalled, *'cost four shillings and sixpence. We had free travel warrants to Torquay, where Lord Nuffield paid for my honeymoon week. When we left, we discovered that another guest at the hotel had settled Maureen's bill. We were never able to thank them because they had insisted on remaining anonymous.'*

On their Wedding Day, 4 December 1943 in Norwich

On their Wedding Day, 4 December 1943, in Norwich

After the honeymoon, Maureen returned to duty at Dunholme Lodge, and Stevie resumed his new role as a Flying Instructor at Upper Heyford and Barford St John. In 1944 Maureen managed to obtain a transfer to RAF Abingdon, so that she and Stevie could be nearer each other and meet when they were off duty. Stevie would go to Abingdon to see Maureen, *'or she came to Banbury. Sometimes we stayed at the Whately Hall Hotel, but often more comfortably at a cottage in Bloxham.'* Corporal Rudge, a fitter at Barford, remembered Stevie *'flying over to Abingdon and calling up your wife in the Control Room (I was with you one day). I had been cheeky enough to twit you about being with a WAAF in Banbury, and you informed me it was your wife!'*

Maureen left Abingdon and was discharged from the WAAF on 29 January 1945, after it was confirmed that she was expecting her and Stevie's son Adrian. On her Certificate of Discharge, the Station Commander at Abingdon, Group Captain King-Lewis, noted:

> *'The above-named airwoman has performed her duties as an NCO very satisfactorily and has shown interest and ability in her work. Her general conduct has been very good.'* The reverse side of the certificate explained, *'V.G. is the highest character which can be awarded in the Royal Air Force.'*

After the hundreds of hours Maureen had spent doing an essential job as an R/T Operator in Flying Control at airfields across 5 Group, it was an accolade that was richly deserved. By any standards, she had 'done her bit'.

> *'I left the WAAF in January 1945,'* she recalled later. *'I was expecting our son Adrian by then, and I came out with £12 10s, which wasn't even enough to buy a pram!'*

Maureen returned to live with her parents in Norwich, and Adrian was born on 11 August 1945 — according to Maureen, a month after he was due. Stevie was preparing to leave Oakley and continue instructing with No. 10 OTU at Abingdon when news of Adrian's imminent arrival reached him:

> *News had come through from Maureen's family doctor in Norwich that she might give birth that day. I managed to get 48 hours off, jumped on the train at Didcot Junction, and went up to Norwich. Maureen's father met me at the station and handed me his bicycle, saying he thought I might need it as the baby was due any time. I pedalled off to the Maternity Home and found Adrian waiting for me, looking very pleased with himself for timing his landing right.*

Adrian was born in Earlham Hall, now part of the University of East Anglia, but then a Maternity Home. He was delivered by Dr George Day, who had

With son Adrian in a family picture, taken in 1947

served in the Royal Army Medical Corps in the First World War, and had long been Maureen's family GP. When Maureen's father, John Miller, was serving as a Recruiting Sergeant for the Royal Marines in Norwich in the years before the First World War, he had got to know Dr Day's father, and they had done business together. John Miller earned a guinea for every man he recruited, but since new recruits had to be given a medical examination before they could be signed up, he would pay 'Old Dr Day', as he was known in the family, half a crown for each recruit he certified fit.

By the time Adrian was born, Stevie had decided to take up a new life and train as a school teacher. The RAF pressed him to stay, delayed his release, and offered him a permanent commission with the prospect of further promotion, but his mind was made up. He had volunteered in 1941 in response to the emergency. He and Maureen did not fancy the prospect of spending their married life being posted from one RAF station to the next, and Stevie had witnessed enough tragic accidents during his years as an Instructor to wonder whether his luck might run out if he carried on flying.

WINNING THE PEACE

After his demobilisation, Stevie trained for a year at Leavesden Green Training College in Hertfordshire under the Emergency Training Scheme for Teachers. He evidently made a very favourable impression on the Principal of the College, whose Final Testimonial, written in December 1948 when Stevie completed the course, was both complimentary and perceptive:

> *Mr Stevens is a man stable and balanced in outlook, and has an excellent sense of humour. Smart and alert in appearance, his cheerful, smiling approach gains him the sympathy and affection of those with whom he comes into contact. He has played a considerable part in the social life of the College as a member of the various athletic societies and as Secretary of the Science Society. His War experience as a commissioned pilot in the RAF and his work with the ATC and with Scouts should be great assets to him in teaching and should make him a popular and valuable member of staff.*

After qualifying as a teacher, Stevie taught Science and Maths at two secondary schools in Norwich: the Norman School at Mile Cross, and the Avenue Road School.

Avenue School 1956 – Staff vs. Boys Football Match. Stevie, standing centre left, is wearing his War Eagle Field top.

Stevie moved to the Earlham School when it opened, and was appointed Head of Maths there. Drawing on his RAF training, he devised and examined a course in Navigation which was unique in the UK. It harvested plaudits from the GCSE Examining Board by which it was validated, and Stevie gained the reputation of being the most original Maths teacher in Norfolk. When the Earlham School became a Comprehensive and acquired a Sixth Form, pupils studying Maths began gaining places at Oxford and Cambridge. *'I loved teaching,'* Stevie remarked.

> *I found Maths difficult at school myself, so I found useful ways of learning it because it was essential to flying, and I made use of those methods when I came to teach. I found teaching to be a very privileged and totally demanding vocation. Children are very good at sorting out the teachers who really care from those who merely look on it as a job.*

Stevie went on to serve as a School Governor at Earlham, and retired in 1986, after a long and successful career as a teacher spanning 38 years. Wherever he went in Norwich later in life, former pupils would come up and shake him by the hand and say, *"Mr Stevens, you taught me Maths,"* and often add remarks like: *"I wouldn't have got where I am now if you hadn't helped me."*

Stevie and Maureen maintained a strong association with the RAF throughout their working lives and the long years of their retirement. Stevie was instrumental in setting up the 57&630 Squadrons' Association, and he and

In the pilot's seat at RAF Coningsby, with S/Ldr Reid in the Battle of Britain Memorial Flight's Avro Lancaster PA474

Stevie in the cockpit of Avro Lancaster 'Just Jane', NX611, at East Kirkby 27 February 2003

Maureen never missed its annual reunions at the Petwood Hotel near East Kirkby. Stevie was on friendly terms with many of the post-war COs of 57 Squadron, and in June 1973 he and Maureen took part in the celebrations at RAF Marham in Norfolk to mark the Squadron's fifty-seventh anniversary, when the last airworthy Lancaster from the Battle of Britain Memorial Flight flew overhead in salute. In July 2005, that same Lancaster flew over London as part of the WW2 national commemoration events. Stevie was invited to RAF Coningsby to inspect it, and was photographed in the *Horncastle News* sitting in the cockpit next to its pilot, Squadron Leader Stuart Reid, smiling broadly as he passed on tips on flying Lancasters.

Stevie and Maureen also helped to support the Lincolnshire Aviation Heritage Centre, located at old RAF East Kirkby airfield from where Stevie had flown his last operational missions. The Heritage Centre, which opened in 1988, was founded by the Lincolnshire farmers Fred and Harold Panton, whose older brother, Pilot Officer Christopher Panton, was shot down and

Stevie lays a wreath at East Kirkby at the 57/630 Sqn reunion on 4 July 2010 [Photograph: Richard J. A. Taylor]

killed while serving with No. 433 Squadron RCAF in 1944. It is both an aviation museum and a memorial to the young men of Bomber Command who gave their lives in the War. The Centre features the Control Tower, a chapel, portions of the runway and a hangar which formed part of the airfield. It is home to the meticulously restored Lancaster bomber 'Just Jane' (NX611), which currently offers taxi rides to visitors, and which, if things go according to plan, may one day take to the skies again.

Stevie and Maureen were friends of Fred and Harold Panton, and of Andrew Panton, who runs the Centre. They made recordings which are still played in the Control Tower, and Stevie provided instruction on running and taxying 'Just Jane' as it underwent restoration. He also used to visit East Kirkby to give talks to schoolchildren about its history and the history of Bomber Command. No wonder Maureen was moved to remark: *'We still live the RAF!'*

Stevie was also closely involved in the work of the Royal British Legion in Norwich. He marched as a standard bearer well into his eighties, and served as the President of the small but fiercely independent Lakenham Branch for over 25 years until most of its members passed away, and it was disbanded.

On 23 July 2010, Stevie and Maureen were thrilled to be invited as guests of honour to the RAF College at Cranwell, where they took part in the Wings

Eric Blanchard and Stevie together at the East Kirkby Memorial, July 1995

presentation ceremony for No. 3 FTS (Flying Training School). No. 3 FTS provides basic flying training for all three of the UK armed services, and 57 Squadron, now a training squadron, forms part of it.

Stevie wrote a moving account of the ceremony shortly after he and Maureen returned to Norwich:

> *Maureen and I were surprised, honoured and delighted to be invited to take part in a Graduation Ceremony at Cranwell on Friday 23 July 2010. We were there to represent members of the RAF from previous generations and to give an idea of Service continuity.*
>
> *In 1918 pilots often used a silver sixpence to pad out the silk brevets they were awarded. This tradition has been continued by No.3 Flying Training School, and now the sixpence is awarded to other aircrew specialists as well. After the AOC No. 1 Group, Air Vice Marshal Greg Bagwell, had presented the brevets to the Graduates, it was my job to hand each one a sixpence and congratulate him or her on their well-earned success. The AOC was kind enough to make some complimentary remarks about Maureen and me in his speech following the presentation. It was 68 years ago that I was awarded my own brevet at War Eagle Field, and I will never forget that day, even though the ceremony in wartime California was not as impressive as the one at Cranwell.*
>
> *After the ceremony, we adjourned to meet and chat with the new Graduates and their proud parents, relatives and friends. We went to the top table in*

Stevie in front of NX611 'Just Jane' in 1996

the superb Dining Hall for a sumptuous lunch followed by a toast to 'The Graduates', to which a graduating student replied, and gave light hearted introductions to each of his fellows.

We were then taken to the airfield to watch a flying display in which many aircraft took part. For Maureen and me, the most nostalgic moment was a flypast by the Lancaster. Tears came to our eyes as we stood for a wonderful moment between our past and the future of those who were chatting to us.

Maureen was able to talk about life in the old Watch Office (later Flying Control) from which she gave the final instruction to 'Pancake' to so many aircraft returning from ops. And I was able to talk to some of the new women pilots, which was a new experience. It was also a delight to talk to the RAF pilots of the present and try to describe what it was like to take off a Lanc with a full bomb load.

At the end of the afternoon, Group Captain Waddington and his wife took us to 'York' Mess to unwind. We sat outside the Mess and watched the aircrews relax with their friends and children. Such is the pull of history and continuity of the RAF community that Maureen and I felt like proud grandparents of a wonderfully progressive and successful family. We were deeply indebted to Group Captain Waddington and his wife, Claire, for a uniquely unforgettable day. His salute as we were driven from the College steps moved us to tears. Needless to say, we were so excited we did not sleep much that night.

No 3 FTS Graduation
Royal Air Force College Cranwell
23 July 2010

Stevie and Maureen as guests of honour at No. 3 FTS Graduation at RAF College Cranwell, July 2010

Two years later, on 28 June 2012, Stevie's and Maureen's son Adrian and his wife Janey attended the ceremony to mark the unveiling of the Bomber Command Memorial in Green Park. Adrian was introduced to Air Vice Marshal Bagwell, showed him a picture of Stevie, and asked him if he remembered meeting him at the Wings presentation ceremony:

> *AVM Bagwell looked at me and grinned. "Of course, I remember your father," he said. "I was really looking forward to that Wings presentation, but I might just as well not have been there. It was your father who was the centre of attention, and all eyes were on him and your mother. As I stood next to him, there was a surge of respect and affection, and I don't mind saying that I felt humble in his presence. He represents all that is finest about the Service."*

On 4 December 2013 Stevie and Maureen celebrated their seventieth wedding anniversary. Their story took up the whole of the front page of the *Eastern Daily Press* under the headline, *'Love Is In The Air: Calming voice*

Stevie and Maureen celebrate their Platinum Wedding Anniversary in December 2013 [Photograph: Archant]

Maureen with Pip Beck, reunited at East Kirkby in 1989

captured the heart of a wartime pilot'. There was a photograph of them holding a large bouquet of red, white and blue flowers presented to them by the editor of the newspaper, and the story of how they met at Scampton in 1943 was told in detail across the next two pages. In the next day's edition, it was continued across two further pages under the headline, *'Steve didn't think he'd live, but Maureen knew he'd come back'*.

The national newspapers were quick to catch on, and the story went viral across the internet, with extended versions of it appearing in the digital editions of the *Daily Mirror*, the *Daily Express*, and the *Daily Mail*. Stevie and Maureen were invited to appear on the BBC Breakfast News programme, but Maureen, feeling that all the publicity had got out of hand, declined the invitation. *'They just don't understand,'* she explained, *'people of our generation didn't join the RAF to become media celebrities. We were just doing our job.'*

Maureen passed away four years later, on 3 December 2017, a day before what would have been her and Stevie's 74th wedding anniversary. She had spent her last days in the Nursing Home at Saxlingham Hall in Norfolk, and passed away peacefully after debilitating weeks spent in hospital. *"In her last moments,"* Stevie said, *"I kissed her. She was quite beautiful to the last."*

Maureen with Dambuster survivors George 'Johnny' Johnson MBE DFM (Bomb Aimer on AJ-T) and Les Munro DSO DFC (Pilot of AJ-W) at Aces High

For all her dislike of publicity, Maureen's story once again went viral. The *Sun* ran it under the headline: '*WW2 HEROINE DEAD: Unsung heroine of the Dambusters raid who guided Lancaster Bombers out of Nazi territory after they dropped bouncing bombs dies*'. The *Daily Mirror* followed suit: '*Radio operator whose cool and calm voice guided the Dambusters home after German bombing raids dies at 97*'. But the most inventive headline was the one that appeared in the *Daily Mail*: '*Angel of the airwaves! Radio operator whose voice guided the Dambusters back to Britain after the famous raid over Germany dies aged 97*'.

Even *The Times* took notice. On 21 December 2017, the day of Maureen's funeral, it printed a half-page obituary under the heading: '*Maureen Stevens: Voice of ground control at RAF Scampton who captured the heart of a bomber pilot as he flew back from a raid over Germany*'. The obituary rehearsed the story of Maureen's meeting with Stevie, and drew an interesting parallel with the 1946 film *A Matter of Life and Death*, in which the hero, Squadron leader Peter Carter, played by David Niven, declares his love for his ground controller mid-flight. The writer captured Maureen's character well when he noted that beating Hitler was, in her view, simply a job that had to be done, and that having helped do it did not make her a celebrity.

Maureen's funeral, at St Margaret's, the beautiful medieval church in the village of Hempnall in the heart of Norfolk, was packed, and the Norwich Branch of the RAF Association laid on an honour guard. Standing next to her coffin draped in the RAF flag, Stevie spoke for twenty minutes or so, fluently, and without notes. *"We were children of the dark,"* he said, painting a vivid picture for the mourners of the hazards of landing in the dark of wartime England, touching down on runways marked by a thin line of Goosenecks to the welcoming sound of Maureen's voice over the R/T:

> *"I was worried she would be on her own,"* he went on, *"but then it came to me that she wouldn't be on her own. All those pilots and their crews she had talked down when they came back exhausted from ops would be waiting in the Control Tower, eager to welcome her to her new station."*

In January 2018, a few weeks after Maureen's funeral, Stevie's son Adrian and his daughter-in-law Janey drove him to Lincoln, where he was one of the WW2 veterans given early access to the IBCC (International Bomber Command Centre). Located on Canwick Hill, overlooking the city of Lincoln, the IBCC has been set up to commemorate Bomber Command and its veterans. Lincoln was chosen as its site because twenty-seven RAF Bomber Command stations (over a third of the total) were based in Lincolnshire during WW2. It is just two and a half miles from RAF Waddington, where Maureen had trained as an R/T Operator. The evening before the IBCC event, Stevie had sat quietly in the Airmens' Chapel in Lincoln Cathedral, remembering the friends and comrades who never returned whose names are recorded on the Roll of Honour, and saying a prayer for them.

2018 marked the hundredth anniversary of the founding of the RAF, and Stevie was in demand. As part of the centenary celebrations, Stevie featured on 12 April on the RAF's Facebook and Twitter platforms as one of the *RAF 100 Heroes*. The RAF also arranged for the broadcaster Dan Snow to interview Stevie in his home in Norwich, and Dan subsequently posted two podcasts about Stevie on his *History Hit* website under the title: *'The Unheard Tapes of Bomber Command with Steve Stevens'*. They make for compulsive viewing and listening. One of the podcasts contains Dan Snow's wide-ranging interview with Stevie, while the other posts the recording Stevie made at Scampton in 1943 describing the Essen raid.

Thanks to the help and support of his neighbour, friend and carer Clair Ling and her family, Stevie was able to live independently at his home in

Stevie with his devoted long-term carer Clair Ling, November 2019

Norwich until he was 97. But in January 2019, he suffered a stroke, and he spent the last year of his life in the Nursing Home at Saxlingham Hall in Norfolk, where Maureen had been so well cared for as her life drew to a close. Although the stroke made it difficult for Stevie to walk unaided, it caused no mental impairment, and he was as mentally alert and verbally fluent as ever. Knowing that he was a gregarious man who loved company, Clair Ling put out an appeal in the local press, and on television and social media, outlining Stevie's service in Bomber Command, and calling on people to visit him. The response was overwhelming. Letters poured in, and so many visitors arrived that Saxlingham Hall struggled to cope with the numbers.

When Stevie's son Adrian arrived from London a few days after the appeal was launched, he found Stevie still in bed, although it was lunch time. Visitors were queuing up the stairs and along the corridor leading to his rooms with their beautiful views over the Norfolk countryside. They

Stevie with son Adrian and David Houghton, celebrating his 98th Birthday at Saxlingham Hall

had started coming early in the morning, and the nurses had been unable to get Stevie dressed. Some of the visitors were RAF buffs; others had fathers who had served in Bomber Command; many of his former pupils came, as did people who wished to interview him. When Adrian went into Stevie's bedroom, he spoke to a couple who had driven all the way from Southampton just to shake his hand. *"It's such an honour to meet your father, it's something we'll always remember,"* they said as they were leaving.

Stevie celebrated his 98th Birthday on 14 December 2019 at Saxlingham Hall with friends and family. Group Captain David Houghton, the President of the 57&630 Squadrons' Assocation with whom he had been close for many years, brought him a bottle of the malt whisky that had become his preferred tipple, and a local pilot who owned an American P-51 Mustang flew over Saxlingham Hall to pay his own very special tribute.

Four months later, on 11 April 2020, Stevie made his final take-off. The Coronavirus pandemic was raging, and Saxlingham Hall was in lockdown, but he remained cheerful and communicative till the end. With the help of the devoted team of nurses who were caring for him, he continued talking to his son Adrian over the telephone until his strength failed. *"Remember that passage from St John, 'My Father's house has many mansions', I still firmly believe that,"* he said to Adrian, drawing on the reserves of faith and courage that had taken him through so many missions, *"I know we'll meet again."*

His passing generated yet another a media storm. The local BBC Television News broadcast a lengthy tribute, which ended with the weather forecaster dedicating a picture of a particularly glorious sunset '*to Stevie*'. The *Eastern Daily Press* ran an extended obituary under the headline, *'From Lancaster bomber hero to beloved teacher: the remarkable life of Stevie Stevens'*. The main daily newspapers followed suit, and Stevie's story was retold in local papers across the UK. The *Times* carried an extended tribute across a whole page, deliberately held back for the edition published on 8 May 2020, the 75th anniversary of VE Day. Its heading was, *'Stevie Stevens: Lancaster bomber pilot, survivor of 28 sorties and smitten suitor to the "angelic-voiced girl in the control tower" at RAF Scampton'*. The author was the same man who had written Maureen's obituary in 2017. He gave a heart-warming account of Stevie's life that delighted his readers, referring again to the story of the bomber pilot and his ground controller told in the 1946 film *A Matter of Life and Death* starring David Niven.

Stevie with his log book in his room at Saxlingham Hall in May 2019

Tributes also flooded the social media, many of them from men and women he had taught in Norwich. Here is a representative sample:

> *The first day he arrived at school, he roared in the gate on a huge maroon motor bike, and we all looked at each other wondering who he was. He was a great teacher, and we could always have a laugh with him, especially when he was standing in for the Science master. There was always bangs and smoke! If you got lines off him for messing about, and then made him laugh, he would always cancel them. He would never tell us why he won a DFC. A very modest man!* (John Garrett)

> *I will always be indebted to Mr Stevens for his bravery during WW2, which helped give us the freedom and liberty we have enjoyed in our own lives. But in my case especially, for his wonderful encouragement, always on tap, and unfailingly given with such patience. He showed me how interesting the world of Mathematics can be. It had not seen him for 50 years when I went to visit him ... but 50 years could have been 50 days. So much was still the same, and the smile and the laugh told me I'd found the right man!* (Peter Palmer)

I remember Mr Stevens from the 60s. I hated school, but I remember well I was in his Maths class. I was hopeless at Maths, but I kept my head down and tried. At the end of term, he stood in front of the class and said he had a gift for the best pupil in the class. When he said my name, I thought he had made a mistake, but he said "No, I do mean you, because though you are not very good at Maths, you have been well behaved, and that's just as important a thing in life." I never forgot that. He made me realize you did not have to be anything great — you were liked for how you were. He left that with me, and for that, Mr Stevens, I thank you. God bless you, Sir. I am still rubbish at Maths, but you taught me something far greater. (Dawn)

A true gentleman and an unsung hero. RIP, Mr Stevens, fond memories of you as my Maths teacher at the Earlham School. (Kim Castle)

Mr Stevens, you were a truly inspirational man. You made my maths lessons so much more fun. I loved to listen to your stories. You have more than earned your wings. God bless you. (Sarah Hesch)

Best teacher and a lovely man. RIP Mr Stevens. (Debbie O'Shea)

Steve was such a wonderful man, the story of how he met his beloved wife still inspires me. He once emailed me one of his accounts of the War, and wow, what those heroes went through! (Ian Mousley)

What a great man, always full of life and love with many stories to share. It was a privilege to get to know him. (Joe Cousens)

I remember him teaching me Maths at High School. What a joyful man with such compassion! (Anita)

Thank you, Steve, for always being a true gent and a positive force in the world. You are deeply missed, but I'm glad I got to know you. Fly safe. (Sean Page)

Such an amazing man who had so many stories to tell. He left a lasting impact on so many friends, and his name will live on for years and years to come. (Sam Rowe)

An incredible, amazing man with a sparkling sense of humour, and I feel very honoured to have met him. (David Bloor)

His colleagues from the Maths Department at Earlham remembered him with equal respect and affection. John Pountain wrote the following tribute:

I was a colleague of Steve's at Earlham for just over eight years in the 1970s and 80s, and what a wonderful colleague he was. I had joined the staff having previously taught in a selective school, and Steve's advice, based on many decades of experience with less able and more challenging pupils, was invaluable to me, and after a difficult first year, my time at Earlham became the most enjoyable of my years of teaching.

Steve was, of course, great fun, and much of his humour involved pricking the pomposity of those who believed themselves rather grand. He loved sending up HMIs. He was understandably sceptical of new ideas and proposals that didn't ring true to his experience. He was never afraid to let his feelings be known. I remember him being fed up with senior management's constant use of the word 'hopefully', and standing up in a staff meeting and challenging them to go through the new school year without using it! I'm sorry that he didn't reach his 100th or get to today's 75th VE Day anniversary, but he lived a long and productive life, and I feel privileged to have known him.

Stevie lies with Maureen in the heart of Norfolk, by the beautiful medieval church in Hempnall. His funeral took place on 23 April 2020, St George's Day. The restrictions put in place because of the lockdown meant that it had to be a graveside burial restricted to five people. The pallbearers had the option of placing his coffin on a cart, but they said to the mourners, *"He was a hero, and we shall bury him like one."* Arms linked, they carried the coffin, draped in the RAF flag, to the grave, and laid him to rest in it. The Rector of Hempnall, the Rev Michael Kingston, who had prayed with Stevie at his bedside in his last hours, performed the traditional Anglican

57 & 630 Sqn veterans and relatives pictured in front of 'Just Jane' at the 2010 annual reunion [Photograph: Richard J. A. Taylor]

burial rite in accordance with Stevie's wishes. The sun shone, birds seemed to be singing from every tree, and the man who had fought to preserve the liberty of the country he loved, the man who had brought light to the lives of so many, and inspired so much love and affection, seemed no more than an arm's length away. The motto of 57 Squadron, which he always quoted with such pride, might have been composed for the occasion: *Corpus non animum muto,* 'I change my body, not my spirit'.

If those words are a fitting epitaph so, too, are the words he had written two years earlier, in celebration of the hundredth anniversary of the RAF. Inevitably, he had his tour of operations and the men who had flown with him from Scampton and East Kirkby in 1943 very much in mind:

> *At that time, only one in five of 57 Squadron's aircraft completed a tour of operations, and neither I, nor the men I flew with, expected to survive. My Bomb Aimer made the long journey from Chile, and my Mid Upper Gunner was French. The world we did our bit to bring about is, for all its problems, an infinitely better place than the world subjected to Nazi tyranny. That is Bomber Command's legacy to the young men and women of today, and its true memorial. They laid down their lives so that you could live yours in peace and freedom.*

STEVIE'S PRAYER, RAF SCAMPTON 1943

Before flying on ops, it was Stevie's practice to find a quiet corner of the airfield in which to pray. A padre at Scampton gave him a small leather-bound copy of the New Testament which he carried with him when he went into battle. In its flyleaf, Stevie inscribed a prayer which he composed himself. His copy of the New Testament was always marked at the passage from St John 14: *'Let not your heart be troubled'*. Adrian read that passage at his funeral, as Stevie had wished. Stevie prepared for his last flight in the firm belief that in his end was his beginning.

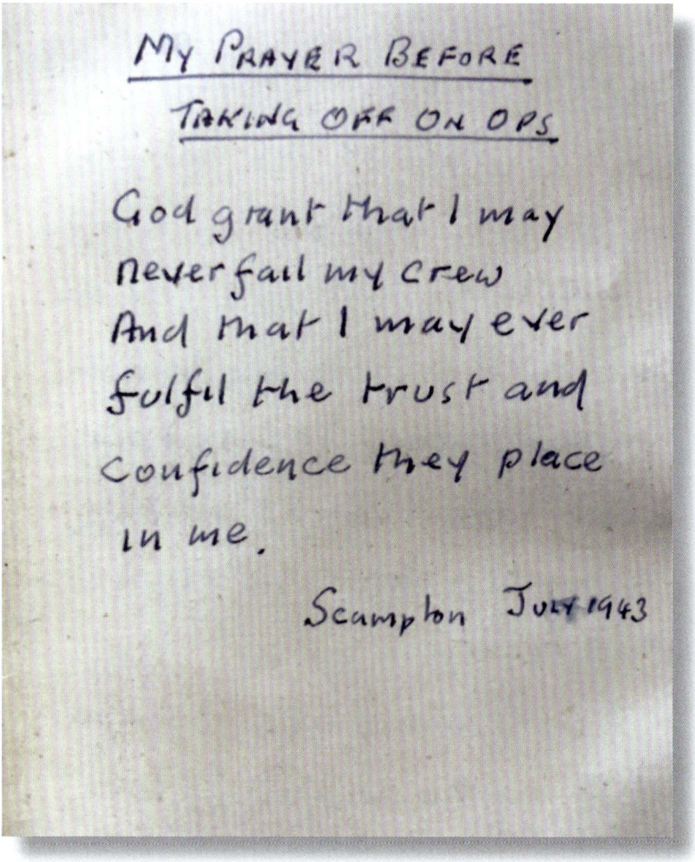

MY PRAYER BEFORE

TAKING OFF ON OPS

God grant that I may
never fail my crew
And that I may ever
fulfil the trust and
confidence they place
in me.

Scampton July 1943

ACKNOWLEDGEMENTS

Thanks are due to the many people who have helped and supported Adrian Stevens and myself while we worked on this book.

I should like to place on record my gratitude to my good friend Mark Postlethwaite. He knew and admired both Stevie and Maureen, and offered to publish this book because, like me, he thought their story deserved to be told. His technical expertise and depth of knowledge, made so readily available, has turned this book into a work of art.

The book has been very much a joint endeavour over the past 20 months. Adrian and I have written it together, and the constraints imposed by the pandemic, rather than hindering us, have actually been conducive to our work, giving us ample time and opportunity to see it through to completion. We were able to draw on the rich archive of photographs, documents, and letters Stevie and Maureen had assembled over many years. They form the basis of this book and which Stevie himself was very actively involved in during the early stages of its preparation. It was his wish that it should tell as much of his story as possible in his own words, and we have done our best to comply.

Stevie's devoted carer and friend Clair Ling deserves a special mention. With her and her family's unstinting help and support, Stevie was able to live at home until January 2019, when he suffered a stroke which left him mentally unimpaired, but unable to walk unsupported. When he was admitted into Saxlingham Hall Nursing Home in Norfolk, Clair launched an appeal on social media for visitors. Her appeal was taken up by the local press and television news, and the response was overwhelming. Letters and messages flooded in, and people came from across the country to shake his hand and hear his stories. It was through Clair's appeal that I came to know Stevie myself. But for her and her extraordinary media campaign, this book would never have been written.

I would like also to express my sincere appreciation of the staff at Saxlingham Hall Nursing Home who cared for Stevie with such exemplary kindness and good humour. Whenever I visited him, they would bring tea and biscuits up to his room, and there would be joking and laughter. Stevie had nothing but praise for them. In the end, when old age and frailty claimed him shortly after the start of the pandemic, a team of nurses tended to him night and day, ensuring that he was in no pain, and keeping his telephone line open so that Adrian could to speak to him as he prepared to take his last flight. They, in their own way, served on the front line, just as Stevie and his friends had done so many years before, and they drew on similar reserves of courage and dedication.

Thanks are due also to Group Captain David Houghton, Stevie's close friend and President of the 57&630 Squadrons' Association. He contributed the Foreword to this book, made helpful comments on the first draft, and went to great lengths to explain the protocols governing reproduction of the 57 Squadron crest. In addition, I should like to mention Air Commodore Wendy Rothery, Andrew Panton and the Lincolnshire Aviation Heritage Centre, Richard Taylor, David Kavanagh, The International Bomber Command Centre, and The Battle of Britain Memorial Flight. They have all in their various ways offered help and support, provided information, and contributed valuable material. Last but not least, Therese Bennett, an experienced publisher whose own father served during the War with distinction as an officer in the Tank Corps in North Africa, Sicily, Italy, and Northern Europe, spent many hours editing the draft manuscript. Her expertise has been invaluable, and we have benefited immensely from her suggestions, corrections and comments.

It gives me particular pleasure to acknowledge the help and support offered by the sons and daughters of Stevie's aircrew and his wartime companions and friends. Douglas Gray, the son of Stevie's friend Len Gray, read through his father's diary and answered a series of questions concerning the months Len and Stevie spent in California. Sheelagh McCrae, Bill McCrae's daughter, gave us permission to quote from her father's beautifully written memoir *A Chequer-Board of Nights*. Diana Perkins, the daughter of Eric Blanchard, responded to queries about the interviews her father recorded for the Imperial War Museum. Eve Janocko, the daughter of Tony Gobbie, Stevie's fellow pilot on 57 Squadron, kindly provided photographs and letters. Gerald Smith, the son of Squadron Leader Smith, with whom Stevie flew as Second Pilot on his first mission, also provided photographs. David Allen, the son of Sergeant Christopher Allen, who replaced George Martin as Stevie's Mid-Upper Gunner on the Berlin sortie of 23 August 1943, provided helpful context. Jane Liddle, the wife of Stevie's solicitor Alisdair Liddle and daughter of Ivor Davies, Stevie's fellow trainee at War Eagle Field, supplied us with photographs and material from the diary her father kept in California. They have all helped us to bring Stevie's story graphically to life, and Adrian and I hope that they will see this book as a tribute not only to Stevie, but to their fathers, who braved the same dangers.

I am, of course, sad not to be able to present this book to Stevie in person. The hours I spent in his company will always remain treasured memories. He reminisced easily and entertainingly, and answered my many questions with the good humour that endeared him to everyone who knew him. We shared many laughs as I sat making notes, often over a glass of cider! It was a privilege, and a humbling experience, to get to know this most unassuming and self-deprecating of heroes; and it is my honour and good fortune to have had the opportunity to tell his inspirational story.

Jonny Cracknell

Jonny Cracknell with Stevie in his room at Saxlingham Hall in May 2019

STEVIE'S OPERATIONAL LOG BOOK ENTRIES

Every wartime RAF pilot kept a log book in which he recorded every flight, accompanied by other details such as date, aircraft type, crew, etc. Each log book entry would be written shortly after the flight and thus provides the most authentic historical record of what actually happened. The following pages show Stevie's log book entries for his 31 operational sorties. Entries in red are night flights.

'Bullseye' was a simulated raid where the crews would have to navigate their way along a preset course to a British city and then carry out a simulated bombing run, usually taking a photo to determine their accuracy. **'Bombing'** was simply dropping practice bombs on the bombing range. **'Boomerang'** was when they were forced to return without completing the op and **'NFT'** was a night flying test.

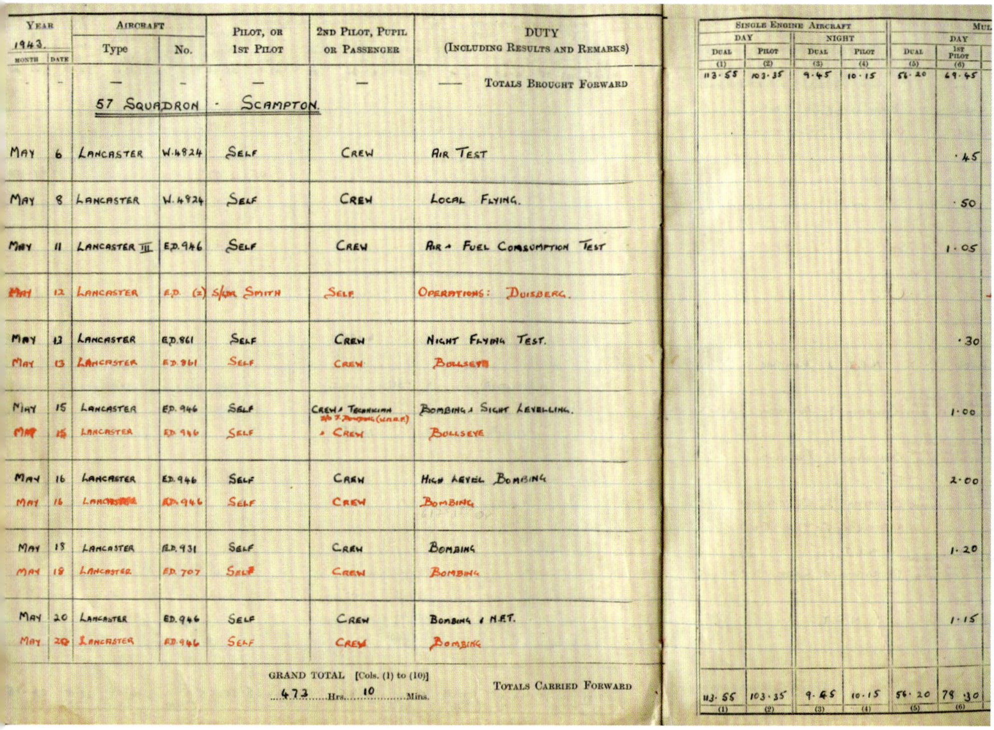

Year 1943 Month	Date	Aircraft Type	Aircraft No.	Pilot, or 1st Pilot	2nd Pilot, Pupil or Passenger	DUTY (Including Results and Remarks)	Single Engine Aircraft Day Dual (1)	Single Engine Aircraft Day Pilot (2)	Single Engine Aircraft Night Dual (3)	Single Engine Aircraft Night Pilot (4)	Mul[ti-Engine] Day Dual (5)	Mul[ti-Engine] Day 1st Pilot (6)
-	-	—	-	—	—	— Totals Brought Forward	113.55	103.35	9.45	10.15	56.20	69.45
		57 Squadron · Scampton.										
May	6	Lancaster	W.4824	Self	Crew	Air Test						.45
May	8	Lancaster	W.4924	Self	Crew	Local Flying.						.50
May	11	Lancaster III	ED.946	Self	Crew	Air + Fuel Consumption Test						1.05
May	12	Lancaster	E.D. (?)	S/Ldr Smith	Self	Operations: Duisberg.						
May	13	Lancaster	ED.861	Self	Crew	Night Flying Test.						.30
May	13	Lancaster	ED.861	Self	Crew	Bullseye						
May	15	Lancaster	ED.946	Self	Crew + Technician [illegible] (W.A.A.F.)	Bombing + Sight Levelling.						1.00
May	15	Lancaster	ED.946	Self	+ Crew	Bullseye						
May	16	Lancaster	ED.946	Self	Crew	High Level Bombing						2.00
May	16	Lancaster	ED.946	Self	Crew	Bombing						
May	18	Lancaster	ED.931	Self	Crew	Bombing						1.20
May	18	Lancaster	ED.707	Self	Crew	Bombing						
May	20	Lancaster	ED.946	Self	Crew	Bombing + N.F.T.						1.15
May	20	Lancaster	ED.946	Self	Crew	Bombing						
				GRAND TOTAL [Cols. (1) to (10)] 473 Hrs. 10 Mins.		Totals Carried Forward	113.55	103.35	9.45	10.15	56.20	78.30

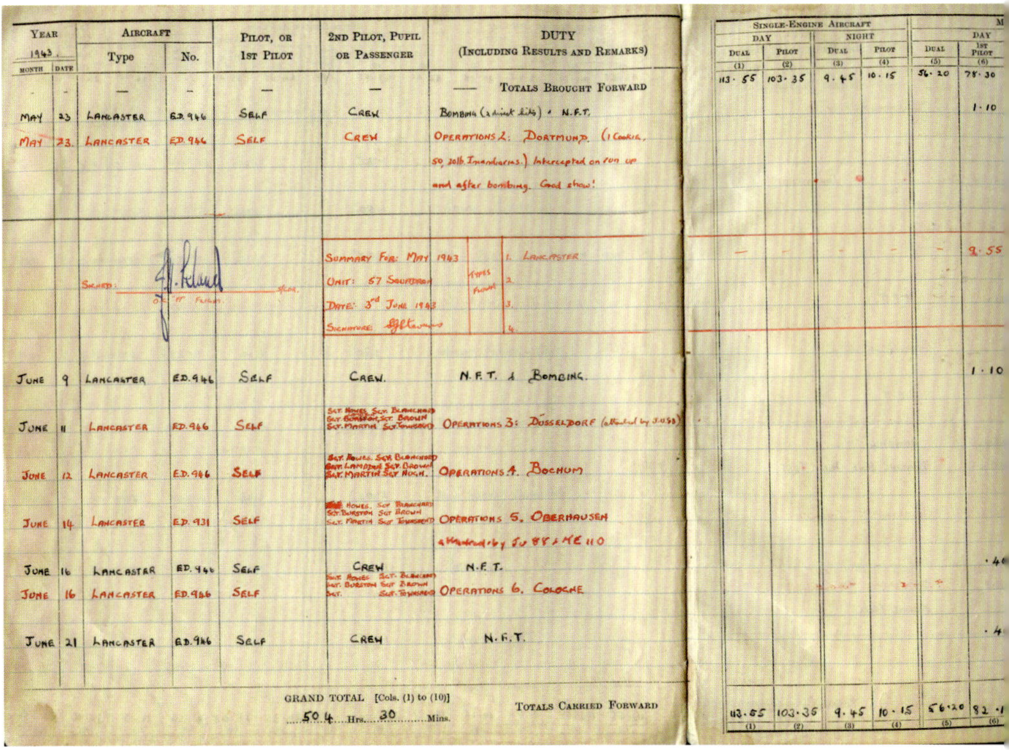

Year 1943 Month	Date	Aircraft Type	Aircraft No.	Pilot, or 1st Pilot	2nd Pilot, Pupil or Passenger	Duty (Including Results and Remarks)	Day 1st Pilot (6)
-	-	—	-	—	—	— Totals Brought Forward	78.30
May	23	Lancaster	E.D. 946	Self	Crew	Bombing (2 direct hits) + N.F.T.	1.10
May	23.	Lancaster	E.D. 946	Self	Crew	Operations 2: Dortmund. (1 Cookie, 50, 30lb. Incendiaries.) Intercepted on run up and after bombing. Good show!	
						Summary for: May 1943. Unit: 57 Squadron. Date: 3rd June 1943. Signature: [illegible]. Types Flown: 1. Lancaster 2. 3. 4.	9.55
		Signed: [signature] O.C. 'A' Flight S/Ldr.					
June	9	Lancaster	E.D. 946	Self	Crew.	N.F.T. & Bombing.	1.10
June	11	Lancaster	E.D. 946	Self	Sgt. Howes, Sgt. Blanchard, Sgt. Burston, Sgt. Brown, Sgt. Martin, Sgt. Townsend	Operations 3: Düsseldorf (attacked by J.U. 88)	
June	12	Lancaster	E.D. 946	Self	Sgt. Howes, Sgt. Blanchard, Sgt. Lamdon, Sgt. Brown, Sgt. Martin, Sgt. Hugh.	Operations 4. Bochum	
June	14	Lancaster	E.D. 931	Self	Sgt. Howes, Sgt. Blanchard, Sgt. Burston, Sgt. Brown, Sgt. Martin, Sgt. Townsend	Operations 5. Oberhausen attacked by Ju 88 & ME 110	
June	16	Lancaster	E.D. 946	Self	Crew	N.F.T.	.40
June	16	Lancaster	E.D. 946	Self	Sgt. Howes, Sgt. Blanchard, Sgt. Burston, Sgt. Brown, Sgt., Sgt. Townsend	Operations 6. Cologne	
June	21	Lancaster	E.D. 946	Self	Crew	N.F.T.	.4[illegible]

Grand Total [Cols. (1) to (10)] 504 Hrs. 30 Mins.

Totals Carried Forward

Single-Engine Aircraft					
Day Dual (1)	Day Pilot (2)	Night Dual (3)	Night Pilot (4)	Day Dual (5)	Day 1st Pilot (6)
113.55	103.35	9.45	10.15	56.20	78.30
113.55	103.35	9.45	10.15	56.20	82.1[illegible]

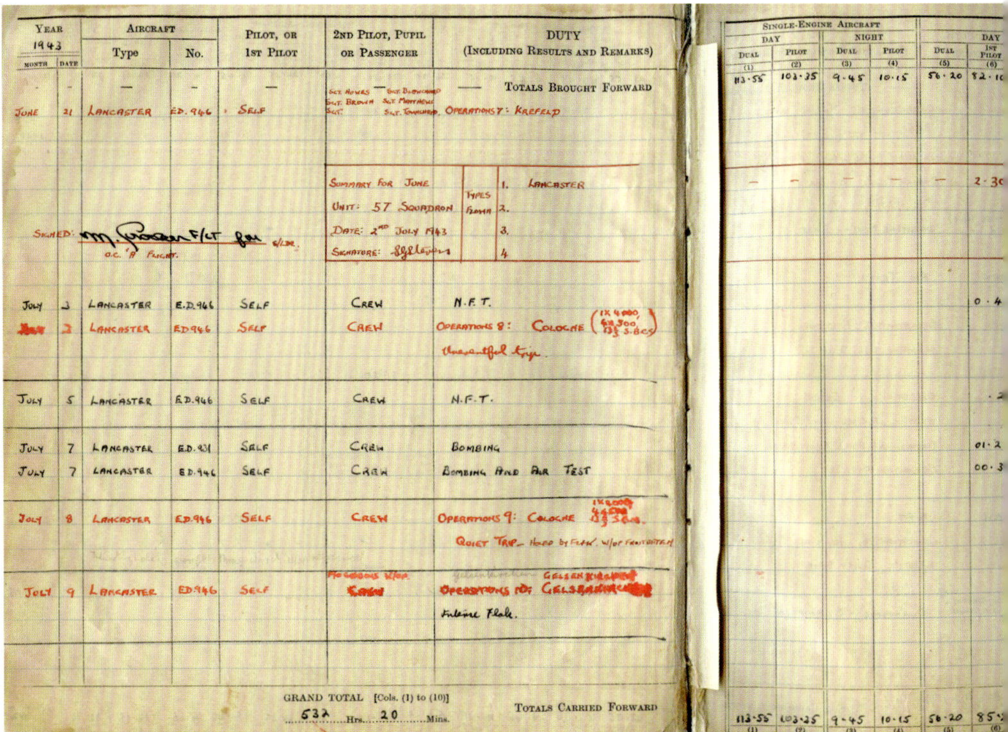

Year 1943 Month	Date	Aircraft Type	Aircraft No.	Pilot, or 1st Pilot	2nd Pilot, Pupil or Passenger	Duty (Including Results and Remarks)	Day 1st Pilot (6)
-	-	—	-	—	—	— Totals Brought Forward	82.1[illegible]
June	21	Lancaster	E.D. 946	Self	Sgt. Howes, Sgt. Blanchard, Sgt. Brown, Sgt. Matthews, Sgt., Sgt. Townsend	Operations 7: Krefeld	
						Summary for June. Unit: 57 Squadron. Date: 2nd July 1943. Signature: [illegible]. Types Flown: 1. Lancaster 2. 3. 4.	2.30
		Signed: [signature] F/Lt for O.C. 'A' Flight S/Ldr.					
July	3	Lancaster	E.D. 946	Self	Crew	N.F.T.	0.4[illegible]
[illegible]	3	Lancaster	ED 946	Self	Crew	Operations 8: Cologne (1x4000, 48x300, 13½ S.B.Cs) Uneventful trip.	
July	5	Lancaster	E.D. 946	Self	Crew	N.F.T.	
July	7	Lancaster	E.D. 931	Self	Crew	Bombing	01.2[illegible]
July	7	Lancaster	E.D. 946	Self	Crew	Bombing and Air Test	00.3[illegible]
July	8	Lancaster	E.D. 946	Self	Crew	Operations 9: Cologne 1x4000, 44x300, 13½ S.B.Cs. Quiet trip – [illegible] by flak. W/Op [illegible]	
July	9	Lancaster	ED 946	Self	[illegible] W/Op. Crew	Operations 10: Gelsenkirchen. Intense flak.	

Grand Total [Cols. (1) to (10)] 532 Hrs. 20 Mins.

Totals Carried Forward

Single-Engine Aircraft					
Day Dual (1)	Day Pilot (2)	Night Dual (3)	Night Pilot (4)	Day Dual (5)	Day 1st Pilot (6)
113.55	103.35	9.45	10.15	56.20	82.1[illegible]
113.55	103.35	9.45	10.15	56.20	85.[illegible]

Year 1943 Month	Date	Aircraft Type	Aircraft No.	Pilot, or 1st Pilot	2nd Pilot, Pupil or Passenger	Duty (Including Results and Remarks)	Single-Engine Day Dual (1)	Single-Engine Day Pilot (2)	Single-Engine Night Dual (3)	Single-Engine Night Pilot (4)	Multi-Engine Day Dual (5)	Multi-Engine Day 1st Pilot (6)
–	–	—	–	—	—	— Totals Brought Forward	112·55	102·35	9·45	10·15	56·20	85·20
July	12	Lancaster	ED.944	Self	Sgt. Helmore (F/O Gibson W/O) Crew	Operations 11: Turin. (4×1000, 4,000 Is) 1/10 Cloud to target. Landed in Cornwall at Davistone Moor. Johnny Pickett missing. W/Cdr Nettleton V.C. killed						
July	13	Lancaster	ED.944	Self	(Sgt. Helmore W/Op) Crew	Davistone Moor – Base.						01·45
July	16	Lancaster	ED.946	Self	Crew	Air Test						00·45
July	24	Lancaster	ED.920	Self	Crew	Operations 12: Hamburg 11,300 lbs. Good trip						
July	25	Lancaster	ED.920	Self	Crew	Operations 13: Essen 11,300 lbs. F.W.190 shot down in flames. A.T. Ariel shot away. S/O on fire over sea.						
July	27	Lancaster	ED.946	Self	Crew	N.F.T.						01·00
July	27	Lancaster	ED.946	Self	Crew	Operations 14: Hamburg. 11,600 lbs. Quiet trip. Landed at Dunholme						·20
July	28	Lancaster	ED.946	Self	Sgts. Howes, Martin & Blanchard + ground crew.	Dunholme – Scampton						
						Grand Total [Cols. (1) to (10)] 563 Hrs. 35 Mins. — Totals Carried Forward	112·55	102·35	9·45	10·15	56·20	89·10 (~~85·20~~)

Year 1943 Month	Date	Aircraft Type	Aircraft No.	Pilot, or 1st Pilot	2nd Pilot, Pupil or Passenger	Duty (Including Results and Remarks)	Single-Engine Day Dual (1)	Single-Engine Day Pilot (2)	Single-Engine Night Dual (3)	Single-Engine Night Pilot (4)	Multi-Engine Day Dual (5)	Multi-Engine Day 1st Pilot (6)
–	–	—	–	—	—	— Totals Brought Forward	112·55	103·35	9·45	10·15	56·20	89·10
		Signed [signature] F/Lt. O.C. "A" Flight				Summary for July '43 — Unit: 57 Squadron — Date: 29th July 43 — Signature: [signature] — Type: 1. Lancaster 2. 3. 4.	–	–	–	–	–	7·00
Aug	9	Lancaster	ED.946	Self	Crew	N.F.T. + Bombing						1·20
Aug	9	Lancaster	ED.946	Self	Crew	Operations: 15 Mannheim 12,300 lbs. Quiet trip						
Aug	10	Lancaster	ED.946	Self	Crew	Operations 16: Nuremburg. Hit by flak. Landed Aldermaston						
Aug	11	Lancaster	ED.946	Self	Crew	Aldermaston – Base						01·00
Aug	12	Lancaster	ED.946	Self	Crew	N.F.T.						0·45
Aug	12	Lancaster	ED946	Self	Crew	Operations 17: Milan						
Aug	14	Lancaster	ED946	Self	Crew	Air Test						0·40
Aug	14	Lancaster	ED946	Self	Crew	Operations 18: Milan						
						Grand Total [Cols. (1) to (10)] ....Hrs........Mins. — Totals Carried Forward	112·55	102·35	9·45	10·15	56·20	92·55

Year 1943 Month	Date	Aircraft Type	Aircraft No.	Pilot, or 1st Pilot	2nd Pilot, Pupil or Passenger	Duty (Including Results and Remarks)	Single-Engine Aircraft Day Dual (1)	Day Pilot (2)	Night Dual (3)	Night Pilot (4)	Day Dual (5)	Day 1st Pilot (6)
—	—	—	—	—	—	—— Totals Brought Forward	113·55	103·35	9·45	10·15	56·20	42·55
Aug	19	Lancaster	ED 946	Self	Crew	N.F.T.						·45
Aug	22	Lancaster	ED.946	Self	Crew	N.F.T.						
Aug	23	Lancaster	ED946	Self	Crew	Operations 19. Berlin Bomb Load 10,300.						
Aug	27	Lancaster	ED.946	Self	Crew	N.F.T.						
Aug	27	Lancaster	ED946	Self	F/Lt. Winyard vice Sgt. Townsend Crew	Operations: 20 Nurenburg Landed Swinderby.						
Aug	28.	(ED.946 Pranged by another pilot while being ferried from Swinderby) FW.190 destroyed										
Aug	31	Lancaster	ED.920	Self	Crew	Operations: Berlin. Early return due to oxygen shortage 1st						
					Summary for Aug. 1943 / Unit: 57 Squadron / Date: 1/9/43. / Signature:	Types Flown: 1. Lancaster. 2. 3. 4.	–	–	–	–	–	4·40
		AHJobbins F/Lt. OC 'A' Flight										
						Grand Total [Cols. (1) to (10)] 615 Hrs. 00 Mins. — Totals Carried Forward	113·55	103·35	9·45	10·15	56·20	94·30

Aug 28th BERLIN

Defences very active. Numerous searchlights over target. Very heavy flak en route. Night fighters plenteous and many combats seen. Rear gunner passed out over target to 3° East. Gee unserviceable shortly after leaving base. 1300 tons of bombs reported dropped on City. Target well alight when we left it. 58 of our bombers missing.

Written by Chas Allen my NUG on that raid

Year 1943 Month	Date	Aircraft Type	Aircraft No.	Pilot, or 1st Pilot	2nd Pilot, Pupil or Passenger	Duty (Including Results and Remarks)	Single-Engine Aircraft Day Dual (1)	Day Pilot (2)	Night Dual (3)	Night Pilot (4)	Day Dual (5)	Day 1st Pilot (6)
—	—	—	—	—	—	—— Totals Brought Forward	113·55	103·35	09·45	10·15	56·20	94·30
Sept.	2	Lancaster	ED920	Self	Crew	Base - Syerston - Wigsley - Base						01·30
Sept	3	Lancaster	W 7479	Self	Crew	Operations: Berlin 2nd Boomerang: P.O. engine U/S, M.U. Turret U/S, M.U. & B.A. heating U/S.						
Sept	5	Oxford	AT 664	Self	F/Sgt. Howes	Base - Topcliffe - Base						03·30
Sept	5	Lancaster	(S)	Self	Sgt. Smith (132) R.G. Crew Sgt. Yates 2nd P.	Operations 21: Mannheim						
Sept	8	Lancaster	ED.944	Self	Crew	N.F.T.						00·30
Sept	24	Lancaster	JB. 311	Self	Crew	Air Test						01·50
Sept	25	Lancaster	JB 236	Self	Crew	N.F.T. (This was the new E. subsequently given to F/Lt. Eagles for operations & aircraft lost)						01·10
Sept	27	Lancaster	JB 311	Self	Crew	Operations 22: Hannover (Diverted Waterbeach)						
Sept	28	Lancaster	JB 311	Self	Crew	Waterbeach - Base						00·50
Sept	29	Lancaster	JB 311	Self	Crew	Operations 23 Bochum (Navigator too sick to cope rest of crew perved)						
						Grand Total [Cols. (1) to (10)] 643 Hrs. 55 Mins. — Totals Carried Forward	113·55	103·35	09·45	10·15	56·20	103·5

Year 1943 Month	Date	Aircraft Type	Aircraft No.	Pilot, or 1st Pilot	2nd Pilot, Pupil or Passenger	Duty (Including Results and Remarks)	Single-Engine Aircraft Day Dual (1)	Day Pilot (2)	Night Dual (3)	Night Pilot (4)	Multi- Day Dual (5)	Day 1st Pilot (6)
–	–	—	–	—	—	— Totals Brought Forward	113·55	103·35	09·45	10·15	56·20	103·50
					Summary for Sept 1943 / Unit: 57 Squadron / Date: 1·10·43 / Signature: [signature]	Types flown: 1. Lancaster	—	—	—	—	—	5·50
						2. Oxford	—	—	—	—	—	3·30
						3.						
						4.						
Signed: [signature] F/Lt. S/Ldr. O.C. "A" Flight.												
Oct.	1	Lancaster	JB.235	P/O Josling	Self (Flight Engineer)	N.F.T.						
Oct.	1.	Lancaster	JB·236	Self	Crew	N.F.T.						·30
Oct.	1	Lancaster	JB 311	Self	Crew	Operations 22nd Hagen						
Oct	2	Lancaster	JB.311	Self	Crew	Operations: 24 Munich						
Oct.	7	Lancaster	JB 311	Self	Crew	Operations: 25 Stuttgart i/c completely u/s bombed Amiens-Glissy Airfield. Sortie Counted.						
Oct	9	Lancaster	JB 311	Self	Crew	Operations: 26 Hannover						
Oct	13	Lancaster	JB 232	Self	F/O Munday	Bombing						1·20
Oct	16	Lancaster	JB.311	Self	Crew	N.F.T Bombing						1·30
Oct	18	Lancaster	JB 311	Self	Crew	N.F.T.						·40
					Grand Total [Cols. (1) to (10)] 672 Hrs. 25 Mins.	Totals Carried Forward	113·55	103·35	09·45	10·15	56·20	107·50

Year Month	Date	Aircraft Type	Aircraft No.	Pilot, or 1st Pilot	2nd Pilot, Pupil or Passenger	Duty (Including Results and Remarks)	Single-Engine Aircraft Day Dual (1)	Day Pilot (2)	Night Dual (3)	Night Pilot (4)	Multi- Day Dual (5)	Day 1st Pilot (6)
–	–	—	–	—	—	— Totals Brought Forward	113·55	103·35	09·45	10·15	56·20	107·50
Oct	18	Lancaster	JB 311	Self	Crew	Operations: 27 Hannover						
Oct	20	Lancaster	JB 311	Self	Crew	N.F.T						·20
Oct	20	Lancaster	JB 311	Self	Crew	Operations: 28 Leipzig. (Severe icing A.S.I. u/s) (P.4.S.I. u/s on return)						
					Summary for Oct. / Unit: 57 Squadron / Date: 1·11·43 / Signature: [signature]	Types flown: 1. Lancaster						4·20
						2.						
						3.						
						4.						
					Grand Total [Cols. (1) to (10)] 688 Hrs. 15 Mins.	Totals Carried Forward	113·55	103·35	09·45	10·15	56·20	109·50

Signed: [signature] S/L
O.C. "A" Flight.

[signature] W/C

END OF FIRST TOUR OF OPERATIONS

CREW.

Navigator: E. J. Howes. (D.F.C)
Bomb-Aimer: R.W. Newcomb. Killed (Also Sgts. Lamludin Killed, Burston ?nd & Matthews Killed. - Missing)
Flight Engineer: E. Blanchard. (D.F.C. on second tour)
Wireless Operator: K.D. Brown. (Also F/O Gibbons, F/k Hellmore)
Mid-Upper Gunner. G. J. Martin (D.F.M) - Missing - Killed
Rear Gunner B.A.K. Townsend - W.F. Smith Killed (Also F/Lt. Wynyard D.F.C.)

Last Post: Stevie remembering his friends, Hempnall War Memorial, Norfolk, Remembrance Sunday, 2019. This was Stevie's last public appearance. He laid the wreath at the invitation of the Rector of Hempnall, the Rev Michael Kingston. Before and after the service, the villagers queued to shake his hand and thank him for all he had done.